Also by Arnold Krupat

FOR THOSE WHO COME AFTER   (1985)

I TELL YOU NOW   (1987)
(edited with Brian Swann)

RECOVERING THE WORD   (1987)
(edited with Brian Swann)

THE VOICE IN THE MARGIN   (1989)

Ethnocriticism

Ethnocriticism

ETHNOGRAPHY
HISTORY
LITERATURE

–

Arnold Krupat

–

University of California Press

BERKELEY LOS ANGELES

OXFORD

University of California Press
Berkeley and Los Angeles, California
University of California Press
Oxford, England
Copyright © 1992 by The Regents of the University of California

Library of Congress Cataloging-in-Publication Data

Krupat, Arnold.
 Ethnocriticism : ethnography, history, literature / Arnold Krupat.
  p. cm.
 Includes bibliographical references and index.
 ISBN 0-520-07447-5 (alk. paper). — ISBN 0-520-07666-4 (pbk. :
alk. paper)
 1. Ethnology—Methodology. 2. Ethnology—Authorship.
3. American literature—Indian authors—History and criticism.
4. Indian literature—History and criticism. 5. Literature and
anthropology. I. Title.
GN345.K78 1992
305.8′001—dc20   91-35142
                 CIP

Printed in the United States of America
1 2 3 4 5 6 7 8 9
The paper used in this publication meets the minimum requirements
of American National Standard for Information Sciences—Permanence
of Paper for Printed Library Materials, ANSI Z39.48-1984

FOR

CARTER REVARD

AND

GERALD VIZENOR

Acknowledgments

For all that "acknowledgments" have become so much de rigueur as to risk rigor mortis, I usually read them in other people's books, and so I dare hope other people may be interested in reading them in mine. It's a pleasure in any case to thank at least some of the many who have helped with this book.

Donald Bahr, David Brumble, Paul John Eakin, Dell Hymes, Anthony Mattina, Julian Rice, and Brian Swann have provided friendship and encouragement of a variety of kinds over a good many years and I am much in their debt. Thanks are also due my Sarah Lawrence colleagues Tara Fitzpatrick and Peter Whiteley, both of whom read early drafts of several of these chapters and not only offered pointed criticism, but kept me up to date in areas I might otherwise have ignored. I am grateful as well for talks with Betty Bergland, Marla and William Powers, Jana Sequoya, and Shamoon Zamir. Mellon Foundation grants for research help at Sarah Lawrence—a very labor-intensive place—helped pay for the services of my student assistants Jess Buckley, Brian McCreight, Erica Metzger, and West Moss, services without which I would, at the least, still be waiting to use the copying machine. A Summer Stipend and a Grant for College Teachers from the National Endowment for the Humanities gave me time to patch parts of the book I might otherwise have left even more leaky than they may still be. Without the help of Janet Alexander and Judy Kicinski of the Sarah Lawrence College Library, I would have been severely constrained in all aspects of research. My appreciation for the warmth and wisdom of Carter Revard's reading of these chapters and for Gerald Vizenor's advice and friendship is indicated by the dedication of this book. Finally, I offer special thanks to Roy Harvey Pearce whose support has long encouraged me in this work.

A.K.

Gardiner, New York
October, 1990

Contents

The central criterion of a critical viewpoint is very simple: Any scientific theory or position which looks like a metaphor of the social ideology, or which can be construed as contributing to the psychological, social, or material alienation of any class or group in the society is automatically suspect.

—ANTHONY WILDEN

—

Tell them all
we won't put up with your hard words
and low wages one more day.

Those meek who were blessed
are nothing
but meat and potato eaters,
never salsa or any spice.

Those timid are sagging in the soul
and those poor who will inherit the earth
already work it
so take shelter
take shelter you
because we are thundering and beating on floors
and this is how walls have fallen in other cities.

—LINDA HOGAN

Ethnocriticism

INTRODUCTION:

Ethnocriticism

*. . . the creation of alternative cartographies, a
ferocious critique of the dominant culture . . . a
proposal for new creative languages . . . the bor-
derization of the world. . . .*

—GUILLERMO GÓMEZ-PEÑA

I

In referring to the studies in this book as *ethnocriticism*, I
take up again a concept I tentatively offered more than a
decade ago in my first awkward attempt to say something
about Native Americans as subjects and producers of varieties of American discourse. *Ethnocriticism* is the name I
give to a particular perspective as this is manifested on the
level of critical writing. On the pedagogical or curricular
level, the ethnocritical perspective manifests itself in the
form of *multiculturalism*, a term I take to refer to that particular organization of cultural studies which engages otherness and difference in such a way as to provoke an interrogation of and a challenge to what we ordinarily take as
familiar and our own. On the level of what I will call cognitive ethics, the ethnocritical perspective is consistent with
a recognition and legitimation of heterogeneity (rather than
homogeneity) as the social and cultural norm. My term for
this recognition and legitimation—and I take my particular
sense of it from Paul Rabinow—is *cosmopolitanism*. Ulti-

mately, ethnocriticism, multiculturalism, and cosmopolitanism are all oriented toward materializing their values on the sociopolitical level, contributing to the possibility of institutionalizing what I have elsewhere called the *polyvocal polity*.[1] I will return to multiculturalism, cosmopolitanism, and the politics of polyvocality in my conclusion. Here, by way of introduction, I want to define, explain, and, so, inevitably, defend *ethnocriticism*.

Ten years ago I found terms for the sort of critical perspective I had in mind most particularly in the historical subdiscipline of *ethnohistory*. "Although ethnohistory is a scholarly strategy with a long pedigree," as James Axtell has written, "it was given academic prominence in 1946 when Congress created the Indian Claims Commission" (Krupat 1979 142), which called upon *anthropologists* to examine *historical* sources in order to determine whether specific tribes had occupied specific lands, and whether they had received fair value for those lands at the time of cession. The American Indian Ethnohistoric Conference was formed, and the journal *Ethnohistory* first published in 1954 to fill scholarly needs in studying Indian-White relations in the history of this country. Twenty-five years later, in 1979, it seemed to me that an "ethnohistorical literary criticism," as I referred to it then (1979 142), an interdisciplinary mix of anthropology, history, and critical theory, was equally needed for the study of Indian-White relations in the literature and culture of this country.

Central to ethnohistorical work is the concept of the *frontier*. The frontier for the modern ethnohistorian is not defined in the progressivist-evolutionist manner of Fred-

1. See my "The Dialogic of Silko's *Storyteller*," in particular pp. 64–5 for my sense of the "polyvocal polity" as a term for imagining the institutionalization of Bakhtinian dialogic values in some form other than "carnival."

erick Jackson Turner[2] as the farthest point to which *civilization* has advanced, a series of those points apparently marking a clearly discernible line between "us" and "them." Rather, in a more relativist manner, the frontier is understood as simply that shifting space in which two *cultures* encounter one another. In James Clifton's recent formulation, "a frontier is a social setting," not a fixed or mappable, but, rather, "a culturally defined place where peoples with different culturally expressed identities meet and deal with each other" (24).

Of course, the two cultures which met and dealt with each other at the various frontiers noted by Western history were almost never two cultures of equivalent material power, so that an ethnocriticism founded upon ethnohistorical descriptions of the frontier must involve a recognition that the topics it takes up from an anthropological, historical, or literary perspective all must be set against the backdrop of a pervasive Western imperialism. For the study of Native American materials, this means attention to the domestic imperialism, which, sometimes intentionally, sometimes not, operated on this continent against indigenous peoples everywhere, and which, regardless of intentionalities, continues to operate to this day.

But inasmuch as the conceptual categories necessary to ethnocriticism—culture, history, imperialism, anthropology, literature, interdisciplinarity, even the frontier—are Western categories, the objection may be raised that ethnocriticism is itself no more than yet another form of imperialism, this time of a discursive and epistemological kind, and one which, by its very foundation in these cate-

2. Turner's enormously influential essay, "The Significance of the Frontier in American History," was originally read at the World's Columbian Exposition, in 1893.

gories cannot help but falsify the lived experience and worldview of any nonwestern people, *translating*, in Eric Cheyfitz's broad understanding of the term,[3] "their" incoherent jabber into an eloquence of use only to ourselves. It seems to me that at the ultimate horizon, this objection is true, or at least unanswerable. Just as anthropology, in an absolute sense, cannot engage innocently with any culture—because anthropology, that is to say, turns *people* into cultural *subjects* (of inquiry, at the least), *objects* of its knowledge—so, too, can there, in this absolute sense, be no nonviolent *criticism* of the discourse of Others, not even an ethnocriticism. The question is whether, short of this absolute horizon, it is worth pursuing certain projects of inquiry in the interest of a rather less violent knowledge.

Objections to the imperialism of criticism, as it were, have been raised not only by Native American critics such as Leslie Marmon Silko, and Gerald Vizenor, but as well by non-Native critics such as Calvin Martin and Robin Ridington, who have urged a turn to "Indian" modes of thinking about culture, history, and literature[4]—a call which, as I have had occasion to say before, parallels a most decidedly Western turn to "postmodernist" approaches to literature, history, and ethnography. Best known among these latter are Stephen Tyler's call for anthropologists to abandon their production of "documents of the occult" and turn their efforts instead to the production of "occult documents"; Jean Baudrillard's denunciation of "Marxist Anthropology" for its inevitable "Domination of Nature"; Jean-François Lyotard's

3. See *The Poetics of Imperialism: Translation and Colonization from "The Tempest" to "Tarzan."*

4. See Silko's "An Old-Time Indian Attack . . . ," and all of Vizenor's critical work, including that in Martin's volume, *The American Indian and the Problem of History*, where Ridington is also to be found.

rejection of the *grands récits*, the overarching explanatory narratives of historicism, philosophy, and science as no more than discourses of legitimation; Richard Rorty's neo-pragmatic demotion of philosophy to the position of just another speaker in an ongoing conversation with no claim (philosophy's historical self-justification) to be anything more than *interesting*; and Gerald Vizenor's explicit linkage of what he calls the "trickster" mode to variants of these latter postmodernist positions.[5] Although I am critical of much of traditional Western disciplinary theory and practice as these have operated in relation to Native American subjects in all the senses of that word, I continue to be in substantial disagreement with "evocative" (in Tyler's term) or "biological" (in Calvin Martin's term), or, quite simply, postmodernist orientations for criticism. The relativism of ethnocriticism is not, as these positions are, a radically epistemological relativism. For all that, ethnocriticism's self-positioning at a great many frontiers, as I hope will become clear, consciously and intentionally courts the questioning of any premises from which it initially proceeds.

For any who believe, however, that it is indeed possible to say an unequivocal "no" to the Western episteme and still do work of a specifically critical and pedagogical type, much of what follows will seem disappointing at best, fraudulent

5. I've taken phrases, here, from the title of Tyler's essay, "Post-Modern Ethnography: From Document of the Occult to Occult Document," where Tyler speaks for a post-scientific, postmodern anthropology committed to "evocation" (123); from chapter 2 of Baudrillard's *The Mirror of Production*, "Marxist Anthropology and the Domination of Nature"; from Lyotard's *The Post-Modern Condition: A Report on Knowledge*; from Rorty's several books, all cited in the bibliography; and from Vizenor's "Postmodern Introduction," and his conclusion, "Trickster Discourse: Comic Holotropes and Language Games," to his edited collection, *Narrative Chance: Postmodern Discourse on Native American Indian Literatures*. More recently, there is also his "Trickster Discourse."

at worst. Nor is it likely to placate the absolutist in these matters to point to the fact that ethnocriticism, *like any analytic discourse*, cannot help but be implicated in what Gayatri Spivak, in a brilliant recent discussion of "post-coloniality," has (re)defined as "the deconstructive philosophical position," one "in which one offers an impossible 'no' to a structure which one critiques, yet inhabits intimately" (794). It may be that ethnocriticism is engaged in a type of catachrestical project (a rather different one, however, from that of Boas, as I discuss it in chapter 2), in Spivak's terms, one which offers "concept metaphor[s] without an adequate referent" (794); if so, I would claim, as Spivak does for what she calls "the study of a globality not confused with ethnicity" (795), that ethnocriticism may—paradoxically, to be sure—turn out to be a project particularly worth pursuing.

2

Although this topic has, of late, been much considered, it may not be amiss, here, to outline more specifically my own "discontents" with postmodernism, the better to situate the ethnocriticism I want to offer in its place.

As Jean-François Lyotard has written, "Simplifying to the extreme, I define *postmodern* as incredulity toward metanarratives" (xxiv). "Metanarratives" are those discourses which, at least from the time of the Enlightenment, have either made truth-claims analogous to those of "science," or, have made claims to "philosophical" status, offering themselves as more inclusive or comprehensive than so-called "first-order" or "natural" narratives. Philosophy has always aimed, in Christopher Norris's phrase, to operate on "a higher plane of understanding," where the subject under discussion "would yield up its true . . . significance" (15), if nothing else, a determination to sustain the Aristotelian distinction between logic, or dialectic, and rhetoric. It is the postmodernist's insistence, however, that philosophy's claim to produce just this sort of metadiscourse ruled by reason and logic is always trapped in the prisonhouse of rhetoric and ideology; thus any would-be explanatory account in the interest of truth or knowledge is inevitably just another occasion-bound story (rhetoric).

As it is for philosophy, so, too, is it for social science, most particularly, history and ethnography: we always tell just another story, inevitably *our* story. Now it would be absurd to pretend that there is not a good deal of truth to this; from the pessimist's perception of the eternally half-empty rather than half-full glass, we must either imperialistically "tell our own story" *as* the other's, or imperialistically speak *for* the other, violent translation or insidious ventriloquism, the only alternatives. But this kind of either/or reasoning, as I shall take considerable pains to argue, is itself a pure product of Western logic, and leads to the practice of what I will call philosophy and social science in the ironic mode, most particularly, as I shall explain further in chapter 2, in the mode marked by the rhetorical trope of *catachresis*, the figure of *abusio* or misuse.

This postmodernist position has, of course, been "scientifically" and "philosophically" contested, most powerfully, perhaps, by the continuing meditations on the subject of Jurgen Habermas.[6] I offer my own version of an epistemological critique, one deriving from my interest in a frontier perspective, later. Here, however, I want to argue against the politics of postmodernism—once more in the interest of ethnocriticism's very different politics.

6. See, for example, *Communication and the Evolution of Society.*

To reduce all discourse to voices in occasional conversation, in the Rortyian postmodernist mode, or to equivalent stories, à la Lyotard, is, as Rorty wholeheartedly admits, to privilege the paradigm of a liberal, bourgeois consensus society—one, unfortunately, that either does not anywhere actually exist or is not nearly so amiably consensual as claimed. Lyotard, as I understand him, would go much further than this;[7] he seems to see his radically relativist view as consistent with such things as justice and liberation. The logic here—for all that logic is a discredited category for postmodernism—has to do with the notion that once all metanarrative aspirations are either abandoned or undermined, then, as David Carroll writes, we will have

> Hundreds, thousands of little dissident narratives of all sorts . . . produced in spite of all attempts to repress them, . . . circulat[ing] inside, or even initially, outside the boundaries of the totalitarian state. (75)

Carroll continues, extrapolating from Lyotard:

> The importance of these little narratives is not only that they challenge the dominant metanarrative and the state apparatus that would prohibit or discredit them, but that they also indicate the possibility of another kind of society. (75)

But what can the social referents of such ostensibly descriptive commentary actually be? Are Carroll, and, in his own way, Lyotard thinking of what was called *samizdat* publi-

---

7. My understanding of Lyotard's position is predominantly derived from his *Post-Modern Condition . . . .*, not, to be sure, his most recent work. But a quick read through (for example) the new *Lyotard Reader* suggests that recent statements are not inconsistent with earlier positions.

cation in and out of Russia? If so, I would challenge them
to name *specifically* not even "Hundreds, [or] thousands of
[the] little dissident narratives" they have in mind but even
a couple of dozen that have had any social effectivity whatsoever *except* to the extent that, "challeng[ing] the dominant metanarrative" of one "state apparatus," they supported the metanarrative and state apparatus of antagonist
states to those in which they originated. I applaud the cour-
age of dissident speakers and writers everywhere, but
surely we need to distinguish between speaking opposition-
ally and toppling the state. In America, as Paul Goodman
used to point out, we let everybody say or publish whatever
they choose; we just restrict access to the microphones,
controlling not the production of counterstories but their
distribution.

As I have worked on this book over the past two years, I
have many times taken a break by looking out the window,
at Tomkins Square Park. From perhaps the summer of 1989
until their removal on December 13, 1989, there were a
very great many speakers to be seen and heard in the park.
Mostly black and Hispanic, mostly homeless, some down
on their luck, some severely disturbed, or badly addicted,
the park people audibly told stories to each other; to the
working class young cops who, for a while, at least, were
gathered here thicker than thieves;[8] to the Yuppies who,

8. Early in the summer of 1988, the Lower East Side was involved in what was
then called Operation Pressure Point, ostensibly an exercise in the escalating "war
against drugs." To residents of Loisaida who were not deaf, dumb, blind, and
incapable of rational thought, what this meant was that on any given day or night
drug dealers would move to streets unpatrolled by the young, rookie cops assigned
in overwhelming numbers to the area. (As one of these young cops told me, they
were to pay the costs for their deployment by writing as many traffic tickets for
infractions such as U-turns or busted headlights as they could.) After the violence
of late summer 1988, when cops, with badges taped over, beat and busted anyone

hurrying to their new renovations, didn't stop to listen. Until the 1988 police riot, the homeless most thickly congregated at the south end of the park, at Seventh Street; after, most of them moved their tarpaulin, box, and board shelters over to Tenth Street, the north end of the park, where I lived. The population density of the park people increased as the summer of 1989 ended. The smell of urine was strong on the southerly breeze; then it grew prematurely cold in the "big shitty," and the foremost smell was wood smoke from the "fire barrels," the garbage cans used as makeshift stoves and heaters. Walking in the park (it is quite safe by day), having Rorty and Lyotard and Carroll in mind, I tried to listen to the stories being told; I tried, too, to see these "*petits récits,*" the "wisps of narrative" unquestionably produced by the people in the park as "dissident" in some meaningful way, a "challenge [to] the dominant metanarrative or the state apparatus that would prohibit or discredit them." But it is their marginality and complete containment that most strike me; only the TV news, which translates for them, is widely heard.

Now, at the end of the summer of 1990, most of the park people are gone—gone from Tomkins Square, that is; doubtless they continue to produce their narratives elsewhere. Who hears them? Where are they to be heard? Of course, this is not the sort of thing that Carroll and Lyotard

---

who was unfortunate enough to be near them, the police presence simply evaporated, the drug dealers returning to their familiar places, so that the local yuppies and the drive-ins from Jersey could score without driving all around the area, a victory, I suppose, for pollution control. An official police investigation of the Tomkins Square riot interrogated more than two hundred officers, not one of whom could recall seeing any covered badges or any use of unnecessary force, both of which had been clearly recorded on videotape. So much for one episode in the ongoing saga of "New York's Finest." (These words were written before the Los Angeles Police Department played "hardball" with Rodney King.)

are talking about. True, no doubt, but then, why aren't they talking about these things? Now that Germans from the east and west are sharing their stories, their currency, and, apparently, their commitment to the Natopolitan world; now that Violeta Chamorro has nominally taken over Nicaraguan politics, and Islamic fundamentalists have taken power in Algeria and the Sudan; now that the Poles have followed an American whizkid economist's recommendations and lifted price controls on food and other staples, and Russians and Americans revel in the luxury of a common "enemy" like Saddam Hussein: do we look out upon a more consensually democratic, liberated world?

Is Lyotard's Paris *that* different from New York? Is it independent of all the rest of the world? What is Carroll's Irvine like, I wonder, that he can write what he does. So far as they "respect the alterity of the other . . . and the conflictual diversity of the social space itself" (Carroll 72), comfortable, middle-class, male, white academics can offer an example that has, perhaps, a certain value. But unless they—we—engage in something more than catachrestic narrative politics, it's all just a "language game" for the privileged, and, so far as I can see, no model for anyone, anywhere.

3

To return specifically to the level of critical discourse—and it will have been obvious already that it is not possible to do more than foreground one level rather than another— the problem of the postmodernist position is not just that, as many have noted, it has been far easier to call for a non-Western, "Indian," "biological," or postmodern ethnography and historiography than actually to produce them. Nor is it even that when these have appeared, as, for example, in Gerald Vizenor's "trickster criticism," apart from surface differences of style, tone, and organization (to be sure, these are not negligible), they have not offered interpretations very different from those of more traditional Western criticism.[9] Rather, it is that postmodern positions, regardless of what they call themselves (e.g., trickster, "Indian," biological, evocative, or whatever), are all based upon models *both* of Western "scientific," "social-scientific," "rational," "historical" modes of thought, *and* of non-Western "religious," biogenetic, "mythic," or vaguely specified "Indian" modes, that are grossly overgeneralized—overgeneralized, so that they may be reified as categories presumptively in (binary) opposition to each other. This insistence upon what Frantz Fanon years ago called a "manichean allegory,"[10] as I shall argue in a moment, is as largely useless as a framework for understanding specific ethnographic, historical, and literary instances as it is, to my mind, politically dangerous.

For Native American materials, as Thomas Biolsi has written in a fine review of Calvin Martin's recent work proposing monolithic dichotomies between "Indian" "biological" worldviews and Western "anthropological" worldviews, "the obvious distortion is the liquidation of the astounding intertribal diversity present at any one time in North America, as well as historical change within tribes, both before and after contact" (262). A persistent attachment to the notion that Indians are inherently "natural" or "biological" people, always and everywhere in perfect harmony with their environment, or to the notion that Western "scien-

9. See, in particular, Vizenor's "Trickster Criticism."

10. See Fanon's *The Wretched of the Earth*, especially pp. 42ff. The topic is also broached in Fanon's *Black Skin, White Masks,* and developed most recently in Abdul JanMohamed's "The Economy of Manichean Allegory: The Function of Racial Difference in Colonialist Literature."

tific" and "anthropological" desire must inevitably foul whatever it touches leads to nothing more than "sermoniz[ing] about 'the Indian mind' " (Biolsi 262), or the evils of "Western civilization."

An ethnocritical frontier orientation, however, soon shows that one of the things that occurs on the borders is that oppositional sets like West/Rest, Us/Them, anthropological/biological, historical/mythical, and so on, often tend to break down. On the one hand, cultural contact can indeed produce mutual rejections, the reification of differences, and defensive retreats into celebrations of what each group regards as distinctively its own—William Bennett and Allan Bloom are available as current illustrations of this option on the Western side of the frontier—for, as Fredrik Barth, in a classic study showed, the maintenance of "ethnic distinctions do[es] *not* depend on an absence of social interaction and acceptance" (10, my emphasis), and that "cultural differences can persist despite inter-ethnic contact and interdependence" (10). On the other hand, it may also frequently be the case that interaction leads to interchange, what A. I. Hallowell, in a term borrowed from Fernando Ortiz and intended to emphasize the dual directionality of cultural contact, has called "transculturalization" (in Clifton 289).

Further, whatever "cultures" or "peoples" do or don't do, particular persons—as the studies in Clifton's book, as well as work by Sherry Ortner, Peter Whiteley, and other anthropologists have shown[11]—react to the new and other with all the range of human response possible. This is not at all to reinstantiate the discredited category of the "free," "au-

11. See, in particular, Ortner's "Theory in Anthropology Since the Sixties," and Whiteley's "Naming, intentionality, and personhood in Hopi society: a critique of Mauss."

tonomous," "individual"; it is to remark that there may be a greater rather than a lesser number of variations within whatever discursive and epistemic limits one may note as prevailing. As just one example of which I am aware, let me cite the case of the Brulé Sioux historian, Clyde D. Dollar. In a paper called "Through the Looking-Glass: History and the Modern Brulé Sioux" (1972), Dollar anticipated some of the recent objections of Martin and others to traditional Western historiography as applied to Native American materials. According to Dollar,

> the idea of an historical fact . . . from the Indian side of the looking-glass, is something one has been told by his elders and therefore is not to be questioned. Indeed, among the High Plains people, there is little interest in the subject matter of history per se beyond the repeating of its stories, and a deeply searching pursuit of data and facts on which to build veracity in history is frequently considered rather pointless, perhaps ludicrous, decidedly nosy, and an occupation closely associated with eccentric white men. (In D. Tyler 1)

Then a historian at the University of South Dakota, Dollar became a Ph.D. candidate at the University of Arkansas, where, I assume, in full consciousness of how "pointless," "ludicrous," "nosy," and "closely associated with eccentric white men" his studies might seem to Brulé people, he must nonetheless have engaged in something like "a deeply searching pursuit of data and facts on which to build veracity in history." Cognizant and respectful of the ways in which traditional High Plains Indian people conceptualize history, Dollar nonetheless chose to pursue researches into Western historiography. So far as this is true, Dollar would have been engaged in an exemplary ethnocritical project, attempting to see whether he could accommodate elements of Brulé historical theory to that of the West, and/or to accommodate elements of Western theory to that of the Brulé. Dollar's efforts to move back and forth across border lines, as I imagine them, seem far richer in their potential for criticism, pedagogy, and politics than any turn to an exclusively defined, monolithically "Indian" or "Western" way. These remarks, I hope it will be understood, do not in the least presume that the mere attempt to mediate such things as the Plains view of history and the view of history of the American graduate school must, as a function of the intensity of its desire, achieve success. Not at all. Indeed, as I shall note in detail later (chapter 5), the difficulties of mediating the view of literature held by traditional people and the view held by the modern West is something particularly vexing, to the point, it may well be, of incapacitating the full practice of the ethnocriticism I nonetheless propose.

Criticizing the European and Euramerican's "culturally patterned system of assigning individual and group identity by race" or "blood" (Clifton 12), James Clifton points out that

> Originally, no native North American society subscribed to the idea of biological determination of identity or behavior. Indeed, the most common identity question asked of strangers was not, "What nation do you belong to?" or "Of what race are you?" Instead, when confronting unknown people, they typically asked, "What language do you speak?"(11)

Not only may language serve as a major determinant of identity as Native American people would "originally" seem to have thought, but, as I want to suggest, in a very particular sense, language may serve as a model for culture as well.

I mean to indicate here a similarity although not an identity between the way Mikhail Bakhtin describes language[12] and the way—one way, at least—I would want to describe culture. This particular analogy was remarked some years ago by James Clifford (but only in a footnote!), and although Clifford has, I believe, worked out some of its implications in practice, he has not, to my knowledge, taken up the matter in an explicit theoretical fashion. So I believe something remains to be said on this matter.

What I want to instantiate, here, is Bakhtin's claim that language in society is always and inevitably a plural construct. As is well known, for Bakhtin, the language of any single speaker, one's "own" speech, can never be absolutely and exclusively his or her own, never some sort of inalienable private property. Rather, real speech—speech, I assume, as it occurs in the marketplace, in the corridors and the classrooms of the academy—is always shot through with the speech of others. In the same way, it may be useful to see culture in history—culture *after* the Fall, outside the gates of Eden, and so on—as never absolute and exclusive unto itself. Epistemologically, for example, it would appear that no culture could very accurately be described as entirely mythical *or* historical; biological *or* anthropological; from the point of view of social organization, there is no known culture that is or ever has been entirely patriarchal *or* matriarchal; and so on. "Language," Bakhtin writes,

12. The essential texts of Bakhtin are presently available in English, and the anglophone commentaries on them are of voluminous proportions. Bakhtin's *The Dialogic Imagination*, to choose one book to stand for many, most informs my own understanding of his commentary on language.

lies on the borderline between oneself and the other. The word in language is half someone else's . . . the word does not exist in a neutral and impersonal language (it is not, after all, out of a dictionary that the speaker gets his words!) but rather it exists in other people's mouths, in other people's contexts, serving other people's intentions: it is from there that one must take the word and make it one's own. (In Gates 1985 1)

And the same sort of thing is probably true of culture and cultural difference, which, like racial or gender difference, is better conceptualized in dialogical rather than oppositional terms—Fanon's "manichean allegory" of white/black, men/women, us/them, and so on.

It should immediately be added that the dialogical or differential view of culture I am proposing in no way assumes an egalitarianism in regard to its various constitutive elements. For all that the words we speak or the cultural practices we engage in do manifest themselves or "exist . . . in other people's mouths, in other people's contexts, serving other people's intentions" as well as our own, not everyone's words, contexts, and intentions weigh equally. The question is not so much, to borrow a formulation from Gayatri Spivak, whether the subaltern can speak but whether and to what effect she can be heard. Nonetheless, for all the care with which it must be employed in practice, the dialogical view of culture seems to me to have advantages over the oppositional view.

Not the least of these, as Dominick LaCapra has noted, is that the "undoing of binary oppositions" can provide a "critique" of what he calls "the scapegoat mechanism—a mechanism that generates purity for an in-group by projecting all corruption or pollution onto an out-group" (6).

This important "undoing" was earlier proposed in Nancy Jay's deconstruction of dichotomized thinking, in which, extrapolating from Emile Durkheim's presentation of the absolute difference between the sacred and the profane, and, more distantly (but with more general effect), from Aristotle's principle of the excluded middle ("anything, and everything must be *either* A *or* Not-A" [Jay 42]), Jay showed that dichotomized reasoning is

necessarily distorting [in its tendency to take all difference as a matter of presence/absence, existence/non-existence] when . . . applied directly to the empirical world, for there are no negatives there. Everything that exists . . . exists positively. (48)

Just as dichotomized, binary, oppositional, or manichean reasoning once served as a justification for imperial domination, so, too, is it too often retained today to justify that form of postcolonial revisionism that produces what Donald Bahr has called "Victimist . . . history," a very specific form of narrative which "tells how one people was damaged by another" (1989 316). In victimist history, it is, of course, not the first, but the second term of each dichotomous set that is valorized, so that, as Tzvetan Todorov has noted, we still get "manichean writing . . . [but] with good and evil simply having switched places. On your right, the disgusting white colonialists; on your left, the innocent black victims" (1986 178)—or the relentlessly genocidal Euramericans, the innocent and hapless Native Americans.

At the risk of elaborating the obvious, I want to state clearly that my own critique of dichotomous logic as inadequate to the actual complexities of cultural encounter in history is not at all intended to endorse Todorov's or anyone else's notion that it is possible somehow to proceed "neutrally," avoiding not merely the reductionist practices of "scapegoating" and "victimizing," but as well the moral and political implications of any situated discourse. One may grant that not all Euramericans were rapacious, genocidal monsters, and that not all Indians were, in the purest and most absolute sense, their hapless, innocent victims: nonetheless, it seems to me beyond question that—all things considered—the indigenous peoples of this continent, along with African Americans, women, and many other groups, have overwhelmingly been more sinned against than sinning. If this is so, to construct one's discourse on such a premise is not necessarily to engage in the revisionist allegory of victimism. Some people *have* been hurt by others and if that is not the only and the most interesting thing to say, it most certainly remains something that still, today, can probably not be said too often.

4

The defining aspiration of philosophical and scientific discourse in the West has always been to rise above and resolve the contradictions of any particular manifestation of manichean logic. Currently, as I have noted, this aspiration has been condemned as futile, retrograde, and epistemologically imperialistic by varieties of postmodernist thought, for which there is no logic or dialectic, but only rhetoric, discourse clearly bound to specific purposes and occasions. For all my general hostility to the postmodern position, there is, I believe, one sense in which it is, indeed, quite accurate: for inasmuch as philosophical and scientific discourse have traditionally based themselves on the achievement of some totalized or totalizing metanarrative, these discourses, precisely in the extent of their claims, are, indeed, unacceptable for secular criticism today. Not even those of us who are sceptical of the amiability of Rortyian conversations, or the pretensions to effectivity of the Lyotardian thousand bits of talk can quite be comfortable with the prospect of having to (re)assert the *universal* authority of any explanatory paradigm. Yet, as Nancy Hartsock points out, it is intolerable

> to be imprisoned by the alternatives posed by Enlightenment thought and postmodernism: either one must adopt the perspective of the transcendental and disembodied voice of Reason, or one must abandon the goal of accurate and systematic knowledge of the world. (205)

"To put the question differently," as Todorov writes in the essay from which I have already quoted, "is there really no middle ground between worshipping dogmas as immutable truth and abandoning the idea of truth itself?" (1986 180). I don't know that there is such a "middle ground"—although I do believe that ethnocriticism's commitment to a movement between grounds may well offer something as near as one can come to what Todorov seems to be after. The question I want to raise here, however, is this: if one does indeed want to predicate one's discourse on something between truth and dogma (versions of logic or dialectic), on the one hand, and random talk ("only" rhetoric), on the other, how is one to recognize that "something" if and when it presents itself?

For no one is likely actually to admit her or his allegiance to a "transcendental and disembodied . . . Reason," or to "worshipping dogmas." By what means then are we to differentiate between discourses predicated upon the latter and those predicated upon "the goal of accurate and systematic knowledge of the world" (Hartsock), or, indeed, even "the idea of truth itself" (Todorov)? A full consideration of this question is beyond my competence and, in any case, would require at least a full volume in itself. As signposts toward some answers, I will note only the importance I continue to find in Raymond Williams's insistence that the very nature of any epistemic or cultural hegemony is necessarily limited, so that rather than totalities, we always get in practice varying degrees of dominant, residual, and emerging values.[13] Here, too, I would also note the value of Jurgen Habermas's recent appeal to an admittedly ideal(ized) speech situation against which claims to rationality might be measured, and of Christopher Norris's suggestion that the actual process of any *rigorous working through*—be it deconstructive, Marxist, or whatever—can yield results which may make approximate truth-claims.[14]

The feminist philosopher Linda Alcoff calls this sort of working-through a form of doing "metaphysics" that "is conceived not as any particular ontological commitment but as the attempt to reason through ontological issues that cannot be decided empirically" (429). Alcoff proposes what she calls "positionality" as a strategy of self-conscious self-displacement within the epistemological and discursive frames any critic cannot help but inhabit. Alcoff's "positionality" is quite close to my ethnocritical stance and its commitment to testing itself in relation to otherness and difference may provide another route to cognitively responsible understandings, some approximation to Todorov's "middle ground."

13. Williams's *Marxism and Literature* contains most of the essays that inform my understanding here.

14. I refer to Habermas's *Communication and the Evolution of Society,* cited above; Norris's ideas are developed throughout his *The Contest of Faculties.*

The point is to recognize that the difficulties currently in the way of establishing probabilistic claims to explanation, although they may be in the nature of the case, may also be a function, more locally, of our situation: not matters of essence, then, but of time, place, and culture. What *we* cannot see just here, just now, *others* may come to see readily enough. It is not yet certain that every epistemological break, in Foucault's terms, for all that it may newly instantiate the knowledge/power relationship, does so in exactly the same way and in exactly the same degree as those that have gone before; it's possible, indeed, even to read Foucault himself for this conclusion.

And it is particularly interesting for my ethnocritical position that Hartsock's invocation of accuracy, systematicity, and knowledge is in the interest of a move "Toward Minority Theories" (204). "Those of us who have been marginalized by the transcendental voice of universalizing theory," she writes,

> need to do something other than ignore power relations, as Rorty does, or resist them, as figures such as Foucault and Lyotard suggest. We need to transform them. (204)

This transformation of knowledge by the hitherto marginalized in all their "concrete multiplicity" (204), Hartsock notes, is unlikely to reproduce Enlightenment metanarratives, because these various persons "are far less likely to mistake themselves for the universal 'man,' " thereby constructing "another totalizing and falsely universal discourse" (205). Of course, it is important also to resist some equally totalized and false metanarrative of absolute Otherness and the perpetuation of Difference.

This latter danger Todorov properly warns of in the essay

from which I have already quoted, reminding us "that the content of a thought" should not "depend . . . upon the color of the thinker's skin" (177), as it should not depend upon the thinker's gender, class, ethnicity, and the like. Yet Todorov's own invocation of "the idea of truth itself," at least in his book *The Conquest of America*, seems to me—whatever its author's intentions—an attempt precisely to defend Enlightenment thought and Eurocentrism, constructing the ideological semiotics of the Other in an entirely manichean, scapegoating, and virtually neocolonialist manner.[15] I have no securely objective criterion for judging Todorov to be *wrong*: nonetheless, any critique of "immutable dogmas" that has the consequence of replicating those "dogmas"—albeit in the name of something more respectable than "dogma"—must, as the epigraph to this book from Anthony Wilden insists, be suspect on the face of it. If Hartsock looks "Toward Minority Theories," it seems to me that Todorov looks toward the reconstitution of (what once were) majority theories. What is needed is some move away from even the majority/minority dichotomy, without, however, denying the differential relations of power it seeks to name.

5

Ethnocritical discourse, in its self-positioning at the frontier, seeks to traverse rather than occupy a great variety of "middle grounds," both at home and abroad. At home, it will try to move between such positions as, for example, a persistent if (properly) contested humanism, on the one hand, and, on the other, a Derridaean/Foucauldian/de Manian virulent anti-humanism; between a Rortyian/Ly-

15. See Deborah Root's penetrating critique of Todorov's book, "The Imperial Signifier: Todorov and the Conquest of Mexico," as well as Cheyfitz's discussion in *The Poetics of Imperialism*.

otardian/Tylerian postmodernist evocative fragmentariness, and a social-scientific aspiration to cognitive adequacy; and so on. This is all quite easy to say. Abroad, however, ethnocriticism is a much less well-equipped traveler, making trips between the best definitions it can construct of an epistemological rationalism that valorizes categories like the empirical and material as "real," and the very different epistemologies of others—ones which, to the Western eye, appear irrationalist, magical, or whatever, but which, indeed, may appear so only because they radically refuse the dualistic and circumferential categories of the West.

Ethnocriticism at home rejects all forms of manichean discourse whether of a traditional and neocolonial or of a revisionist, "victimist" kind. Thus, ethnocriticism, as I have said, is concerned with differences rather than oppositions, and so seeks to replace oppositional with dialogical models. These latter always claim that the logical principle of the "excluded middle" itself excludes careful attention to the varieties of empirical differences discernible everywhere. Ethnocritical discourse regards border and boundary crossings, with their openness to and recognition of the inevitability of interactive relations, as perhaps the best means to some broadly descriptive account of the way things "really" work in the material and historical world. Ethnocriticism thus wishes to develop and refine dialogic models whose claims to accuracy, systematicity, and knowledge would reside in their capacity, in Anthony Wilden's sense,[16] to take in more context.

This is to say that ethnocriticism does not offer itself as a master narrative, while it does not either offer itself as just one position among others. An ethnocritical perspective

16. See the introduction to *System and Structure*, p. xxi and passim.

will certainly invoke reason, philosophy, and science—in full awareness of the ways in which, in their modern Western forms, these have "failed," but also with a modest awareness of the ways in which they have "succeeded" in particular and locally specifiable instances. Given its frontier condition of liminality or betweenness, ethnocriticism by its very nature must test any appeals to "reason," "science," "knowledge," or "truth" it would make in relation to Other or non-Western constructions of these categories, or, for that matter, to any alternative categories Others may propose. As the frontier is "a culturally defined place" (Clifton 24), so, too, will "truth" likely be—so far as we may know it, whatever it may be "in itself"—a "culturally defined" place, a *relative* truth, therefore, but not necessarily in the sense of a full-blown epistemological relativism. Indeed, ethnocriticism seeks a position not quite (in R. J. Bernstein's phrase) "beyond objectivism and relativism,"[17] but instead somewhere between objectivism and relativism.

Just as ethnocriticism must consider other constructions of the categories it would employ, calling its own largely Western assumptions or origins into question, so, too, must it permit all who would articulate those alternate constructions to be heard. It must do this not only as a matter of fairness or decency, important as these are, but (again) as a consequence of its very nature as ethnocriticism, its constitution by the principle that all discourse, like all cultural practice and all actual speech, is inevitably plural, regardless of what is officially permitted. This need not condemn ethnocriticism to any delusively utopian absolute freedom and egalitarianism. Rather, for all the openness it values, it nonetheless admits the fact that any serious discourse pre-

17. The reference is to R. J. Bernstein's *Beyond Objectivism and Relativism*.

tending to effectivity must in some degree be *regulatory*, and thus constrained to argue for and defend those ideas and perspectives it considers more valuable or important than others—while yet refusing to suppress those it considers less valuable or important. Obviously all of this is easier to imagine, even to articulate, than it is to put into practice. But, as I have said, imagining and articulating it, so far as one can, is already to contribute, however incipiently, to its practice and the practices it may found.

Of course, there will always be something paradoxical about a criticism that insists on its betweenness—while seeking a certain privilege or centrality; a criticism that insists upon a commitment to dialogue and the shifting processes of "transculturalization"—in the name of such apparently monologous and fixed categories as accuracy, knowledge, and truth. But this is only to recognize that ethnocriticism is not only *at* but *of* the frontier, its situation and its epistemological status the same. As I have already said, the accuracy, knowledge, and truth invoked by ethnocritical discourse will of necessity be "deconstructive," in Gayatri Spivak's sense; *liminal*, in Victor Turner's term,[18] expressed explicitly or implicitly in the *subjunctive*, mood, domain of *if-I-were-you*, or *should-it-turn-out-that*. The trope most typical of ethnocritical discourse, in the rhetorical terminology I will use at times in this book, is the *oxymoron*, that figure which offers apparently oppositional, paradoxical, or incompatible terms in a manner that nonetheless allows for decidable, if polysemous and complex, meaning. Standard examples of this apparently paradoxical

18. Turner's fullest discussion of the concept of "liminality" occurs in "Betwixt and Between," in *The Forest of Symbols*; a more recent although less fully developed account of the various concepts I have referred to appears in *The Anthropology of Performance*.

but ultimately coherent figure are such things as "thunderous silence," "dark light," "joyful sadness," or Emily Dickinson's notation of "thunders" that *"hurried slow."* As a critical discourse which claims to be both on and of the frontier, traversing middle ground while aspiring to a certain centrality, descriptive and normative at once, it should come as no surprise that ethnocriticism and the oxymoron have particular affinities or, again, in Spivak's very particular sense, that a catachrestical figuration—"concept metaphor without adequate referent" (Spivak 794)—may also come into play.

6

Thus far I have attempted to define ethnocriticism at its broadest, in theory. In the chapters to follow, however, it will be seen that I practice it rather more narrowly (e.g., chapters 4 and 6), or, indeed, that I question the possibility of its full practice (chapter 5). Inasmuch as it seems fairly certain, for example, that a post-colonial, anti-imperialist, dialogical anthropology may well be achieved as a result of the conversation between Western and non-Western perspectives, I hope to have practiced ethnocriticism more or less fully in regard to anthropological discourse in chapters 1–3. In the same way, in chapter 4 I have tried to situate a Cherokee perspective in relation to the dominant American discourse of law in a manner that might question the assumptions of that discourse. Although it is a *Cherokee* perspective that confronts the American perspective, as the reader will see, it is a Cherokee *textual* perspective, one largely produced and expressed by highly acculturated Cherokee persons who may themselves already be seen as ethnocritics of a sort. When we come, however, to Native American oral literatures (chapter 5), and consider the radically different assumptions of Euramerican and Native people concerning the genesis, ontology, transmission, and function of expressive discourse, it is by no means clear that any border encounters between them one might stage will be more nearly productive of a desired reconciliation—some new "invention" or synthesis—than of an altogether hostile confrontation. I have, in this book, as I suppose elsewhere, operated as a sort of perennial optimist in these matters; but I would not want to operate as a fool. I believe there is much already that ethnocriticism can do; I believe there is more it will soon be able to do; and I believe as well, however reluctantly, that there are some things that it probably will never be able (quite) to do.

In every case, the danger the would-be practitioner of ethnocriticism must try to avoid is, as I have to some extent indicated above, to speak *for* the "Indian," "interpreting" him or her, in Michael Castro's term,[19] in a manner that would submit her or him to a dominative discourse. This is a danger both for those (like myself) who can claim no experiential authority (i.e., they/we have no personal experience of being Indian), and also in some measure as well for those who have that experience. That is, it is always possible, as T. S. Eliot's Gerontion discovered, to have had the experience but missed the meaning—or to have provided a meaning that the experience cannot bear. Unwilling to speak *for* the Indian, and unable to speak *as* an Indian (although, as I have just said, simply to be an Indian speaking of Indians guarantees nothing), the danger *I* run as an ethnocritic is the danger of leaving the Indian silent entirely in my discourse. I don't know of any way securely to avoid this danger, for all that I hope it may somewhat be mitigated by a certain self-conscious awareness. It would,

19. See Castro's *Interpreting the Indian.*

of course, be possible simply to keep silent. In going forward with this book, it is obvious that I choose not to keep silent, for all that I have a strong sense that at this particular moment in history (I am working on revisions for this book as an American witness to what we have done to the people of Iraq; on the eve, too, of American celebrations of Columbus's "discovery" of a new world for domination) silence might indeed be the most decent choice. It is surely the best guarantor of safety.

Inasmuch as safety is bought at the price of some small usefulness, I choose not to keep silent in the tentative hope that my self-placement at some very particular frontier points, for all that it risks infuriating people on both sides of the boundary lines, may still in some degree help people on both sides of those lines in their understanding of the cross-cultural encounters I believe will increasingly mark the future.

Although I have argued elsewhere for the usefulness of retaining the category of *literature* as a distinct although not unique type of discourse,[20] these studies in ethnocriticism are very little concerned with specifically literary texts. This is not a change of mind, only an enlargement of interest—an enlargement that requires me to remind the reader on several occasions in the course of my treatment of anthropological or historical texts and subjects what he or she will already have surmised, that I am not an anthropologist, not a historian, and so on. Such disclaimers obviously serve the purpose of mitigating responsibility for error; such disclaimers also serve, I would suggest, as reminders of the position the would-be practitioner of ethnocriticism must inhabit, a position at the various frontier points where the

20. See *The Voice in the Margin*, pp. 34–49ff.

disciplines of anthropology and literature, literature and history, history and philosophy meet and interact.

In *The Conflict of Faculties*, Kant spoke, in a manner common to nineteenth-century German philosophical thought, of interdisciplinary studies as necessary to achieve the whole or totality of knowledge, the only goal sufficiently lofty to justify the existence of the University and lay claim to the scholar's devotion. Yet the actual history of the development of disciplines and fields within the University, as I have already noted—and, indeed, as Gerald Graff's *Professing Literature* abundantly documents—has tended to produce exclusivity and isolation rather than complementarity and community. Current trends toward interdisciplinarity, for all their commitment to community and complementarity of interest and information, do not, I believe, dream of recuperating the Kantian ideal of a totalized body of knowledge, Kant's *ganze gegenwartige Feld*, the whole present field, but, rather, of reconstituting the field, or reconceptualizing its divisions and unities.

This project has clearly engaged the attention of many in the Western disciplines. Consider, for example, Barbara Herrnstein Smith's title for a Modern Language Association Presidential Forum published in *Profession 89*: "Breaking Up/Out/Down—The Boundaries of Literary Study." Contributors to the Forum call their individual essays, "On the Line: Between History and Criticism," and refer to "The Shifting Interaction," "Literary Revisionism," or, as in the text I shall consider just below, affirm that "Being Interdisciplinary Is So Very Hard to Do."[21] This would suggest that

21. E.g., Dominick LaCapra, "On the Line: Between History and Criticism," Janet Swaffar, "Curricular Issues and Language Research: The Shifting Interaction," Donald Lazere, "Literary Revisionism: Partisan Politics and the Press," Stanley Fish, "Being Interdisciplinary Is So Very Hard to Do."

while almost everyone recognizes that hard lines between the disciplines have softened as surely as the Berlin Wall has come down, this recognition has not as yet produced any agreement as to what this all means and whether it is, in general, a good or a bad thing.

I would suggest that commitments to interdisciplinarity —ethnocriticism, multiculturalism, cosmopolitanism, and so on—are, currently, either determined gestures of trust, hopeful preparations for a future that will be very different from the past dominated by white, middle-aged, middle-class males, or, in a less prophetic mode, that they are quite simply sober gestures of realism. In just thirty years, to cite a fairly well-known statistic, thirty percent of the American population will be nonwhite (and women are already a majority). And, I suspect, well before the year 2020, for all that George Bush and William Bennett and Allan Bloom (not to mention a very great many professors of literature) may shout against the sea, it will not fail to break upon the shore—with all sorts of foreseeable and unforeseeable results. So it would perhaps be foolish rather than particularly brave *not* to be ethnocritical, multicultural, interdisciplinary, and so on.

And yet, as Stanley Fish has argued, "Being Interdisciplinary Is So Very Hard to Do." Indeed, Fish has insisted, "more than hard to do; it is impossible to do" (19). Fish's point is that each "imported product," from one discipline to another,

> will always have the form of its appropriation rather than the form it exhibits "at home"; therefore, at the very moment of its introduction, it will already be marked by the discourse it supposedly "opens." When something is brought into a practice, it is brought in in terms the practice recognizes; the practice cannot "say" the Other but can only say itself. (1989 19)

For Fish, there is really no such thing as "traveling theory," in Edward Said's phrase,[22] no complex interaction between the place (and time) of a "product['s]" origin, its final destination, and the vagaries of the voyage. For Fish, things are distinctively what they are only if they stay where they are; should they move, they then become transformed entirely, taking on the characteristics of the place to which they have moved. It is curious to note the parallels between Fish's extreme topological determinism (to call it that) in regard to disciplines, and one version of "melting pot" theories of American culture in the period just after World War I.[23]

Then it was assumed by some that being multicultural was also not only hard but impossible to do: Italian or Polish or Chinese culture, once imported by immigrants to these shores, would be intelligibly American only as these melted down to a monolithically conceived Americanism. The new immigrants would most certainly not "open" American "discourse" or culture, or impart to it nuances or inflections it had not formerly known, for America could not " 'say' the Other but . . . only . . . itself"—nor did it have the slightest intention or desire to try and do so.

Fish, of course, does not say this of persons or cultures, only of disciplinary practices. But his arguments and his conclusions are the same as those of the monocultural purists of the twenties. Philosophy might as well stay home with the philosophers, ethnography with the anthropologists; for, should they decide to emigrate to the literature faculties, they will only be melted down into a literary dis-

22. Cf. Said, "Traveling Theory."

23. See, in these regards, F. H. Matthews, "The Revolt Against Americanism . . . ," and David Hollinger's "Ethnic Diversity, Cosmopolitanism, and the Emergence of the American Liberal Intelligentsia."

course that endlessly "can only say itself." "The American mind," Fish concludes with reference to Allan Bloom, "like any other, will always be closed" (21). The only question, for Fish, "is whether we find the form of closure it [the American mind] currently assumes answerable to our present urgencies" (21). The options seem to be to say yes, the current form of closure is "answerable"; or to say no, the current form of closure isn't "answerable" at all. If we say no, we still can do nothing but wait until the forms of closure change (by what means Fish never indicates)—and in full cognizance of the fact that they may not change in the direction of any greater "answerability."

Politically, this position is very much like Rorty's in its cheerful conviction that, here in the good old U.S. of A., things just go on as they go on—and that's not bad at all. But this position, to invoke an earlier American instance, has its more sinister side in its resemblance to Hawthorne's response to the problem of slavery. Slavery, Hawthorne wrote, is

> one of those evils which divine Providence does not leave to
> be remedied by human contrivances, but which, in its own
> good time, by some means impossible to be anticipated, but of
> the simplest and easiest operation, when all its uses shall have
> been fulfilled, it causes to vanish like a dream. (In Arac 254)

And so we—who are not slaves—just wait, doing exactly what we've always done until change occurs, in God's or history's own good time. As with Hawthorne and slavery, so Fish with the academic disciplines: no change can be brought about by "human contrivances" because any attempt to do differently from what has always been done is inevitably to continue doing just exactly what has always been done. I do not mean to suggest that Hawthorne's complacency about slavery and Fish's complacency about interdisciplinarity are morally equivalent: they clearly are not —although both equivalently recommend a quietism and submission to the status quo that I find wholly obnoxious. In any case, Fish's monolithic and totalized concept of the disciplines has a very bad fit with the actual world of current academic practice where, however much literary critics may domesticate anthropological or philosophical materials, these latter still retain and "say" a certain Otherness which not only can have but in innumerable cases has had effects upon literary practice that would not likely have come about without their "appropriation."

But let me leave Stanley Fish's untroubled denial of the very possibility of interdisciplinary work (and this would also mean denying the possibility of ethnographic work) to consider problems that arise when, in spite of Fish, one nonetheless attempts to engage in such work, not only crossing disciplinary but cultural boundaries as well. One of these is the temptation dilettantishly to *dabble*. Too many Westerners have played carelessly in the realms of Otherness, taking what they wanted—a little of this, a little of that—and blithely moving on, "savagizing" or "orientalizing" the Other.[24] Another danger of transgressing traditional boundaries is illustrated by the work of some of the contemporary French savants who occasionally seem to "savagize" or "orientalize" not the Other, but, rather, the historical record. I am thinking, here, of some of what Michel Foucault has written about the family, the clinic, and the prison, and of Jacques Derrida's accounts of the

24. I refer here, of course, to Roy Harvey Pearce's *Savagism and Civilization* and Edward Said's *Orientalism*.

fortunes of speech and writing in the West. Both of these authors, that is, often proceed so as to force one to accept or reject their arguments independently of the accuracy of the empirical data that is offered—for all that, some, if not always very much, empirical data is, indeed, offered. It is a tribute to the imaginative and rhetorical power of Foucault and Derrida that their work continues to have value even when, as has happened again and again, it is shown to be based on factually dubious or radically incomplete information. Even so, I want the ethnocritic to encourage as much frontier interaction as possible between the empirical and the logical, between concrete practice and abstract theory.

Hard as it is to get the details right in any one field, culture, or period, it is harder still to get them right in several. Still, I believe one ought to try to get as many of the details right as possible—in several fields, if interdisciplinary or ethnocritical work is properly to be pursued at home, and in foreign fields as well. For all the difficulties of the ethnocritical position, I continue to think that boundary-crossing with care, self-positioning, as I have said, at the various frontiers of historical and cultural encounter, in the interest of questioning the culture that constitutes one's "self," remains foremost among nontrivial options for cultural critics today.

7

The lines that one speaks of as marking frontiers, borders, boundaries, fields, and disciplines are very often considered to be real and tangible in their existence, not merely figures of speech. *As* a figure, however, the line and, in particular, its adjectival form, linear, have been used to provide generalized images for what are said to be typically Western ways of constructing reality. Western lines and linearity have then been set against the circles and circularity that are, figuratively, supposedly descriptive of the Native American worldview. Having argued the case against the logic of opposition as useful for cultural analysis, I want now to argue against what I will call the metaphorics of opposition. My aim is further to undo manichean types of cultural representation, here, in their specifically figural form.

There is an abundant available history of metaphorical representation of the Western *logos* as linear, most particularly as this linearity is imaged as a chain or a ladder. Arthur O. Lovejoy's 1936 book *The Great Chain of Being* is perhaps still the best study of and along these lines. Generalizations about the Native American metaphysic or mapping of reality, in contrast, propose an apparently pan-Indian epistemology, which, so far as it may be represented, appears in no linear image, but, rather, as one or another type of the circle or circularity. So far as there is an "Indian" worldview, tribal diversities notwithstanding, it would then most appropriately be figured as a wheel (most typically a *medicine* wheel) or hoop (usually a *sacred* hoop). Sacred hoops and medicine wheels, in their seamless curvature, represent the cyclical, no-beginning, no-end, turn-and-turn-again, "mythic" view of reality of Native American peoples, one that can metaphorically be set against the ladderlike view of *arché* and *telos*, hierarchy and progression, of the Western "historical" view.

Thus, as Paula Gunn Allen has written, in an essay revised and reprinted several times, the Native American

circular concept requires that all "points" which make up the sphere of being be significant in their identity and function, while the linear model assumes that some "points" are more significant than others. In the one, significance is significant, and is a necessary factor of being in itself, while in the other, significance is a function of placement on an absolute scale which is fixed in time and space. (In Chapman 116)

She continues:

> In the Native American system, there is no idea that nature is somewhere over there while man is over here, nor that there is a great hierarchical ladder of being on which ground and trees occupy a very low rung, animals a slightly higher one, and man a very high one indeed—especially "civilized" man. (116)

A variant of such a view also appeared in the seventies in the autobiography of the Lakota traditionalist, Lame Deer, in a chapter called—whether by Lame Deer himself or by his editor, Richard Erdoes—"The Circle and the Square." In the late eighties, the Lumbee professor of law, Robert A. Williams, Jr., began a lengthy article "on the cycles of confrontation between white society and American Indian tribalism," in particular "the structural similarities . . . between the early nineteenth-century Removal era and the modern West today" (237), with these sentences:

> As an eastern Indian moved West, I have become more appreciative of the importance of a central theme of all American Indian thought and discourse, the circle. (237)

It is "the importance of the circle in American Indian thought and discourse," Williams continues, which "particularly alerts [him] to many alarming similarities" (238) between the Removal period and the present. Finally, let me mention a recent essay by the German scholar Hartmut

Lutz, called "The Circle as Philosophical and Structural Concept in Native American Fiction Today." What to make of this curious agreement on the part of Western and Native scholars alike concerning the metaphorical disagreement of their respective cultures?

I should first say that from Lovejoy to Allen and after, these figural accounts of—in a phrase from George Lakoff and Mark Johnson to which I will return in chapter 6—the metaphors Europeans and Indians "live by" seem to me generally accurate—at least insofar as the Native American's worldview is determined by its material base in the seasonal/cyclical rhythms of the agriculturalist's and the hunter's perspective, and the Western Euramerican's worldview is determined by the arbitrary, strictly conventional rhythms of first an industrial and, now, a postindustrial society of consumption, information, and representational exchange. For the Native American situation, Carter Revard's astute comment that "We might well be cautious about generalizing too far, but we should not shiver inside unnecessarily narrow limits either" (92) seems to me very much to the point. And yet, for all its importance to current Indian critics and scholars, the metaphorical allegory of opposition, like its logical counterpart, seems to me devoid of any but the most general explanatory usefulness.

Just as Sam Gill's recent *Mother Earth: An American Story* has shown that only at an extremely high level of generalization can it be said that Native American people traditionally viewed the earth as their "mother"—something that is also taken, by now, as a virtual truism among Indians and non-Indians—so, too, only at an extremely high level of generalization might it be said that circles are, in Robert Williams's formulation, "a central theme of all

American Indian thought and discourse" (237). It is my suspicion that just as Native people and whites equally came to accept as useful to their mutual and antagonistic purposes what Tecumseh (in Sam Gill's analysis) and, later, Seathl (in Rudolf Kaiser's analysis)[25] may not ever have said, in the same way, both Native and non-Native scholars have been avid to generalize the Plains camp circle, tipi shape, and medicine wheel as providing a master trope governing the thought of all Indian peoples.

As Allen, whose background is Laguna, must certainly know, Pueblo people do not live in round houses—although, to be sure, the shape of the kiva is round (but, then, Hopis dance in lines as well as circles). Robert Williams currently works in Pima and Papago (Tohono o'odham) country and these tribal peoples' dwellings were not and are not circular. (Although as an eastern Indian, and so—I merely guess here—one closer to economies that are currently somewhat further away from hunting and agriculture, he may well have been impressed by Hopi and Papago economic rhythms.) Neither are Navajo blankets and rugs round; the most prized of these—highly valued, I mean to say, by the weavers themselves as well as by their Indian and non-Indian owners—have linear designs worked into them. And what of the Iroquois, people of the Longhouse? Their wampum belts and strings, it should be noted, are not worn in a circle around the waist or neck, but may depend vertically or extend horizontally. And so on. One might also go on to point out that if Euramericans square dance they also circle round their partners, and ring-

---

25. See Kaiser's "Chief Seattle's Speech(es): American Origins and European Reception."

around-a-rosy, and so on and on. (And, historically, European agricultural economies, at least, were undoubtedly quite "cyclical" in orientation.)

But let me repeat: none of this is to deny that if one *had* to choose a single image to figure the reality-construction of Westerners and Native people, lines for the former and circles for the latter *would*, indeed, be the best choice. (And, once again, partly because even in today's world most Indian communities are a good deal closer to seasonal cycles than most Euramerican communities.) The point is that one does *not* have to choose. Just as reliance upon the manichean logic of civilized/savage, lettered/unlettered, or its victimist revision as biological/anthropological, primary/secondary, etc., imposes a hierarchy that both hurts people and constrains understanding, so, too, does reliance on manichean metaphorics. Further, by imposing totalized stereotypes that insist not merely upon the difference but the opposition of the images invoked, such a reliance threatens to doom Native Americans and Euramericans to repeat the past. If lines and circles can meet only *tangentially*, a figural or geometric imperative acting, as it were, in the place of fate, then frontier encounters between the peoples submitted to that fate must continue to be marked by misunderstanding and conflict.

Yet, as I have said, both Indians and non-Indians who participate in American, academic, critical culture seem to have a deep-seated attachment to metaphors of this kind, and so for all my sense that explanations in terms of hoops and lines, and the like, are both potentially dangerous and, as well, essentially helpless before the complex facts of Native American and Western cultural diversity, I will nonetheless take the time to suggest ways in which these figures might be construed so that they would be capable of relations to one another that are not merely oppositional or tangential. Consider what follows as an ethnocritical exercise in subjunctivity.

If it were the case that these figures could effectively be deployed for explanatory purposes, *then* it might be noted that inasmuch as a line is a potentially infinite series of points, it could not strictly be said that lines have beginnings and endings, but only that segments of lines do. Nor are lines always straight; one definition of the line is "a continuous extent of length, *straight or curved*" (Random House Dictionary, my emphasis). Lines, thus, need not be seen as necessarily the opposites of circles, but, rather, they may be seen as parts of circles, the line as *arc* ("any unbroken part of the circumference of a circle *or other curved line*" [R. H. Dictionary, my emphasis])—or like a chain arranged in a *loop*. I will not pursue this *line* of reasoning, which courts a certain *circular* logic, any further just here. In the realm of metaphor, as in the realm of speech and culture, differential interaction may be proposed both as more "realistic" and as politically more egalitarian than oppositional conflict.

8

An adequate ethnocriticism for Native American culture, history, and literature, so far as it may be established at all, I have argued, will not come about by means of a monolithic orientation to hoops and wheels, and ladders and lines, nor to dichotomized references to "biological" or "anthropological" conceptualizations of reality, and the like. Rather, such a criticism, which does not yet exist and, to repeat, may never fully exist in other than tentative, oxymoronic, or catachrestical forms, will only be achieved by means of complex interactions between a variety of Western discursive and analytic modes and a variety of non-Western modes of knowing and understanding. The Western modes are quite well known, and I continue to think that, in spite of some inevitable distortions, they are still, at least in some measure, useful for an encounter with Native American literary materials—more so, of course, for the written than the oral. Native modes of knowing and understanding are not well known, and that is in large measure because they have not been formulated *as* analytic or critical modes *apart* from the verbal performances they would know and understand. This is something I directly address in chapter 5 of this book.

Traditional Indian expression has many stories about stories, about aspects of language, about various words and phrases. But there are no traditional essays on the nature of language, no rule-governed explicit definitions of the various genres of oral performance, and the like. This is not, of course, to suggest a deficiency or lack, only a difference. Just as, according to Clyde Dollar (see p. 16), modern Brulé Sioux consider the "pursuit of data and facts on which to build veracity in history . . . rather pointless, perhaps ludicrous (D. Tyler 1), so, too, have Native people sometimes considered the questions ethnographers ask about why they sing or tell a song or story this, that, or the other way, and why they begin and end with certain words, and so on, rather pointless, perhaps ludicrous. (It should also be noted, however, that Native people have many times themselves become fascinated by such questions and pursued them in rich and ingenious ways.) But what might be called an "indigenous" criticism for Indian literatures remains to be worked out. Until it is worked out—and there is, as again I note below, no guarantee that it *can* or even *should* be worked out—the adequacy of the ethnocriticism I have envisioned must remain at an early stage of development. Thus it cannot help but be the case that the essays in ethnocriticism I offer in the pages to follow, my own limitations aside, will be marked by this incipiency, liminality, and indeed, paradoxicality. Still, one must begin somewhere; and I hope these particular beginnings may prove of use—not only for the understanding of Native American culture, history, and literature, in themselves and in relation to the dominant culture, but perhaps as well for other frontier or border analyses.

PART I

Into each life, it is said, some rain must fall. Some people have bad horoscopes, others take tips on the stock market. . . . But Indians have been cursed above all other people in history. Indians have anthropologists.

—VINE DELORIA, JR.

—

It wasn't that long ago, you know, that the average Cheyenne family had five people in it: the mother, the father, two kids, and an anthropologist.

—LANCE HENSON

1. ETHNOGRAPHY

AND LITERATURE:

A History of Their Convergence

I

"For the first time in the long and fruitful relationship between literature and science," David Porush writes, "literature actually has the means to meet science on its own territory in a contest concerning which epistemological activity does a better job of telling the truth" (373). The context for this "contest" is "postmodernism." For Porush, "*literary postmodernism* and *scientific postmodernism* [are best seen as] two aspects of a single enterprise" (376–7), an "enterprise," moreover, in which currently the balance has tipped in literature's direction. This is because, as Porush continues,

> First, postmodernism places the self-conscious activities of the human observer/scientist/teller—and consequently the making of narratives—in the center of things. Second, postmodernism stresses the paradoxical power of structures of information and codes. That is, while the postmodern position states that *codes create reality*, postmodernism does not trust codes to tell the whole truth. . . . they do a good job of delivering information, but they are less successful at capturing an underlying inexpressible, inchoate, silent realm where meaning resides. (377)

As Rorty and others have cheerfully submitted philosophy to literature, finding it advantageous for one reason or another to abandon the hopes—as I have said above—of a variety of logics and dialectics to the situation of an all-pervasive person- and occasion-governed rhetoric—so, now, Porush will bring science into (what he understands as) literature's empire. I will only a little worry the question of what "truth" can possibly mean in comments like these.[1] For if one really does believe that *"codes create reality,"* it is difficult to see how "truth" would be an operative term at all. How could such a view establish criteria for determining "which epistemological activity does a *better* job of telling the truth" (373, my emphasis), or for distinguishing "the *whole* truth" (377, my emphasis) from what James Clifford calls "partial [truths]—committed and incomplete?" (1986 7) "Truth" for Porush predictably elides to "meaning," but even so, it may be worth noting that, so far as literary aspirations in these regards are concerned, *secular* literature has only occasionally (and mostly from the latter eighteenth century forward) been interested in incursions into "underlying inexpressible, inchoate, silent realm[s]," in the interest of "capturing"—but I must here remark the belligerently imperial nature of Porush's discourse—the transcodal, as it were—for all that literature's capacity successfully to colonize such "realm[s]"—may currently be more attractive to "scientists" than it has heretofore been.

Porush does not question the premise that "meaning resides" in the "underlying . . . silent realm" he posits, sim-

---

1. Or how a phrase like "the *center* of things" could be meaningful. As many have repeatedly noted, epistemological radicals cannot attack the language and categories they wish to discredit without employing that language and those categories. This is something Derrida admitted as far back as 1966, at Johns Hopkins, in his paper, "Structure, Sign, and Play in the Discourse of the Human Sciences."

ply taking it as axiomatic that whatever we may mean by meaning does, in point of fact, live *there*. But his assumption, which I would characterize as a turn to mystico-religious and away from secular perspectives, is no doubt shared by many today in the context of postmodernism. Porush's reference to "literature and science" as "*epistemological* activit[ies]" (my emphasis) goes a ways toward explaining why it is that many of the social scientific workers called ethnographers have, of late, become particularly interested in literature. (Literary people have become interested in what the ethnographers do, as well—but less so.)

An obvious starting point for the current convergence is Clifford Geertz's self-interrogation of 1973. Asking, what does the ethnographer do? Geertz answered, he writes.[2] (I assume *she* does, too.) If it is indeed writing that is the ethnographer's central or preeminent activity, then clearly it is to the practice and product of that activity that we must attend, to its "signature" or individual author-specific nature, as Geertz would further state, and its "discourse" or style-specific nature (1988 9). Thus in 1982 we have the publication of an essay by Dick Cushman and George Marcus called "Ethnographies as Texts." Here, Cushman and Marcus, with all the excitement of Molière's *bourgeois gentilhomme* discovering that he has been speaking *prose* all his life, recognized that ethnographies were, indeed, texts, and that therefore "rhetorical analysis is prior to an evaluation of truth claims [the ostensible priority of "science"] because explanation and theory building cannot escape the rhetoric of the language in which they are expressed" (56n).

This implicit acknowledgment of a necessary attention to literary matters came more then fifteen years after Roland

2. See "Thick Description: Toward an Interpretive Theory of Culture," p. 19.

Barthes, Jacques Derrida, and Jacques Lacan, among others, at a Johns Hopkins University conference,[3] had announced to the Americans that just about everything was
texte. And it came nine years after Hayden White's *Metahistory* had denied the possibility of *any* "truth claims" in the
writing of history, so far as these might be evaluated according to more or less agreed-upon standards of verifiabil-
ity or falsifiability. For White, there simply could be no
objectively valid "truth claims" in a discipline like history,
or, for that matter, in a discipline like ethnography "not yet
reduced (or elevated) to the status of a genuine science
[e.g., with agreed upon definitions and quantifiable data,
where] . . . truth remains the captive of the linguistic
mode in which it seeks to grasp the outline of objects in-
habiting its field of perception" (1973 xi). This subordina-
tion of logical and empirical operations to the rhetorical,
for White, meant that we were constrained to base our acceptance or rejection of any social scientific account whatever on strictly esthetic or moral grounds, for "there are no
apodictically certain theoretical grounds on which one can
legitimately claim an authority for any one of the [possible
modes of historiography] . . . over the others as being
more 'realistic' " (1973 xii), that is to say, more scientific. As
White puts it in the epigraph (from Roland Barthes) to his
most recent book, *"Le fait n'a jamais qu'une existence lin-
guistique"*: a fact never has anything but linguistic existence
(1987 n.p.). It should be noted here that the epistemology
of science all these writers use—perhaps unconsciously, or
perhaps strictly for polemical purposes—is essentially a
Newtonian or "realistic"/positivistic one. The relativistic

3. This is the conference alluded to in note 1. The proceedings were published
in 1972 as *The Structuralist Controversy: The Languages of Criticism and the
Sciences of Man*.

paradigms of Einsteinian/Heisenbergian science of the 1920s, the response to relativist science in the cybernetic revolution of the 1940s, and the various ongoing projects of postmodernist science, all go unmentioned.

Fully aware of the radical, or as the poststructural theorists of the period would (cheerfully enough) say, the *abysmal* implications of White's confinement of history to the "prison house of language"—a full-blown postmodernist move—Cushman and Marcus referred their readers to "sources of literary criticism that might be useful to a perspective on ethnographic writing," among these the work of Barthes, Derrida, Michel Foucault, and Raymond Williams. (But Williams's insights, it seems to me, would not easily be consistent with those of his cited French contemporaries.) And Cushman and Marcus briefly surveyed what they called "Ethnographic Writing Experiments" (58) as these seemed to mark a dissatisfaction with what they called "realist ethnography."

In 1986, Marcus, now with James Clifford, used the etymology of the word ethnography itself for the title of their coedited book of essays titled *Writing Culture: The Poetics and Politics of Ethnography*. Although the tone of the introduction and in some of the contributors' essays tends to be one of dismissing or, at least, of passing beyond Geertz, still, the editors and contributors essentially develop and expand upon the implications of Geertz's determination that what is central to ethnographic practice is ultimately the textualization of interpretations deriving from particular experiences/encounters. In 1987, we have the publication of *Anthropology as Cultural Critique* by Marcus, once again, and Michael Fischer, which, among its many inadequately theorized assertions and recommendations, turns to the Russian Formalist critics of literature of the early part of this century, and takes their central concept, *ostranenie*, translated usually as *defamiliarization* or, simply, *making strange*, as authorizing experimentation and innovation in the writing of ethnography—a practice that might or might not (Marcus and Fischer are curiously timid radicals, in these regards, as Marcus and Cushman were earlier) turn ethnographic writing from its traditional status as a "document of the occult" to an "occult document." I have referred once again, here, to the title of Stephen Tyler's essay in *Writing Culture*, one that defines the postmodern project of ethnography as indeed a shift from the production of documents of the occult to the production of occult documents.

Such documents—they would be conformable to Porush's enthusiasms—would subsume all claims to "scientific" realism or "truth" to an essentially "literary" evocativeness. In Tyler's words, a postmodernist ethnography "*describes* no knowledge and *produces* no action," instead transcending these "by *evoking* what cannot be known discursively or performed perfectly." This "Evocation," for Tyler, "is neither presentation nor representation;" it is "beyond truth and immune to the judgment of performance" (123). Occult document to be sure: for if one is to take Tyler seriously, ethnography's postmodern move beyond science (again, a science that is a straw man, one whose positivistic paradigm has long since been abandoned in theory, if not always in practice) here passes beyond all literature except that which specifically attempts to give voice to the mystico-religious "silent realm" of the inexpressible, and inchoate—which, indeed, in David Porush's account, the postmodernist scientist also values.

Of course, by 1973 and 1982, my points of beginning for this subject, a great many other developments had already occurred to prepare the current convergence of ethnographic and literary concerns. No account of this subject ought leave out the extraordinary conference held at Indiana University in 1958, which brought together anthropologists like the young Dell Hymes and Conrad Voegelin, literary critics of international reputation like René Wellek, I. A. Richards, and William Wimsatt, and, of course, linguists like Roman Jakobson, and Thomas Sebeok of Indiana's Research Center in Anthropology, Folklore, and Linguistics. The volume of papers from the conference edited by Sebeok and published in 1960 contained the influential "Concluding Statement" by Jakobson titled "Linguistics and Poetics." In it, Jakobson called for collaboration between the linguist and the literary critic, a call not for the estheticization of science, but, to the contrary, for a certain scientization of literature. Only two years later, Jakobson would collaborate with an old friend, none other than Claude Lévi-Strauss, on an analysis of Charles Baudelaire's sonnet, "Les Chats." The essay was published in the French journal, *L'Homme*. In introducing their essay, the authors acknowledged that

> It will perhaps be found surprising that a review of anthropology should publish a study devoted to a French poem of the XIXth century. Yet the explanation is simple. A linguist and an ethnologist decided to combine their efforts in an attempt to understand the creation of a Baudelairian sonnet, because they had found themselves independently confronted by complementary problems. (In DeGeorge and DeGeorge 125)

These "problems," of course, seemed amenable to solution by the methods of what was called structuralism, methods that, at least for a time, appeared useful equally to linguists, literary critics, and ethnologists. Lévi-Strauss's use of these methods for the study of myth, and, as well, his apparent willingness to intermix such seemingly disparate genres as autobiography and ethnography in texts like *Tristes Tropiques*, appealed for obvious enough reasons to literary critics. One reason for the appeal of linguistic and ethnographic structuralism, such as it was, to American literary critics was a certain fatigue with New Critical textual explication, the dominant critical paradigm from the latter twenties into the fifties.

There is no doubt that the New Criticism, whatever else it did or didn't do, taught generations of American students of literature to *read* carefully, and to find citable bases in the language of a poem (more rarely of a story or novel) for what E. D. Hirsch, by 1960, was calling its "meaning." It did little, however, to help the critic determine the "significance"—I again cite Hirsch, who attributes his understanding of the distinction between "meaning" and "significance" to Husserl—of that meaning.[4] For help in that regard, prior to the appearance of structuralism (which, indeed, offered no help at all in these regards), the alternatives to New Critical close reading were Northrop Frye's version of myth criticism, announced in *The Anatomy of Criticism*, in 1957, and a variety of contextualist, historicist approaches, either Leavisite or more homegrown. (I am thinking of the work of Roy Harvey Pearce and a number of Americanists, particularly.) The first of these seemed to lead directly to religion, the second to sociology, or even—dreaded fate—to *politics*. (This is, recall, the late fifties and

4. See Hirsch's "Introduction: Meaning and Significance," to his *The Aims of Interpretation*.

earlier sixties.) No wonder, then, that imported linguistic and anthropological structuralism might be appealing.

So appealing that Susan Sontag, in 1966, could call her essay examining Lévi-Strauss's early work, "The Anthropologist as Hero." What Sontag did not like about Lévi-Strauss's work, interestingly enough, was its refusal to relinquish claims to some kind of scientific status—a status Frye's own system most certainly courted. Throughout the fifties and sixties, I would suggest, there was an ambivalence—reactions, that is, of attraction and repulsion—on the part of literary people to science, but a clearly growing attraction to literature (with a concomitant rejection of science) on the part of social scientists.

Thus, for the student of literature in the sixties there were a number of anthropologist heroes—or at least ethnographers who worked in ways that (themselves influenced by literary study) appeared congenial to literary critics. I will mention only Victor Turner's dramatistic and performative studies of ritual, and Clifford Geertz's exposition, essay by essay, of an interpretive ethnography, anthropology as "thick description," in the phrase Geertz took from the philosopher Gilbert Ryle. By 1973, in "Thick Description: Toward an Interpretive Theory of Culture," Geertz could explicitly announce, "The concept of culture I espouse . . . is essentially a semiotic one . . . and the analysis of it to be therefore not an experimental science in search of law but an interpretive one in search of meaning. It is explication I am after" (5). It is one of the ironies of anthropology's recent history in America, I suppose, that Geertz should specifically criticize, for his espousal of an "ethnoscience, componential analysis, or cognitive anthropology" (1973 11) still "in search of law," none other than

Stephen Tyler, whose attraction to a transcendent and evocative ethnography has all the passion of a recent conversion.

Of course Tyler, in his earlier enthusiasm for truth and law in anthropology, along with a number of other ethnoscientists or philosophers of the social sciences such as May Brodbeck,[5] was only carrying forward a call to make anthropology a bona fide science that was little more than a half-century old. And as these people did so, in the fifties, they encountered what I have remarked in Geertz, a strong reaction against claims to science and law in anthropology and a turn to semiotics, hermeneutics, and interpretation. This, to repeat, occurred at exactly the moment when literary people themselves became fascinated by semiotics, hermeneutics, and interpretation, most particularly of a structuralist sort—which, paradoxically enough, they partly valued for the scientific authority or at least the scientific aura structuralist methods appeared to bestow on literary studies. To employ Raymond Williams's useful terms once more, we have a curious mix of "residual," "emergent," and "dominant" values, where "science," as I believe, is the dominant disciplinary value of the period, and where (vaguely defined) esthetic values—"thickness" in description serving to indicate what once (as we shall see just below) had been called "atmosphere," and which would in our time be called evocativeness—have both a residual and emergent function. This would help explain the appeal of the Canadian Frye and the Frenchman Lévi-Strauss to Americans, inasmuch as both of them invoke scientific categories (for literary criticism and ethnographic explanation) while privileging the study of myth. It would help explain as well the

5. See the large volume edited by Brodbeck called *Readings in the Philosophy of the Social Sciences.*

attraction to semiotics on the part of literary people, for whom this study appears to be far more scientific in its methodology than anything they are used to, while for social scientists, it seems to open the door to interpretive/explicative rather than explanatory results.

I will only add that these disciplinary developments occur in the context of independence movements in the colonized worlds of Africa and Southeast Asia, movements which present the most direct sorts of challenges to "scientific" models of knower and known as epistemological justification for the maintenance of differential power relations, and in the context of American post-Sputnik anxiety, spurring aggressive hard-scientism in the most traditional mode. More needs to be said about both of these, apparently contradictory, developments. Nonetheless, I will, with all necessary, if inadequate, apologies, turn to a more distant history—and an essentially cultural rather than materio-political history.

2

Inasmuch as the term literature, from Latin, *littera*, letter, for years in the West referred to whatever information a given culture wished to preserve and transmit by the technology of writing, it might be said that ethno-*graph*-y in its earliest manifestations was inevitably a part of literature. Thus, there was a time when all who were literate, who knew their letters, knew also the Latin of Caesar's account of the tripartite nature of Gaul and his descriptions of the Gauls themselves. It seems reasonable to say that in one form or another, ethnography most certainly existed in the classical period. Indeed, Tacitus's *De Germania*, a study of Teuton people appearing in the year 98 of the Common Era was, as one writer has called it, a political ethnography, for

Tacitus was concerned about the threat that restlessness among the Germans might pose to the Empire's borders. If one wished to show anthropology's relation—perhaps an inevitable, most certainly a very longstanding relation—to imperialism, one could easily begin with Tacitus. (But Tacitus, like Thucydides, was also in some measure offering a criticism of the direction his own society was taking; so if his name may signal an early instance of imperial anthropology it may also signal an early instance of "anthropology as cultural critique.")

Although all writing, almost until the latter eighteenth century, was, as I have said, nominally literature, there did nonetheless exist a distinction between what was then called poetry—or *poesie*—the term for imaginative and affective writing (literature) and the discourses, most particularly, of history and philosophy. That epistemological distinctions among these types of writing were, or ought to be, clear and well-defined does not seem to have been nearly so important to ancient thought as it was to become later. In Foucault's useful terms, it was not so much whether statements were true ("scientific"), *vrai*, but whether they were *dans le vrai*, whether they met the appropriate conditions, epistemologically but also socially—"discursively"—to be taken seriously as making "truth claims." The operative distinction was not between truth (e.g., real, scientific, actual, empirically verifiable, etc.) and fiction (made up, invented, wished, dreamed, imagined, etc.) but, rather, between truth and error; rudely, to mix Foucault with Lévi-Strauss, between what was thinkable or "good to think" as opposed to *impensable*. At least until the late Renaissance, the blurring of genres that Geertz has remarked upon as particularly a development of our time was more nearly the rule than the exception.

Thus the "voyage narratives" of the sixteenth century re-
counting European explorations of the New World, are an
extraordinary mix of "ethnography" and "literature," of
what probably appears to the modern reader as careful observation and description—the truth—on the one hand,
and of the wildest assertions, which, from our present perspective, couldn't possibly be true. Yet what strikes us as
inevitably "poetical" or fantastic imaginings in these texts—
encounters with people ten feet tall, with four arms, or
breathing fire—are also offered on the "ethnographic authority," in James Clifford's justly celebrated phrase, of the
author's own experience, an experience which, for all our
conviction that it "couldn't really have been that way," by
conforming to the epistemic assumptions of its age, may
perfectly well present "truth claims." (Hence the logic of
the Church's rejection of Galileo's "discovery" of sun spots,
and the refusal to accept an invitation to look through the
glass and "see for oneself" as in any way relevant to the
subject at hand.) There were enough of these narratives by
the latter sixteenth century to spur the Reverend Richard
Hakluyt—for purposes, it should be noted, that were not
strictly those of a disinterested curiosity—to begin editing
and collating them, a task taken up, after Hakluyt's death,
by the Reverend Samuel Purchas, who published his massive *Hakluytus Posthumus, or Purchas His Pilgrimes* in
1625. As Mary Louise Pratt has recently shown (1986),[6] the
mix of personal "narration" and cultural "description" established in these narratives continues to shape the presen-
tational strategies of ethnographies from early in the twentieth century up to the present, for all that they operate
with different epistemic premises than their predecessors;

6. See "Fieldwork in Common Places."

for all that, at least until the current postmodern reaction, they might claim to see things "as they really were," scientifically, realistically, and so on.

Responses to the seventeenth-century voyage narratives prompted what may be the earliest, or at least they are the best known, enunciations of what we would now call positions of cultural relativism and cultural absolutism or evolutionism, and both are by authors firmly established as "literary." I refer, first, to Michel de Montaigne, whose celebrated essay on the cannibals rhetorically asks how a people who punish by use of the rack and execute by drawing and quartering (this latter practice seized upon by Foucault for the beginning of his *Discipline and Punish*) can denounce as "primitive" those who merely eat their slain enemies. And I refer to William Shakespeare, whose play *The Tempest*, known to have been performed in 1611, anagrammatizes the term cannibal for the character of Caliban, who is presented as man in the state of nature, a filthy, lustful brute, far inferior to the cultivated human products of civilization.[7]

Perhaps the first self-conscious attempts to separate literature and ethnography, rigorously to distinguish between art and science, the imagined and the real, fact and fiction occur in the eighteenth century. Broadly speaking, these define science in the ways we continue to know it best, in terms of its commitment to sequential ratiocinative steps, quantitative and methodological documentation, and to procedures that are at least theoretically replicable. This is to say that although the observer's unique personal experience could convey upon her account a certain *ontological*

7. On Montaigne and Shakespeare, see Eric Cheyfitz, *The Poetics of Imperialism . . .* , in particular, chapter 7, "Eloquent Cannibals."

authority—the *être là*, or simple fact of her "being there"—
its *scientific* (epistemological) authority would depend precisely upon the absence of its uniqueness; had others been
there, they would have seen and concluded the same. To
offer a single, well-known American example, I will mention Thomas Jefferson's celebrated reply, in his *Notes on the
State of Virginia*, published in the latter 1780s, to the
Comte de Buffon, concerning the "productions mineral,
vegetable, and animal" of the New World. In this text, Jefferson refuses to speak of anything he has not seen himself—and he invites other interested parties to come and
see for themselves. It is not the richness of his deductive
powers that is to be celebrated but, as it were, the richness
of the material itself—material, he is proud to imply, that
is peculiar to America.

This is hardly an adequate account of Jefferson as
naturalist-scientist. I mean my few words to indicate the
way in which, from Jefferson forward, America will stand as
one of the world's foremost laboratories for anthropological
science, a science Americans proceed to establish upon the
basis of detailed first-hand study of the Indian. Through the
nineteenth century, in the researches of Cadwallader Col-
den, and, particularly, of Henry Rowe Schoolcraft, a massive amount of information (some of it accurate, some of it
not) on the languages and cultures of Native peoples began
to be assembled, culminating, from the middle of the nineteenth century forward, in the work of Lewis Henry
Morgan.

Morgan was an amateur or freelancer, a retired lawyer
inspired by enthusiasm and a growing curiosity; he was not,
that is, like the older voyager, or missionary, or entrepre-
neurial writer, an ethnographer only as an accident of his
employment by a church or government, a land sale or fur-

trading company. Morgan might, therefore, claim for his work the sort of disinterestedness that was to become one of the cornerstones of the new commitment to objectivity and science in American ethnography toward the end of the nineteenth century. Thus, those like James Mooney who did work for interested parties—government agencies or the great museums—still could demonstrate their commitment to science by the suppression of subjective commentary of an ethical or esthetic nature, by the assemblage of massive quantities of detail observed firsthand, and by a tone or rhetorical stance in their published texts that confirmed the distance between themselves and the subjects of their researches. It seems to me that it is a failure or a refusal to respect most of these criteria that still makes Frank Hamilton Cushing, for example, a rather enigmatic figure in the history of American ethnography. (David Murray's *Forked Tongues* has much to say about this—as it does about translation, autobiography, and other matters I discuss. Murray's fine book appeared while this one was in press so that, except for this parenthesis, I do not make reference to it.)

A fuller account of these matters than I can give here is to be found in such volumes as the 1974 Proceedings of the American Ethnological Society edited by John Murra and called *American Anthropology: The Early Years*; in the studies of Regna Darnell; in Robert Bieder's *Science Encounters the Indian*; and in George Stocking's masterful *Victorian Anthropology.*[8] What cannot be left out, of course, is the advent of Franz Boas, whose name—probably more accurately than not (for all that I interrogate the nature of

8. For Darnell's work, see Works Cited.

Boas's contribution to anthropology as a science in the chapter that follows)—is synonymous with the scientization of anthropology, according to a largely positivistic model intended to parallel if not quite mirror the meaning of science in pre-Einsteinian physics. Of course, in the years of Boas's mature production, Einsteinian relativism (if not Heisenbergian uncertainty) was very much part of the intellectual climate, and cultural relativism was from the first a cornerstone of the Boasian program. But I see not so much as a hint of epistemological relativism among the Boasians. This is yet another subject I can only glance at here. Suffice it to say that Boas's privileging of fieldwork over library work; his insistence upon some fair degree of competence in the language of his or her "people" on the part of the ethnographer; his rejection of the broadly deductive generalizations indulged in by the evolutionist practitioners of the so-called "comparative method," in favor of an inductive, particularist, and rigorously relativist method: all of these were linked to attaching to ethnographic work the authority of the hard sciences.

The scientization of ethnography under Boas paralleled its professionalization as this was directly linked to its academicization, its institutionalization, in the University. Boas, to be sure, began his career with the Berlin museum and had associations in this country with the Field and the American museums, but his enormous influence is directly associated with his almost half-century-long tenure (1896–1942) at Columbia University—during which time the government ethnologists (particularly in the Bureau of American Ethnology under Major John Wesley Powell) and the museum ethnologists declined in influence. Only Clark Wissler, so far as I know, was both a Boasian and a "museum man." By 1926, as George Stocking has noted, every academic department of anthropology in the United States was headed by one of Boas's students.[9]

Now, for all that was gained by the linkage of anthropological professionalism and anthropological academism in the name, to be sure, of anthropological science, there was one important loss, the consideration of which will bring us back to literature. I mean to point to the fact that the professionalization and academicization of anthropology were achieved at some cost to what I will simply call its public significance and utility. Most of the collections made by the museum anthropologists were, after all, available for public viewing; the ethnographic data gathered by the anthropologists attached to the government bureaus were available for use in making public policy. And, with whatever qualifications we might want to add, Americans did actually go to the museums, did actually feel the government was in some substantial measure "theirs."[10] But to whom did the data gathered by the Columbia University anthropology department belong? Of what use was it to anyone but the academic anthropologist and his or her students, a number of whom would themselves perhaps become anthropologists, and study and teach, turn and turn again. It is exactly the success of anthropological science in achieving the status of disinterested professionalism that threatens to render it trivial or irrelevant. The issue to be addressed here is not epistemological so much as sociopolitical. Boasian social scientists, as I shall have further occasion to explain in the following essay, are secure, or, at the least, highly optimistic

9. See *Race, Culture, and Evolution* . . . , p. 296.

10. A fascinating account of the ideology of the organization of museum exhibits is to be found in Donna Haraway's "Teddy Bear Patriarchy: Taxidermy in the Garden of Eden, New York City, 1908–36."

about the anthropologist's ability to arrive at the scientific truth; what they decently wonder about is the social uses of such truth.

Two sorts of response to the problem of academic anthropology and social significance seem to have developed. One was given in Boas's own citizenly practice. For although Boas pretty thoroughly avoided the statement of theoretical implications or the suggestion of practical applications in the vast majority of his published work, some of that work vigorously deployed scientific findings to combat, for example, racism and anti-Semitism in American society. Boas believed in the public role of the academic, professional scientist; he wrote letters to editors, and spoke out on behalf of his beliefs and principles, never *as* a scientist—for Boas took for granted, in a way I think we cannot any longer, the value-free nature of science—but always as a citizen informed by science. Academic anthropology, then, could show the way toward a more clear-sighted society, founded upon the best modern scientific information rather than upon ancient prejudice. The career of Margaret Mead, Boas's student, may, in the future, remain most interesting to us precisely as developing this line of response; that is to say, whatever the academic-scientific status of Mead's data from Samoa, the social force of her prescriptions ostensibly based upon that data was substantial.

Another sort of response to the separation of academic science from public significance came in the attempt on the part of some anthropologists to engage the interest of an audience not strictly professional by attempting literary forms of writing, couching some of their observations about Native people and cultures in autobiographies elicited from them, and, most particularly, in fictional narratives about those cultures and people. Whatever the philosophical in-

fluences on Boas's thought and on that of his students, I
believe that the view of literature they had would have in-
clined them toward the traditional capacity of literature to
provoke the reader to moral imagination, and thence to
moral action. They would not, if I am at all correct, have
seen the function of literature as merely to entertain or
amuse, not even to put one transcendentally in touch with
the "beautiful." If this is so, then the esthetic of the Boasian
milieu would have been as old-fashioned as its epistemology, for—as I shall have further occasion to note—it would
be based upon romantic-realistic perspectives at just the
moment when these were being abandoned for modernist
perspectives. To say this, I hope it is clear, is not to say that
either the esthetic or the epistemology was hopelessly mistaken. Fuller biographical work on Boas, Radin, and Kroeber is necessary to determine whether the speculative intuitions I have offered are more accurate than not.

As early as 1913, Paul Radin, of the first generation of
Boas's students, had published "The Personal Reminiscences of a Winnebago Indian"; this was followed by "The
Autobiography of a Winnebago Indian" in 1920. In the introduction to that text, Radin noted that "For a long time
most ethnologists have realized that the lack of 'atmosphere'
in their descriptions is a very serious and fundamental defect," a defect, according to Radin, that "could only be properly remedied by having a native himself give an account of
his particular culture" (1920 1)—which account, to be sure,
would be edited and actually published by the anthropologist. But Radin had published both "The Personal Reminiscences" and "The Autobiography" in scholarly journals, not
the best way to reach a broad audience. Accordingly, he
revised and expanded the 1920 "Autobiography," composed
an introduction which began with the acknowledgment that

"the common-sense man, the man in the street, has always been good-naturedly skeptical of the academically trained scholar" (xv), and published it as *Crashing Thunder: The Autobiography of an American Indian* in 1926 with the commercial publisher D. Appleton and Company of New York.[11] Although Boas himself, late in his life, was to deny the scientific usefulness of Indian autobiographies, noting them as good only for documenting "the perversion of truth by memory" (1943 335), a great many anthropological life histories continued to be recorded.

The other important linkage of ethnography and literature I want to mention comes through what I will call ethnographic fiction, a literary genre with ostensibly wider public appeal than the (developing) genres of professional ethnography. Here the example of Adolph Bandelier's novel *The Delight Makers*, published in 1890, serves as an important precursor. In his preface, Bandelier wrote that he

was prompted to perform the work by a conviction that however scientific works may tell the truth about the Indian, they exercise always a limited influence upon the general public; and to that public, in our country as well as abroad, the Indian has remained as good as unknown. By clothing sober facts in the garb of romance I have hoped to make the "Truth about the Pueblo Indians" more accessible to the public in general. (xxi)

11. All three autobiographies were based on the life histories of two brothers, whose English surname was Blowsnake. For accounts of Radin's autobiographical work, and his intentional confusion of names and details—his fictionalization, in the interest of science, as it were—see David Brumble's *Annotated Bibliography of American Indian and Eskimo Autobiographies*, and his *American Indian Autobiography*. My foreword and appendix to the reissue of *Crashing Thunder*, as well as my account in *For Those Who Come After*, may also be useful here.

We may compare this statement to that of Boas's student Elsie Clews Parsons, in her preface to a volume she edited in 1922 called *American Indian Life*. In that book, Parsons offered no less than twenty-seven short fictional pieces by professional anthropologists focused on the cultures about which they had formerly published scientific papers. The final text is by Boas himself, his unique attempt, so far as I am aware, at writing fiction. Parsons asks:

> Between these forbidding monographs [by the scientific anthropologists] and the legends of James Fenimore Cooper, what is there to read for a girl . . . or, in fact, for anyone who just wants to know more about Indians? (1)

It was "From these considerations," Parsons explains, that "this book was conceived." Like Bandelier before her, Parsons, like Boas's students generally, firmly adhered to a rigorous separation of literary "legends" from ethnographic "science," while being attracted to the possibility that science might use the novel's (apparently predictable and foreknown!) form and manner for its own purposes, purposes which might, indeed, be "just . . . to know more," for all that I would again propose that knowing more implies doing better. The important thing, as Alfred Kroeber, the first to take a Ph.D. in anthropology with Boas at Columbia, remarked in his introduction to Parsons's book, is to adopt "The method of . . . the historical novel, with emphasis on the history rather than the romance" (Parsons 13). In that introduction, Kroeber went on to praise Bandelier's *Delight Makers*—for all that Bandelier himself referred to his book not as a "historical novel" but as a romance.

What may be interesting to note from the point of view of literary history is that the anthropologists in their elevation of the novel over the "romance" or "legend" as the literary genre most congenial to—although still quite clearly distinguishable from—the realism of their science, are taking positions in a battle that long ago had been won. From somewhere around the time of Henry James's brief study called *Hawthorne*, in 1879, the realistic novel in this country began to take on an authority vastly superior to the romance in American literature. Bandelier's accommodation of his text to the romance is, in this regard, similarly belated; by 1890, romance means Cooper and Longfellow, if not necessarily Hawthorne, as they represent a tradition thoroughly out of fashion in an age ready to admire William Dean Howells, Henry James, and Edith Wharton. And by 1922, when Kroeber indicates his own approbation of the novel over the romance in his introduction to Parsons's book, even the realistic novel is in eclipse; 1922 is the year James Joyce's *Ulysses*, that masterpiece of a modernism bent on subverting the pretensions of realist fiction, was published. But it is also the year Bronislaw Malinowski's *Argonauts of the Western Pacific* was published, a text which has been said to instantiate a "modernist" anthropology, which, here, means a "scientific" anthropology, in line with a largely abandoned realism in the novel (not to say a realist/positivist science that atomic physics with its relativist findings also eclipses). To complicate matters further, we may note that 1922 is also the year T. S. Eliot's "The Waste Land" was published. Eliot's poem owed much to the work of Sir James Frazer—whose particular sort of "armchair anthropology" Malinowskian anthropology supposedly superseded.

This "out-of-phaseness,"[12] as the anthropologist Edwin Ardener has called it, between literature and ethnography,

12. See "Social Anthropology and the Decline of Modernism."

even as literature and ethnography importantly influenced one another all through the twentieth century, currently continues in Marcus and Fischer's turn to the Russian Formalists and to their encouragement of what they (Marcus and Fischer) call modernist experimentation in contemporary ethnographic writing. To call for modernism today is quite as belated as Bandelier's turn to the literary romance or Kroeber's to the historical novel, inasmuch as the experiments of modernism have themselves, for many, become old hat, monumentalized and stultified, so that the genuinely new appears to take form in a postmodernism that is itself already more than two decades old—a postmodernism that may be the continuator of a modernism whose revolutionary potential has been more nearly occluded than ended, for all that most of the present-day ethnographers— Tyler, and others—interested in it have embraced only the postmodern *break* with modernism (see chapter 2).

Not only Parsons, but Ruth Underhill and Ella Cara Deloria, among anthropologists in the Boasian milieu, wrote ethnographic novels, always marking these off, as Boas insisted they could and should be marked, from their truly "scientific" work. Thus in 1939, Underhill published a scientifically proper Papago ethnography, the *Social Organization of Papago Indians*, and followed it, in 1940, with a novel about these people, *Hawk Over Whirlpools*. Deloria, a Dakota from the Yankton Reservation, who had worked with Boas in 1915 and 1928, after a great many years devoted to the scientific study of Dakota language and culture, sometime in the 1940s set to work on the novel that would be called *Waterlily* (1988). According to Raymond De-Mallie, in his afterword to the book, it was Boas and Ruth Benedict who suggested she attempt the work. Other of Boas's students, in particular Ruth Benedict and Edward Sapir, also had a strong penchant for literary work, both of them writing and exchanging poetry (some of which Benedict published under the name of Anne Singleton). Sapir's book of poems, *Dreams and Gibes*, appeared in 1917.

All of those I have named, whatever their attraction to literary pursuits, did keep their art distinct from their scientific pursuits, pursuits which, for the most part, defined their working lives. Nor is it clear whether—or how much—the injunction to keep literature and ethnography, art and science apart caused these second-generation Boasians pain. This is not the case with the last of Boas's students I must mention here, Zora Neale Hurston. Hurston studied with Boas and with Benedict at Barnard College, from which she graduated in 1928. Although she admired "Papa Franz," whom she referred to as the greatest anthropologist alive, Hurston's major was English, not anthropology; and her major achievement came in the writing of literature, not ethnography. Thus a text like Hurston's novel, *Their Eyes Were Watching God*, for all that it is rich in ethnographic detail, could not fairly be categorized strictly as ethnographic fiction—an appropriate enough appellative for *The Delight Makers*, *Hawk Over Whirlpools*, or *Waterlily*, all of which, to be sure, are books I admire. Unlike these latter, Hurston's novel is more nearly modernist in its esthetic—its commitment to verbal and linguistic richness and ingenuity, and a "poetics" very different from realist poetics or prosaics—and in its intentionality, at least partly animated by the concern of her friends associated with the Harlem Renaissance, to show that the "negro" may be the subject of "high" literary culture.

To call *Their Eyes Were Watching God* a "masterpiece" rather than a "mere" example of "ethnographic fiction" would require an excursus on evaluative standards that would take us too far afield just here. Perhaps it may be all right, if not quite adequate, to say that the range of its possible interest to the reader—its portrait of Florida's rural black culture, its version of a highly elaborated vernacular speech with a determinedly poetic narrative style privileging the spoken over the written, and, of course, its questioning of accepted gender relations—qualify it for comparison to the most interesting American novels, and make a strong claim for its inclusion in the canon of American literature.

Even in the ethnography she published, Hurston regularly threatened to collapse what was still seen as the hard-won distinction between science and art. Her *Mules and Men*, a study of southern black folklore published in 1935, was legitimated as "science" thanks to a single-page preface provided by Boas—after he had authenticated all the facts. Hurston's *Tell My Horse*, of 1938, an account of visits to Jamaica and Haiti (where she wrote *Their Eyes Were Watching God*), received no such legitimation—indeed, its manner of proceeding did not permit that—and as a result, as late as 1977, Robert Hemenway, Hurston's first (and, to date, her only) biographer could call *Tell My Horse* Hurston's poorest book. It is exactly this book, however, that seems to me likely to be of special interest to ethnographic and literary theorists. Hurston's persistent discomfort with the stance of detached, scientific, professionally disinterested observation, a stance upon which Boas insisted, now may be seen as contributing to a redefinition of ethnography, one that places it more comfortably in our present moment of ethnographic and literary convergence than in its actual historical moment.

3

The most recent convergence of ethnographic and literary concerns, to return to the point from which I began, does indeed take place within the context of postmodernism. Scientific claims to truth are threatened not only by rhetoric and ideology but by indeterminacy and interconnectedness, these latter two terms reminding us of David Porush's description of the milieu of postmodern science. The Heisenberg indeterminacy principle,[13] it would seem, operates not only at the subatomic levels of physics, but everywhere, with the consequence that even as would-be disinterested observers we inevitably enter into relation with and have effect upon whatever it is that we observe. And now, beyond Heisenberg, there is Bell's Interconnectedness Theorem implying that—I know this only in Porush's account—local operations have nonlocal effects: everything we do and say, perhaps everything we think, alters the universe, an exhilarating or a frightening prospect.

The postmodern perception of a world organized in terms of signal/noise or figure/ground relations that are constantly shifting doesn't only blur genres, as Geertz might have it; rather, as I have several times noted, it blurs epistemological distinctions, asserting a kind of cognitive egalitarianism on the part of literature, ethnography, and even—at least at the highest theoretical level—the physical sciences. This particular sort of equivalence between truth and beauty is not at all of the sort apparently sanctioned by Keats's great lines, " 'Beauty is truth, truth beauty,'—that is all / Ye know on earth, and all ye need to know." For Keats, as indeed for Shelley in his *Defence of Poetry*, the identity of truth and beauty resided not in an equivalence

13. Werner Karl Heisenberg published his indeterminacy principle in 1927. It held, as I understand it, that certain pairs of variables in quantum physics affected one another in such a way that each could not simultaneously be given an independent and exact value, e.g., an exact position and an exact momentum. The philosophical implications of indeterminacy seem to have been felt early on.

in the type of knowledge/experience each produced, but in a potential equivalence of *function*; both truth and beauty were, each in its own way, conducive to the achievement of that more capaciously informed consciousness which—so it was hoped—might result in more just and generous living.

David Porush observes that the postmodern privileging of literary discourse comes as the result of literature's traditional ability to express "a vision of the beauty not only of order but of disorder" (388), something that is more difficult for the physical or social scientist. Porush further notes as "cybernetic laws" that humans 1) find it compulsory to interpret or disambiguate uncertainty—uncertainty I take as synonymous with a perception of disorder—and that 2) one man's noise is another man's signal, as, indeed, one person's figure is another's ground (396). But this latter observation makes problematic Porush's earlier claim: if anyone's figure may be ground for anyone else, how, then, to establish a distinction between "order" and "disorder" stable enough to support "a vision" of one or the other? How to determine that that vision does indeed express the "beauty" of order or disorder, inasmuch as "beauty" would have to be defined differentially in contradistinction to something that could be called ugliness, or some such? In the same way, Porush's overexcited suggestion that "any exchange of information creates a narrative" (379) seems to me also mistaken. For the term "narrative," like "beauty," or "order" represents a determination as to what counts as signal or figure; narrative, beauty, and order are sociolinguistic constructs, which is to say that only those exchanges of information we take as fulfilling the conditions we posit for narrativity can be taken to constitute a narrative.

I say all this by way of instantiating the importance of human agency. This is not, as I have had occasion to remark earlier, to reinvoke humanistic claims to autonomous individualism or a fully self-present subjectivity. Rather, it is to centralize the observation that inasmuch as figure and ground, signal and noise may, indeed, be constantly shifting; inasmuch as no "apodictically certain grounds exist" (H. White 1973 xii) for our determinations as to which is which, that each of us must bear the responsibility at any given moment for our choices in these matters. (The influence of an older and currently largely disregarded existentialism should be obvious here.) In the same way, although it is no longer possible to believe that we can literally represent "reality," "history," or "truth," it still makes a difference whether one chooses or refuses to take it as axiomatic that there is, nonetheless, an aprioristic material reality, of whose history we can more or less speak, in a manner positing truth as a value.

I will here only repeat what I have said earlier, with reference, however, to anthropological theorists particularly. I believe, that is, with the anthropologist Jacques Macquet,[14] that if we cannot be objective, we can still be scientific in ways that allow that word coherent meaningfulness—by specifying the methods and procedures we have followed, by indicating the empirical as well as logical components of our arguments, and so on. I believe with Marvin Harris in "the struggle for a science of culture,"[15] whether that science is defined solely in Harris's terms or not. No one can doubt that such a science will be more modest and very different from what science has heretofore been in the West—but that strikes me as a good thing. I am reluctantly convinced, mostly by the work of Hayden White, that at

14. See Jacques Macquet, "Objectivity in Anthropology."
15. See, among other texts, *Cultural Materialism: The Struggle for a Science of Culture.*

the highest levels of interpretation there are no *secure* epistemological grounds for preferring one account of sociocultural phenomena as more "realistic," hence more nearly "true" or "scientific," than another. For White, therefore, our preferences have the authority only of choices, truth becoming now not a matter of proof but of value, of our own sense of the beautiful or the good. While this may be the case at some ultimate theoretical horizon of these matters, where rhetoric rules with totalized effectivity, and the linguistic circle has no break in its circumference, I return, again and again, to Raymond Williams's sense of the way in which the very nature of cultural hegemony is such that it cannot help but permit breaks, blanks, holes, areas weakly (or un-) colonized, with room, thus, for "residual" and "emergent" elements to have a certain play. I suggest, at least by way of analogy, that a similar situation prevails in the epistemological realm, with the result that there may indeed be a good deal of practically occupiable space— short of the absolute theoretical horizon of cognitive and esthetic equivalences—space in which probabilistic and tentative statements that offer themselves as more nearly true than others, if not absolutely true, might yet be made effectively.[16]

Curiously, even Porush admits that at a practical, day-to-

16. Thus, as I remarked in the introduction, I believe with Habermas that a domain of rationality can indeed be posited, which, although in its absolute form must finally be "transcendental" (e.g., one cannot actually show "reason" free of its entangling rhetorical and ideological contexts), nonetheless can have proximate and mediate traces of concrete effectivity sufficient for me, at least, to accept its existence as a force if not an essence. Compare, in this regard, P. Steven Sangren's observation that our failure fully to encompass or represent social reality in no way logically entails denying the existence of that reality. "Individuals' perceptions of the world are encompassed within the world, but they do not exhaust the world within which individuals live" (Sangren 415).

day level, scientists operate and, indeed, achieve results in spite of the constraints imposed by the highest theoretical findings about an increasingly slippery and "undecidable" physical universe. In the same way, authors and readers achieve the communication of more or less "decidable" meanings, for all the poststructuralist insistence on the infinite semantic possibilities of the signifier's free play. In all these instances we have—and Anthony Wilden's work of twenty years ago is absolutely essential to an understanding of this matter—an unfortunate but typical Western capitalist insistence on digitalizing what is in fact a matter of the analog.

Let me return, by way of closing, to what I only passingly mentioned at the outset, that it is among the ethnographers more than among the literary people that some of these issues are most hotly being debated. No doubt this is because it matters immediately and materially to ethnographic work whether one believes that—I return to the quotation from David Porush—"meaning resides" in some "underlying [realm of] the inexpressible, inchoate, [and] silent" (377), and wishes to evoke that meaning in one's ethnographic writing; or whether one believes, however tentatively—and here I return to Nancy Hartsock—in "the goal of accurate and systematic knowledge about the world" (205), attempting, by whatever moves or means, to approximate to such knowledge. That these things do matter more to the ethnographer, to offer at least one bit of empirical evidence, I'd mention that the number of sessions devoted to literary theory and practice at the American Anthropological Association Convention of 1988 (the last I attended) was proportionally much greater than the number of sessions devoted to anthropological theory and practice at the 1988 Modern Language Association Convention. "New historicist" literary critics, to judge from a recent collection of essays,[17] have only gotten as far as Geertz; they seem not yet to have discovered Clifford, Marcus, Tyler, Fischer, Rabinow, and others—although it is the case that these just-named students of anthropology, all of whom are fascinated by postmodern developments, seem (more or less) up on the latest in literary theory. Now that literary studies are enjoying a certain return to history, a return by no means limited to "new historicism," it remains to be seen what the anthropologists will do. As the literary canon opens itself and expands, and critics see the necessity of attending to multiple canons, most particularly what I have referred to elsewhere as local, national, and cosmopolitan canons of literature,[18] they—we—will need the expertise of ethnographers, not so much, to my mind, as colleagues in the decipherment of, and meditation upon, codes, but as providers of data for the understanding of other worlds.

17. See H. Aram Veeser's *The New Historicism.*
18. See "Local, National, Cosmopolitan Literature," in *The Voice in the Margin.*

2. MODERNISM, IRONY, ANTHROPOLOGY:

The Work of Franz Boas

That ethnographic and literary concerns currently converge strikes me, as I have tried to indicate in the preceding chapter, as an encouraging development—but not at all because, to pick up David Porush's capitalist metaphorics in a gently satiric vein, as a specialist in literature, I rejoice that my literary stock, in a postmodern epistemological (and disciplinary) market, has appreciated in value. Rather, I am pleased to have the anthropologists closely attending to what the literary specialists are doing because, as I have just said, I believe we literature professors increasingly need them to help us achieve varieties of "multicultural literacy." This is to say that we will need to become more sophisticated in understanding how the cultural concerns of Others, formerly marginalized, inform a proliferating number of new texts, and, additionally, how those concerns bear upon and can illuminate the canonical texts we may now have to reread in a new light.

So far as this is the case, it becomes natural enough for the would-be practitioner of ethnocriticism to study not only the general history of anthropology, but, on occasion, the careers of particular anthropologists. And I think it is reasonable to say that, in the twentieth century, the preeminent anthropologist in America was Franz Boas. If the basic foundation of American anthropology was laid by Morgan, and its edifice initially raised by the likes of Mooney and Cushing, among others, it was elaborated by such powerful figures as Kroeber, Sapir, Radin, Benedict, Lowie, and Mead—all of whom were Boas's students. From the last years of the nineteenth century until almost the mid-part of the present century it is virtually impossible to discuss American anthropology without reference to the work of Franz Boas.

Boas began his academic career with interests in physics and geography. After an arduous field trip to Alaska as a young man (with a manservant—whose story remains to be told!), Boas came to America and to anthropology as a profession. I have already indicated aspects of his contribution and will comment further on this later. His work, as Thomas Jefferson foresaw would be true for any American anthropologist, would focus on the peoples indigenous to this continent, and the data he gathered are simply mind-boggling in their quantitative richness. But what has always seemed difficult to understand was the potential use and theoretical implications of that data, both in terms of their sheer quantity, and, as well, in the "raw," uninterpreted quality of them. How does Boas's work fit into the history of anthropology as a *science*, and how does it fit into the intellectual context of literary and critical *modernism* in which it developed?[1]

1. In an early version, this essay first appeared in *Social Text* 19/20 (1988), 105–18. I am grateful to the editors for permission to reprint parts of it. A later version, one fairly close to what I give here, appeared in *Modernist Anthropology: From Fieldwork to Text*, ed. Marc Manganaro. I am grateful to Princeton University Press for permission to reprint.

I

Born in Minden, Westphalia, in 1858, Franz Boas was clearly an extraordinary figure, not only a teacher, but a *maître* in the grand sense, whose students often became disciples, and, in several cases (Kroeber, Mead, Sapir, Benedict, Radin), virtual masters themselves. Boas published extensively on linguistics, folklore, art, race and, of course, ethnography, a fabled "five-foot shelf" of materials on the Kwakiutl. Yet, Boas did not, like his contemporaries Sigmund Freud and Ferdinand de Saussure, found what Foucault refers to as a field of discursivity, a written discourse which gives rise to the endless possibility of further discourse, or a discipline, like psychoanalysis or structural linguistics. The exact nature of Boas's achievement yet remains to be specified.

In 1888, Boas went to Clark University where he taught anthropology until 1892. He held positions with the World's Columbian exposition in Chicago and at the American Museum of Natural History in New York before moving, in 1896, to Columbia University as a lecturer in physical anthropology. He received promotion to a professorship in 1899, a position he held until his retirement in 1936. Boas died in public—in the arms of Lévi-Strauss—in 1942. From his academic base at Columbia, Boas's influence was enormous. By 1926, for example, as I noted earlier, every academic department of anthropology in the United States was headed by one of Boas's students. That the Winnebago were studied by Paul Radin or the Pawnee much later by Gene Weltfish, that Edward Sapir and, after, Melville Jacobs gathered Native texts is largely due to Boas.

Both Boas's admirers, who are many, and his detractors—

they have been fewer—have agreed only on the issue central to their disagreement, the question of Boas's contribution to a *science* of culture. No one can doubt that Boas did much of worth. But can what he did properly be summed up as serving to found anthropology as a *scientific* discipline—moving it, as it were, from impressionism to realism, as Alfred Kroeber, Margaret Mead, Ruth Benedict, and others have insisted?[2] Or is it, rather, as Leslie White and Marvin Harris, foremost, have claimed, that Boas's practice was, finally, no more "scientific" or "realistic" than that of his predecessors, the accidental "men on the spot," and the so-called "armchair anthropologists"; no more "scientific" than his contemporaries, the "museum men," and the fieldworkers of the government bureaus?[3] Moreover, what is one to think when one considers Boas in the context of that cultural development broadly called "modernism," a literary development for the most part. Is modernism in literature or in anthropology consistent with that "realism" generally taken as consistent with claims to scienticity, or, rather, a break with a realist/scientist past?

I read Boas, as I do literary modernists, against the backdrop provided by what has been called the epistemological

2. See, for example, Ruth Benedict, who writes that "having found anthropology a collection of wild guesses and a happy hunting ground for the romantic lover of primitive things; [Boas] left it a discipline in which theories could be tested" (93). Or Alfred Kroeber who claims that Boas "found anthropology a playfield and jousting ground of opinion; he left it a science" (in L. White 67). Or Margaret Mead who affirms that Boas was "the man who made anthropology into a science" (in L. White 67).

3. See, for example, Leslie White, who finds that "Boas came fairly close to leaving [anthropology's] 'chaos of beliefs and customs' just about where he found it" (in Rohner and Rohner xiii). Or Marvin Harris who judges Boas's achievement most impressive for "the amount of effort lavished in proving that chaos was the most salient feature of the sociocultural realm" (1968 282).

crisis of the late nineteenth century, the shift away from apparently absolute certainties—in religion, linguistics, mathematics, physics, and so on—in the direction of relativity. "In the twenty years between 1895 and 1915 the whole picture of the physical universe, which had appeared not only the most impressive but also the most secure achievement of scientific thought," as Alan Bullock has observed, "was brought into question" (34). To recall some well-known contextual markers, I note that these are the years of work in the direction of Godel's proof that certain mathematical problems cannot be solved in terms of the system in which they are formulated; of the Heisenberg Indeterminacy Principle; and finally, of Einstein's relativity equations. These are the years when more than once Freud would speak of psychoanalysis as the third wound to human narcissism, for its demonstration, after the Copernican and Darwinian wounds (e.g., that we are not only not the center of the universe, nor only a little lower than the angels), that we are also not even masters of our own minds. No wonder that de Saussure could look back upon the nineteenth century's solid accumulation of philological data and conclude that in language there are no positive quantities but only differences.

This is also the period in which Thomas Hardy's sense of the haphazardness of fate would be most fully developed (the last novel dates from 1896, but what is ostensibly Hardy's masterwork, *The Dynasts*, was issued from 1903 to 1908). It is the time when Nietzsche's scorn for the unfounded pretenses of religion, logic, or history is felt; the time of fictional experiments with point of view in Conrad, James, and Ford Madox Ford. Consider as a telling image Stephen Crane's "open boat" bobbing precariously in an infinity of ocean, its weary passengers trying to survive and to be good, as all the past had instructed them to do, but as the present made most difficult.[4]

Now, the anglophone writers I have named were almost surely not direct influences on Boas (if they were at all), as, indeed, Nietzsche was probably not. It seems reasonable, however, to suggest that the epistemological and discursive climate in which Boas's work took shape was one in which there was a strong sense of the relative rather than the absolute; of an absence of fixity, of all in flux; of certainty nowhere, uncertainty everywhere. What attitude other than one of scepticism could claim to be appropriate to such a worldview? Irony is the trope identified by the West for the expression of scepticism as a response to uncertainty, and one may imagine either that Boas (1) somehow founded a science entirely against the grain of the ironic temper of his time, (2) founded a science in the ironic mode, or (3) operated according to an ironic paradigm of a sort that was inconsistent with the establishment of any kind of science whatsoever. These latter two possibilities (I reject the first of these as theoretically unlikely and in practice untrue) are what I shall explore in the remainder of this chapter.

I take irony to be the central trope of modernism. But just as "modernism" is no monolith, neither is irony; there are many modernisms and many ironies to consider as well. Among ironic figures, let me name four: *antiphrasis* or negation, *aporia* or doubt, *oxymoron* or paradox, and *catachresis* or misuse. The figure of aporia (it was not invented by Jacques Derrida, Paul de Man, or J. Hillis Miller, but was well known to classical and Renaissance rhetoricians)

---

4. "The Open Boat" was first published 1895–6, when Boas came to Columbia (I wouldn't guess, however, that Boas read it).

is, as I have said, the ironic figure of doubt; the aporitical text, then, is one filled with "doubts and objections" (OED). Antiphrasis is the ironic trope of negation, the central trope, for example, of satirical writing in which prior assertions are denied in the interest of promoting opposite or alternative assertions. The figure of the oxymoron presents apparently absurd or incongruous linkages, but oxymoronic figures may be distinguished from catachrestical figures in that the absurdity or incongruity of the oxymoron is only apparent, not real; however paradoxical the statement on the face of it may be, a fully coherent, rational point may be extracted—e.g., in such phrases as coarse gentleman, or noble savage. The figure of catachresis is one whose force is particularly difficult to convey. The OED defines it as "misuse with a sense of perversion." According to Henry Peacham in his 1593 *Garden of Eloquence*, "Catachresis in Latine is called Abusio," and Peacham gives as one of his examples of catachresis the "water runnes," the abuse consisting in attributing animate capacity to something which does not have life. For us this figure seems, I believe, purely metaphorical. Curiously, the OED describes, but does not provide examples of, catachresis. Would Milton's "blind mouths," or Dylan Thomas's "the long friends" resonate as indicating perverse or abusive misuse? Or perhaps we must turn to something from popular culture, a phrase such as "jumbo shrimp" (some would add "military intelligence")— which might have more catachrestical than oxymoronic force—might present, in Spivak's sense, a metaphor with no adequate referent.

The first three of these figures (antiphrasis, aporia, oxymoron), I suggest, are tropes for the sort of scepticism which founds the "realist"/"modernist" work of writers like Hardy and Stephen Crane, of the early Pound and Eliot, of Joyce at least through some of *Ulysses*. And these tropes may also be found nonfictional writing of a sort that may generally be considered "scientific." The fourth one of these figures (catachresis) I see as the central trope of "modernist" work of a more radical nature, work such as Nietzsche's, perhaps of Henry Adams's *Education*, of Henry James's *The Sacred Fount*, possibly of Joyce's *Finnegans Wake*, and of Virginia Woolf's *The Waves*. The catachrestical text cannot be considered "scientific" according to any of the usual understandings of the term to the extent that it seeks to sustain and amplify the disparity between metaphor and adequate referent (not the case, as I have said, with ethnocriticism which, perhaps impossibly, seeks to close the gap). It is catachrestical modernism of this gap-sustaining type, I believe, which most current forms of postmodernism (as I understand them) may be taken to continue or extend, while it is aporitic (to choose one of the terms possible here to stand for all others) modernism that postmodernism rejects and rebels against, constituting itself by means of a break.

It is my contention that Boas's work is rich in irony, but it remains unclear which *type* of irony—the doubtful, paradoxical, and negational, consistent with some sense of realism and of science, or the perverse-absurd, subversive of any sense of science—dominates in it. On the one hand, essay after essay may be cited as instantiating just the sort of hearty scepticism that clears the field for more securely founded hypotheses; on the other hand, the work as a whole either perversely insists upon conditions for scienticity that are in no way attainable, or asserts positions that so thoroughly contradict one another as abusively to cancel each other out, moving beyond the oxymoronic to the catachrestic, and thus subverting the conditions of possibility for any scientific hypotheses whatsoever.

The case for Boasian anthropology as constituted by the kind of aporitic irony that founds what I will call a modernist realism consistent with science, might focus on the meaning and function of the new relativism in Boas's work. Unlike the late-nineteenth-century historians who, in Hayden White's account, saw the specter of relativism as serving to "undermine confidence in history's claim to 'objectivity', 'scienticity', and 'realism' " (White 1973 33), Boas and his students seemed to find the new relativity not the foreclosure but the promise of "objectivity," "scienticity," and "realism." Relativism, for Boas, was understood primarily to mean cultural relativism, and a stance of cultural relativism (which was not taken, as I have noted, to imply a general epistemological relativism) as enabling a satiric method by which to expose the abundant undocumented generalizations indulged in by practitioners of "the comparative method in anthropology."[5] In page after page of his writing both early and late, Boas shows a real delight in his ability to expose or deconstruct, as we might now say, generalizations that could not stand up to his aggressive ironic scepticism. In its historical moment, this aspect of Boas's intervention most certainly seems to have advanced the project of a scientific anthropology.

But then there is the famous Boasian hostility to theory and to laws. For there are, indeed, many passages in Boas's writing where he warns against the dangers of interposing aprioristic theory between the putatively innocent eye of

5. See Boas's 1896 essay, "The Limitations of the Comparative Method in Anthropology," in *Race, Language, and Culture*.

the observer and the facts or data in themselves (his view of these matters seems positivist in a largely discredited manner).[6] Boas also seems to have given many of his students and readers a strong impression that he was implacably opposed not only to theory but to all statements of phenomenal lawfulness, that for him anthropology was the sort of inquiry that best limits its view to the singularity or particularity of cultural phenomena. Nonetheless, as I shall try to show in only a moment more, one can also cite essays in which Boas asserts that the statement of general laws is, indeed, the ultimate aim of anthropology, as of any science. These latter assertions permit one to wonder whether there is not, at a deep level of Boas's thought, a commitment to sustaining contradiction, a refusal of closure as somehow a violation of the way things "really" are: a refusal, of course, that denies the possibility of science. This seems all the more likely when one considers that even in Boas's explicit remarks approving the possibility of scientific generalization, he insists again and again on impossible conditions for such generalization, for his contention is that laws will legitimately be "discovered" only when "all the 'facts' are in."

So far as there was to be a Boasian science of anthropology, then, its achievement required the collection of "facts" in the interest of the "discovery" of "laws." Facts, for Boas, are not conceptual constructs or even choices on the part of the researcher, but simply out there. And laws, for Boas, in the generalization of his understanding of facts, do not

6. E.g., Marion Smith: "Boas taught his students statistics and phonetics as tools for handling biological series and language, but the greatest lesson we learned was that data had an order of their own" (in Goldschmidt 51). Or, most recently, Irving Goldman, "If I am remembering correctly from 50 years ago or more, this is how the [Boasian] legacy was transmitted in the classroom. First, minimum theory, then hardly anything on methodology, and just about no global statements [?] on anything but race and culture" (in Schildkraut 552).

either have to be formulated or constructed; rather, once all the facts are in, laws will simply announce or dis-cover themselves to the assiduous observer. Boas would not abandon the goal of stating laws because that would be to abandon the project of a scientific anthropology in the strong sense; but he also would not abandon his adherence to impossible conditions for the actual achievement of a strongly scientific anthropology. Inasmuch as it is obvious that *all* the "facts" never will be in, it is not possible ever to satisfy Boas's ironic scepticism, not possible ever to achieve exactly the science he is after. Such a position, I suggest, is not aporitic, but is best figured by the trope of catachresis. But it is surely time to do some reading.

2

In an 1887 text called "The Study of Geography," Boas distinguished between sciences as they derive from one or the other of two apparently invariant tendencies in the mind—or at least the Western mind. The natural sciences, like physics, Boas claimed, spring from what he calls the "aesthetic" impulse, while those like "cosmography," or history, what we would term the social sciences, are the expression of what he calls the "affective" impulse. The first, a sort of "rage for order," is concerned with stating the general laws governing the phenomena under consideration, while the second is more particularistically concerned with the individual phenomenon itself. For the cosmographer, the historian, or, as Boas spent most of his life insisting, the anthropologist, "The mere occurrence of an event claims the full attention of our mind, because we are affected by it, and it is studied without any regard to its place in a system" (644). As opposed to the physicist, who seeks to generalize from "mere occurrences," the cosmographer, Boas writes,

"holds to the phenomenon which is the object of his study,
. . . and lovingly tries to penetrate into its secrets until
every feature is plain and clear. This occupation with the
object of his affection affords him a delight not inferior to
that which the physicist enjoys in his systematical arrange-
ment of the world" (645). It is hard to resist noticing the
erotic dimension of Boas's description of the cosmographical romance. But can such a conception be compatible with
an anthropological *science*? Boas characteristically answers
yes—and no. "Physicists," he writes, "will acknowledge
that the study of the history of many phenomena is a work
of scientific value" (642), and, near the end of his essay,
Boas pronounces both cosmographical and physical inquiry
to be—and it would seem equivalently—"two branches of
science" (646).

What Boas says here of history and cosmography he
would say again and again of anthropology, that it was to
study its object of affection "without any regard to its place
in a system." But he would also say again and again that
anthropology, in this regard now quite like physical science
("aesthetic" as distinguished from "affective" science),
must, indeed, search out systematic laws. Just a year after
the publication of "The Study of Geography," in an 1888
text called "The Aims of Ethnology," we find Boas writing
that "the human mind develops everywhere according to
the same laws," and that "the discovery of these [laws] is
the greatest aim of our science" (RLC 637). As I have noted,
to the end of his life, Boas continued to insist upon the
necessity of reducing the multitudinous phenomenal data
of culture to some kind of lawfulness—to a commitment to
finding its "place in a system"—while appending the condition that more and ever more data would first have to be

examined before the formulation of explanatory generalizations might legitimately begin. Anthropology must ultimately discover general laws of some sort, just as any proper
science must, but such laws cannot be discovered until all
the evidence is in. Since all the evidence never will be in,
the anthropologist, now a kind of "connoisseur of chaos,"
had best stick to particularities and defer concern for pattern or for general lawfulness—although the discovery of
laws is, indeed, the goal of ethnology. It is a simple matter
to quote Boas on both sides of what seem to me antithetical
and—in the form in which they are stated—irreconcilable
positions. But further quotation would not be especially
helpful—nor, indeed, is it necessary, once we note that Boas
himself chose just these two essays—"The Aims of Ethnology" and "The Study of Geography"—with their conflicting
positions, to conclude the last major book of his lifetime,
Race, Language, and Culture, published in 1940.

Writing when he was more than eighty years old, Boas
announced that these two papers, composed some fifty
years earlier, were chosen to conclude his book "because
they indicate the general attitude underlying [his] later
work" (vi). Boas's "attitude" is such as to offer firm support
for both sides of a great many questions, and such an attitude, I suggest, goes beyond the aporitic ironic scepticism
compatible with science to the catachrestical irony that
would subvert any pretense to science.

Now, *Race, Language, and Culture* is a volume of six
hundred forty-seven pages, comprising sixty-three essays
written over a period of forty-nine years. It is a wartime
book, and Boas's preface states his intention that the essays
to come may show anthropology's bearing "upon problems
that confront us" (v). A section called "Race," consisting of

twenty essays, is the first in the book; "Language," with five, is the second; the third section, "Culture," the category of Boas's most substantial contribution, has thirty-five essays.

One might well expect that Boas chose these divisions, representing the three main areas of his work over a long lifetime, and arranged the essays in them in some kind of ascending or progressive order; one might expect, that is, that this large book was organized in such a way as to permit some sort of climactic or at least clear statement of Boas's position. But any such expectation is undercut by the presence of a fourth section, one, that in its structural and thematic effect, is decidedly anticlimactic. For Boas does not end the book called *Race, Language, and Culture* with the section on "Culture" (or, for that matter, with an afterword or conclusion), but instead follows it with something called simply "Miscellaneous." And it is in "Miscellaneous" that Boas places the texts that are indicative, as he states in his preface, of his final position on matters central to his understanding of anthropology. The texts in "Miscellaneous" are not recent writing, but, instead, three nineteenth-century essays that work backward, from 1898 and "Advances in Methods of Teaching," to 1888 and "The Aims of Ethnology" (in which there was a call for the discovery of laws), to "The Study of Geography" of 1887 (in which the discovery of laws was announced as not the aim of social science at all).

To conclude his final book this way is to reveal a deeply ironic sense of structure (*which* irony, again, remains to be seen). For what is true of irony thematically, as an "attitude," is true of irony structurally, as a form, as well: ironic structures achieve their effects by frustrating conventional expectations for climax and closure. Ironic texts may seem to work according to the familiar Western patterns of trag-

edy, comedy, and romance, but in the end they always subvert them. Rather than the revelation and resignation of
tragedy, the reconciliation and reintegration of comedy, or
the idealistic transcendence of romance, the ironic ending
suggests that things just happen as they happen, to no special point, or at least to no clear one. Think of a play like
Samuel Beckett's *Waiting for Godot*, with its last lines,
"Well? Shall we go?" "Yes, let's go," and its final stage direction, "They don't move." Nothing moves for the ironist;
plus ça change, plus ça reste le même. Even more radically,
moving again from aporitic to catachrestic irony, there is the
suggestion that the very idea of an ending is an absurdity
or paradox; no text can ever *end*. Think of Kafka's *Castle*, or
of *Finnegans Wake* whose final words lead back to its first
words. Does the *apparently* contradictory juxtaposition of
"The Aims . . ." and "The Study . . ." really have its
oxymoronic point? Or is it Boas's ultimate instantiation of
the catachrestical figure of perverse misuse, *abusio* that has
the last word?

At this point, I can well imagine that the scientist reader,
if not so hotly the literary reader, may well be asking, what,
after all, do the essays themselves have to *say*? Speaking
from outside the disciplinary borders of anthropology, I
would repeat that the essays on "Race" seem ironic only
insofar as they are sceptical of entirely undocumented, un-
scientific, and self-serving statements about race. Throughout his long career, as I remarked earlier, Boas insisted on
the cultural explanation of cultural differences and pro-
foundly intervened against German racist theories directed
against Jews, and American racist theories directed against
blacks, and these essays lend themselves more readily than
usual in Boas's work to rather direct application and use.

I am not sure what to make of the few (five) essays on

language, although it seems difficult to read them without the double sense of, first, Boas's clear insistence on the importance for the ethnographer of learning Native languages, and, second, of the uncertainty surrounding Boas's own knowledge of Kwakw'ala, the language of the Kwakiutl: of Helen Codere's statements, for example, that Kwakiutl people she interviewed in 1951 remembered Boas speaking their language,[7] and Ronald Rohner's conclusion in 1969 that Boas had learned Chinook jargon but not Kwakw'ala, nor any other "indigenous Northwest Coast language" (xxiv). In a recent essay, Judith Berman accepts Codere's estimate that Boas did, indeed, speak the language of the Kwakiutl—while demonstrating that his translation of at least one story he was told in Kwakw'ala, while it "may not be the worst conceivable, . . . is still a very bad one" (in press).[8]

The many essays on "Culture" divide into more nearly general, theoretical pieces and specific ethnographic pieces. I will look briefly at the major theoretical piece in just a moment. As for the ethnographic work, it seems mostly an immense, even celebratory record of randomness: Boas was there when he was there, he saw what he saw, he left us whatever he happened to leave us. Even Helen Codere, for all her enormous respect for Boas, acknowledged that "it is not possible to present a synthesized account of Kwakiutl culture based upon Boas's works" (in Harris 1968 314–5). Whether Boas purposely worked in such a way as to forestall what he would have considered an inevitably *premature* "synthesis," or, rather, worked in such

7. See Codere, p. xxiv.
8. See "Oolachan-Woman's Robe: Fish, Blankets, Masks and Meaning in Boas' Kwakw'ala Texts."

a way as to obstruct any synthesis whatsoever, must remain, I believe, undecidable.

Ronald Rohner, who found his own attempt to work in the field with Boas's Kwakiutl materials beset with difficulties, has noted that even when Boas "was aware" that some of his texts and ethnographic "materials over time contain[ed] many inaccuracies and inconsistencies . . . he never corrected them in print" (1969 xiii), an observation that reaffirms Alfred Kroeber's statement of 1959 that Boas knew he was wrong in his account of how the Kwakiutl potlatch functioned "but that he never took the time to re-explain the system" (L. White 1963 56). Here, too, it might be that he just "never took the time"; but it also might be that this lack of concern to reconcile conflicting views was a consequence of a radically ironic, catachrestical set of mind.

I turn now to the essay Boas placed first in the section on "Culture," his presidential address to the American Association for the Advancement of Science in 1932, called "The Aims of Anthropological Research." Both the occasion of its original delivery and its placement in this book are such as to suggest it may fairly be taken as representative of Boas's mature thought. What we find all through this text is irony's ability to doubt and deny; the question for science is whether the doubt and denial are, once again, in the interest of alternative affirmations or whether they go so far as to deny affirmative statements of any kind.

Boas begins with a sketch of anthropology's beginnings from a variety of sources; next, he defines "our objective as the attempt to understand the steps by which man has come to be what he is, biologically, psychologically and culturally" (RLC 244). It appears, Boas says, that "our material must necessarily be historical material, historical in the widest sense of the term" (244). Having announced the need for historical data, however, Boas then goes on to show how unlikely it is that sufficient data will ever be forthcoming, and to list the errors and dangers of a variety of positions. He next passes from considerations of race and psychology to those of "cultural anthropology." I will catalog some of his negational figures, without, to be sure, providing sufficient context to understand each of his remarks in itself. My claim is that the sheer number of these figures does the work of establishing Boas's commitment to ironic scepticism. Boas writes: "The material needed for the reconstruction of the biological history of mankind is insufficient on account of the paucity of remains" (250); "Even this information is insufficient" (251); "For these reasons it is well nigh impossible" (252); "This method cannot be generalized" (252); "It may be admitted that it is exceedingly difficult to give absolutely indisputable proof" (252); it "hardly admits of the argument that . . ." (252); "this view is not admissible without proof that . . ." (253); "It is not a safe method to assume that . . ." (254); "Even the fullest knowledge of the history of language does not help us to understand" (255); "The phenomena of our science are so individualized, so exposed to outer accident that no set of laws could explain them" (257); and so on and on.

For all that aporia and antiphrasis structure Boas's text, still, the doubts and negations may yet imply some positive recommendations. Nonetheless, even if this first essay on "Culture" is useful for the project of an anthropological science, *Race, Language, and Culture* will still present us, as its conclusion, the "miscellaneously" juxtaposed and contradictory final essays of the book.

And it does indeed seem to me that Boas's writing, taken as a whole, has a kind of abusive perversity that, as with

Nietzsche, undermines the foundations for any claims to scienticity. At the furthest horizon, I believe Boas was rather anxiously fascinated by cultural and epistemological chaos of the sort with which Richard Rorty, Jean-François Lyotard, and Stephen Tyler, among other postmodernist and poststructuralist thinkers today, are quite comfortable. If I am at all correct, he did, indeed, engage a kind of *abysmal* ironic vision, which I have tried to link to the figure of catachresis. And it is the figure of catachresis, as I have said, which marks postmodernist subsumptions of logic to rhetoric, science to narrative or conversation, as it marks a sense of the constant inconstancy of figure/ground, signal/ noise relations.

If this is so, then, to the extent Boas may have become "unreadable" in the present moment, he might well be re-cuperated as a sort of precursor of postmodernism. But if I seem here to have conducted Boas to just the place Mar-ilyn Strathern, in a recent essay, brought Boas's English contemporary, Sir James Frazer, I want to warn even more strongly than she against any attempt actually to reread these complex figures as postmodernists.[9]

For all that I have claimed to find a powerful attraction to the chaotic possibilities of freeplay and undecidability (to use more or less current terms) at some deep level of Boas's work, nonetheless, it seems to me that for the most part Boas was attracted to the study of phenomena which he probably felt to be more orderly (whatever their order) than chaotic, phenomena which, looked at particularly and care-fully, at least were probably coherent in themselves. This sense of cultural things was tropologically figured in vari-eties of what I have called aporitic irony, the central trope,

9. See Strathern, "Out of Context: The Persuasive Fictions of Anthropology."

to repeat, of a sort of realist/scientist modernism: distanced and distancing, sceptical, tough-minded, sensitive to paradox, self-conscious, and so on.

Like a number of writers of the modernist period—and I think this is true in a historically specific way of writers of the modernist period and not just of writers in general—Boas's work is difficult to characterize as a whole, the whole not at all comprehensible as the strict sum of its parts. In somewhat similar fashion, the Eliot of the "Preludes" or "Prufrock" is not fully consistent with the Eliot of the "Four Quartets," or, to cite an author not always considered as a modernist in manner, the D. H. Lawrence of *The Rainbow* may not be fully consistent with the Lawrence of *Aaron's Rod*, *The Plumed Serpent*, or the *Studies in Classic American Literature*. The same, as I have noted, is true of Henry James, whose *Sacred Fount* of 1901 cannot be understood as simply the "mature" work of the author of the *Portrait of a Lady* (1881).

Yet I will say that for all the powerful contradictions a careful reading of his work may discern, I think Boas today, in our moment, as indeed in his own, is much more useful for the project of a scientific anthropology (however modest and circumscribed current claims for scienticity must be) than for either Geertzian semiotic anthropologies or Tylerian postmodern anthropologies. I, at any rate, would like to see him recuperated for such a project, for all that we must allow to his work its catachrestical component.

3. ETHNOGRAPHIC

CONJUNCTURALISM:

The Work of James Clifford

> *If we are to break out of the nonhistorical fixity of*
> postmodernism, *then we must search out and*
> *counterpose an alternative tradition which may*
> *address itself not to this by now exploitable be-*
> *cause quite inhuman rewriting of the past, but,*
> *for all our sakes, to a modern* future *in which*
> *community may be imagined again.*

—RAYMOND WILLIAMS

In his jacket blurb for James Clifford's *The Predicament of Culture* (1988), Clifford Geertz describes Clifford as "one of the few persons" writing today "who connects history, literature, and anthropology." "He's had an enormous impact," Geertz continues, "because he provides a new perspective on the study of culture that would almost certainly never have been generated from within anthropology itself." The "connections" Clifford makes are, of course, important to my own ethnocritical project (which, I should say, is much indebted to Clifford's work). What I want to examine in this chapter is the nature of this "new perspective" of his.

In his introduction to *Writing Culture*, a collection of essays on "The Poetics and Politics of Ethnography" he coedited with George Marcus in 1986, Clifford called for a "plural *poesis*" (1986 17), noting that "Ethnographic truths are . . . inherently *partial*—committed and incomplete" (1986 7). Most recently, Clifford has written on behalf of "A modern 'ethnography' of conjunctures"—what I have taken the liberty of calling ethnographic conjuncturalism—"constantly moving *between* cultures" (1988 9). Such a "perspective" would seem to have affinities with the perspective I have been calling ethnocriticism. And yet, as I hope to show, for all the similarities between ethnocriticism and ethnographic conjuncturalism, there are some major differences, not the least of which, perhaps, concerns the nature of critical "movement." This chapter consists mostly of a close reading of the introduction to Clifford's *The Predicament of Culture*, a complex and insightful text called "The Pure Products Go Crazy." I will, of course, make reference to other of Clifford's texts, for all that "The Pure Products Go Crazy," as I think, offers the most recent and the most developed theoretical statement of Clifford's "perspective."

"The Pure Products Go Crazy" begins with a commentary on a poem by William Carlos Williams. Clifford quotes Williams's poem in its entirety, and it is probably most convenient for the reader that I take the space to do so as well:

> The pure products of America
> go crazy—
> mountain folk from Kentucky
>
> or the ribbed north end of
> Jersey
> with its isolate lakes and

valleys, its deaf-mutes, thieves
old names
and promiscuity between

devil-may-care men who have taken
to railroading
out of sheer lust for adventure—

and young slatterns, bathed
in filth
from Monday to Saturday

to be tricked out that night
with gauds
from imaginations which have no

peasant traditions to give them
character
but flutter and flaunt

sheer rags—succumbing without
emotion
save numbed terror

under some hedge of choke-cherry
or viburnum—
which they cannot express—

Unless it be that marriage
perhaps
with a dash of Indian blood

will throw up a girl so desolate
so hemmed round
with disease or murder

that she'll be rescued by an
agent—
reared by the state and

sent out at fifteen to work in
some hard pressed
house in the suburbs

some doctor's family, some Elsie—
voluptuous water
expressing with broken

brain the truth about us—
her great
ungainly hips and flopping breasts

addressed to cheap
jewelry
and rich young men with fine eyes

as if the earth under our feet
were
an excrement of some sky

and we degraded prisoners
destined
to hunger until we eat filth

while the imagination strains
after deer
going by fields of goldenrod in

the stifling heat of September
Somehow
it seems to destroy us

It is only in isolate flecks that
something
is given off

No one
to witness
and adjust, no one to drive the car

The first nine of Williams's twenty-two triplet stanzas
provide a context for the particular example of Elsie, who
shares in and, finally, comes to epitomize the craziness of
"the pure products of America." Elsie herself, however, is
not quite one of those "pure products" by virtue, or defect,
of her "dash of Indian blood"—"perhaps."

That is, to say what should be obvious, Williams's "pure
products of America" are *not* the Indians—although,
strictly speaking, who but they might better claim that title?
Rather, Williams's American "pure products" are "devil-
may-care men" and "young slatterns," inhabitants of Ken-
tucky and north Jersey and anywhere along the railroad
lines, transplanted Europeans with congenital historical
amnesia; all they know is their present American restlessness and malaise. Nonetheless, thinking of American "pure
products," and the absence here of "peasant traditions,"
Williams also thinks of Indians—"perhaps." This is not so

surprising because, for one thing, although Native American people have typically been represented in American discourse as possessing hunting rather than (counter to a good deal of evidence) agricultural traditions, still, from the seventeenth century forward, Americans nonetheless managed to think about Indians as remnants, as it were, of America's feudal past, substituting, in Francis Jennings's phrase, "Savage Form for Peasant Function."[1] For another thing, it is worth noting that about the time Williams wrote the "Elsie" poem, he was working on *In the American Grain* (1925), a book of prose meditations on America and American history, in which he seems to have thought of Indians a good number of times.

In *In the American Grain*, Williams wrote, "I do believe the average American to be an Indian, but an Indian robbed of his world" (1925 128). Of course, it is the "real" Indian, the indigenous American, not the "average American," who was robbed—of his lands, at least—for all that he seemed still to be in possession of his "world." "Nowhere [in America]," Williams would further assert, "the open, free assertion save in the Indian" (1925 155).

This is not, of course, the "agent's" view, at least not of Elsie, who, like many a breed or mixedblood before and after her, is perceived as even more "desolate" than her untainted "pure" American coevals, crazy or not. And so she is "rescued . . . . reared by the state," and placed in the quite traditional position not of the peasant but of the ser-

---

1. This is the title of Jennings's chapter 5 in which he demonstrates that the eastern Indians were sufficiently engaged in intensive agriculture to have been seen by the English invaders as indeed "peasants" of some sort. The necessities of "savagist" ideology (see Pearce), however, were such that Indians had to be seen foremost as hunters rather than agriculturalists to qualify for subaltern, "primitive," or "savage" status.

vant to an upper middle-class, suburban, professional family, "some doctor's family." Dr. Williams, at this point, as he moves to the cultural commentary in which Elsie expresses "with broken / brain the truth about us," refers to Elsie as "voluptuous water," attending not only to her "broken / brain" but to "her great / ungainly hips and flopping breasts" and their "address" to "cheap / jewelry / and rich young men with fine eyes." Here, Clifford writes, "suddenly the angry description veers" (3).

So it does—to a vision of the "earth under our feet" as "an excrement of some sky." But what is it that Williams is angry about? Obviously the degeneration of the "pure products of America," the lack of character in the "imaginations" of slatterns and "devil-may-care men," while "*the* imagination" (my emphasis) "strains" for—something else. Yet the brunt of Williams's anger is quite specifically directed at the sloppy and dirty yet clearly unsettling sexuality of working-class women (although "devil-may-care men" are promiscuous with these women, they "lust for adventure"). For if Elsie and her broken brain can come to express the truth about "us" only by way of her ungainly voluptuousness, it has earlier been the "young slatterns, bathed / in filth / from Monday to Saturday" who have specifically led Williams to his observation about the absence of those "peasant traditions" which might "give them / character." Working in the doctor's house, Elsie, like the "slatterns," is also probably bathed in filth a good part of her six-day week. Like the "slatterns" "tricked out . . . with gauds," Elsie also "addresses" herself to "cheap jewelry."

Clifford misses none of this and generously reads Williams's "anger" as an "angry, bleak *sympathy*" (5 my emphasis), claiming that Williams turns Elsie's "personal story toward the general," "turns it all into modern history" (5), in which, seen "in the late twentieth century" (7), "a female, possibly colored body serves as a site of attraction, repulsion, symbolic appropriation" (5)—serves possibly as a representation of "groups marginalized or silenced in the bourgeois West" (5). Of course, to perpetuate a well-documented imperial tradition in which Indians, women, or the "colored body" *serve* as symbols, and symbolically to *appropriate* such persons for the purposes of generalizations useful to "us," is to practice a form of "sympathy" these people might well reject. "To Williams," Clifford writes, Elsie's "story is inescapably his, everyone's" (1988 4). But, here, too, one may wonder about the degree to which Elsie's story is "everyone's," for neither Dr. Williams, nor Clifford, nor I can quite claim ourselves to be "silenced in the bourgeois West," even if our poetic and academic discourse is, indeed, "marginalized."

Still, so far as Clifford's observations are accurate—and in the main I think they are—what we have here is the early, post–World War I Williams in an apparent "revulsion from Americanism," in F. H. Matthews's phrase, "quarrying the national past in search of lost virtue"[2](14): for there is not

---

2. This would seem accurate enough for the "Elsie" poem. But I would suggest that, beyond the "Elsie" poem, Williams's turn to the past is less a "search [for] lost virtue," than for wrong turns and missed possibilities. In "Père Sebastian Râsles," an extraordinary chapter of *In The American Grain*, Williams re-creates a conversation between himself and Valéry Larbaud in Paris. At one point, the highly cultured Larbaud says to Williams, "You wish to uproot history," to which Williams responds, "No, I seek the support of history but I wish to understand it aright, to make it SHOW itself" (1925 116). America's "history," Williams insists, is "Puritan," but "All that will be new in America will be anti-Puritan" (1925 120). It is just because Williams sees America's history as "Puritan" and (rightly or wrongly) sees Puritanism as a kind of death to the imagination and the senses that Americans could not possibly go back to "authentic traditions" or "lost virtue[s]." Indeed, we must go back and see where and how we went wrong—and to learn

much pure or sane in the modern, American world he sees around him. "In the 1920s," the period of this poem and of *In the American Grain*, Matthews writes,

> the revulsion from Americanism and the search for a viable cultural community intensified into a major quest. Intellectuals in a position to assert their identity with some minority now fanned the embers of recently-declining traditions. . . . Writers who lacked a vital region or ethnic minority with which to identify turned instead, like Sherwood Anderson and William Carlos William[s], to quarrying the national past in search of lost virtue. (14)

Consistent with Matthews's account, Clifford takes Williams's lines as presenting a "feeling of lost authenticity, of 'modernity' ruining some essence or source . . . authentic traditions, the pure products, are everywhere yielding to promiscuity and aimlessness" (1988 4). Thus Elsie's story, whether it can be generalized as "everyone's" or not, is, nonetheless, an apparently tragic tale of loss, decline, and fall. As against this tragic vision, Clifford himself "proposes a *different* historical vision" (1988 5 my emphasis), one that "does not see the world as populated by endangered authenticities—pure products always going crazy" (1988 5). Clifford's "different . . . vision" is, it would seem, of a more nearly comic narrative, one that raises, as he puts it, "the political issue of history as *emergence*" (1988 7 my emphasis) to contest the politics of history as decline.

But in Clifford's subtly nuanced reading, it turns out that Williams's story is not strictly tragic—just as, indeed, Clifford's will not be strictly comic. Clifford discerns a certain

---

from the New World history we have chosen to ignore, most particularly, that of the Indian.

contrapuntal line at work in the "Elsie" poem, so that Williams does not only

> resign himself sadly to the loss of local traditions in an entropic modernity—a vision common among prophets of cultural homogenization, lamenters of the ruined tropics . . . [but instead he] claims that "something" is still being "given off"—if only in "isolate flecks." (Clifford 1988 5)

Clifford discovers, then, that Williams also believes, as he himself does, in cultural "invention" (cf. Clifford 1988 17) and not only decline.[3] This hesitancy before *either* tragic *or* comic narratives parallels what Clifford calls Williams's "perpetual veering between local attachments and general possibilities" (1988 4). Under conditions of "ethnographic modernity" (1988 3), the culture critic must "veer," or as Clifford will say later "oscillate" (17), between narrative paradigms—as he must "tack," in Geertz's well-known term, between local/Western and general/global visions, moving back and forth between tragic and comic stories. For "there is no master narrative that can reconcile the tragic and comic plots of global cultural history" (1988 15).

But this veering and oscillating, as I will have further occasion to remark, while it avoids the "pervasive dichotomy" by which "[s]tories of cultural contact and change have been structured" (Clifford 1988 344), for all its proper doubts about the adequacy of strictly tragic or comic emplotments both locally and globally, and its disbelief in the

3. In his introduction to *The Invention of Ethnicity* Werner Sollors notes that "the word 'invention' has become a central term for our understanding of the universe" (ix), and in a lengthy footnote (even lengthier than the one above and than this one), gives thirty-one references (including a quotation from Henry James in 1877) of mostly very recent studies in English, French, German, and Italian that make reference to the concept of invention. Clifford, then, is already working within what can be called the *tradition* of invention.

possibility of any metanarrative *aufhebung* or synthesis of the two dichotomous poles, turns out to be not an "invention" at all, but, rather, simply the choice of a third Western form of emplotment, of—to borrow the words of Hayden White—"an ironic mode of representation" (1989 30). In the most recent formulation of a point he has forcefully made on a number of occasions, White says, "A mode of representation such as irony is a *content* of the discourse in which it is used, not merely a form" (1989 30). And it is irony that is the content and form, newly "invented" or anciently recovered, of James Clifford's discourse about culture.

Thus it seems to me that Clifford provides for the story of culture in history the kind of negative critique that poststructuralism provides for narrativity in general. In a manner typical of the deconstructive mode, Clifford documents the unacknowledged contradictions and the ideological implications of narratives that would commit themselves wholly to tragic or comic emplotments, while largely exempting the equivalently ideological implications (for all that they are equivocal implications) of his own narrative's ironic stance. Clifford "contest[s] the prevailing narratives of Western identity," so far as these have been constructed as narratives of *loss* by raising, as I have noted, "the political issue of history as emergence" (7). He can show, that is, the comic possibilities always subverting ostensibly tragic narratives—as, indeed, he can show the tragic possibilities at work in ostensibly comic narratives. This is the standard methodology of ironists from Socrates to Boas to Paul de Man.

Clifford writes that

> modern ethnographic histories are perhaps condemned to os-
> cillate between two metanarratives: one of homogenization, the

other of emergence; one of loss, the other of invention. In most specific conjunctures both narratives are relevant, each undermining the other's claim to tell "the whole story," each denying to the other a privileged Hegelian vision. (1988 17)

It is all too easy, no doubt, to wonder why and how *some* narratives apparently escape the bivalence of "*most* [but apparently not all] specific conjunctures" (my emphasis)— although, it would seem, some do. In any case, this likely necessity to "oscillate," as I have said, is not so much a contestation of the modes of Western narrative representation as an unacknowledged choice of one of them—a choice not of comedy or tragedy, but of irony.

And this is why Clifford's instantiation of the likely necessity of critical veering or oscillating, although it might seem to be a parallel perspective to ethnocriticism's frontier orientation to border and boundary crossings is, in fact, quite different from it. For the ethnographic conjuncturalist is committed to perpetual ironic free play, or undecidability; to the constant and unending rhetorical subversion of logic and dialectic; to continual rebellion, as it were, with no hope of revolution. And this oscillation without end, this perpetual shuttling back and forth between the privileged Western narrative paradigms of tragedy and comedy, on the one hand, for all that it refuses their allegorization as reified oppositions, and on the other, while it correctly recognizes that they "prevail [. . .] " in "narratives of *Western* identity" (7, my emphasis), nonetheless seeks to extend both their privileged status and the subversion of that status as relevant to the narrativization of "*global cultural history*" (1988 15, my emphasis).

Geertz's "tacking," at least in theory if not always in practice, is indeed between the local and global—which is to

say, between specifically Western ways of knowing and telling and *other* ways of knowing and telling, in the interest
of providing descriptions/interpretations of cultural practice and transformation that, if "thick" enough, might alter,
or at the very least, ambiguate Western narrative and explanatory categories. To alter or ambiguate Western narrative and explanatory categories is, of course, the project of
ethnocriticism, for all that it is (I readily admit) still a project
easier to expound theoretically than to carry out in practice.
To practice ethnocriticism, at any rate, will require real
engagement with the epistemological and explanatory categories of Others, most particularly as these animate and
impel Other narratives. The necessary sorts of movement,
therefore, are not only those between dominant Western
paradigms but also those between Western paradigms and
the as-yet-to-be-named paradigms of the Rest. (And even
then, the deconstructive paradox of a "no" to that which
founds one's discourse still stands.)

Perhaps this is the place to note that the sort of movements Clifford valorizes are not of this kind. He concludes
"The Pure Products Go Crazy" by affirming that "Westerners are not the only ones going places in the modern world"
(17), noting,, "But have not travelers always encountered
worldly 'natives'? Strange anticipation: the English Pilgrims
arrive at Plymouth Rock in The New World only to find
Squanto, a Patuxet, just back from Europe" (17). This is
generous, but a bit too breezy, inasmuch as it makes it seem
as though Squanto had just decided to take off and see a bit
of the Old World rather than having been carried forcibly
to England; that he had just had time to unpack before
hurrying down to the shore to complicate the Pilgrims' vision of the New World.

Indeed, to speak now only of Indians, there is no doubt

that today, as yesterday, many—not all—tribal people are fond of traveling, using their cars and pickups as their ancestors used horses, to go around and visit. But this sort of traveling and visiting is very different from what a phrase like "going places," with its implications of progress and advance, connotes. As William Bevis in an important essay has shown,[4] the typical pattern of Native American fiction is what Bevis calls "homing in" rather than—the pattern typical of Euramerican fiction—moving out, breaking away, searching, seeking, transcending, and so forth. Indians, that is to say, travel a good deal, but they don't "go places." The sense of rootedness seems extraordinarily persistent in Native American peoples today, so there's really no place to go, no matter where one travels for one purpose or another.

Raising the question of place in regard to politics, Willard Gingerich in an essay on "The Southwest as Spiritual Geography" asks, "South of what, and west of whom?"[5] Beginning with a reading of "Blue, the Sacred Lake" by the New Mexican poet Leroy Quintana, and proceeding to an analysis of "Back into the Womb, the Center," a section of Simon Ortiz's "Between Albuquerque and Santa Fe," Gingerich comments that

> It is decisively not regionalist issues that Ortiz wants to raise, but larger, national and historical interests and forces which he sees as the context of those regional issues.

Gingerich concludes his discussion by answering his own question—"South of what, and west of whom?"—as follows:

4. See William Bevis's, "Native American Novels: Homing In."
5. See Gingerich's "The Southwest as Spiritual Geography in the Work of Simon Ortiz, Rudy Anaya, and John Nichols."

By incorporating the images of these centers into his work, Ortiz lays the foundation for a revisionist history, geography, and politics by attacking the east-west axis of manifest destiny at the very roots of its New World, new Adam, new West mythology. South of nothing, west of no one.

This resonates closely with Kirkpatrick Sale's recent sweeping statement that

> The only political vision that offers any hope of salvation is one based on an understanding of, a rootedness in, a deep commitment to, and a resacralization of, *place*. (446)

I would not want unequivocally to endorse the whole of this. Still, to come at these issues from an awareness of Native American perspectives is to be uncomfortable with at least some of the political implications of even a generously intended recognition that "Westerners are not the only ones going places in the modern world" (Clifford 1988 17). I hardly mean to bludgeon Clifford with his phrase; however, as both Gingerich and Sale remark, given the extraordinary persistence of the sense of home among Native American people today, there's really no place to go, no matter how many miles one may drive or fly. Thus it may be that the politics of placement, rather than the politics of travel, are what's needed for the most radical social (re-)inventions.

Ethnocritical movement is, obviously, a form of criticism and criticism is a form of movement. If "civilization," that is, is the product of neurosis (see Freud), then criticism may be considered the product of restlessness; centered peoples don't produce it in forms recognizable to the West (see chapter 5). Thus ethnocriticism cannot strictly be based on the rootedness and sacralized sense of place that the indigenous people of this continent had and continue to have. Its decentered center is indeed the "West," but its movement is not in the interest of going places; rather, it is a tentative feeling-around to encounters with Others who— for whatever reasons, less securely centered than some of their contemporaries or their ancestors—are also feeling their way around.

The movement Clifford recommends, however, as I have tried to show, is pretty exclusively a movement between Western narrative paradigms (so, too, in my view, was any movement Williams might be taken to recommend, his modernist irony here overlapping Clifford's postmodern irony), between narratives that are quite specific to Western culture, and which, even in dialogized form, may have little use as providing paradigms for the understanding of the variegated narratives of identity of other cultures. I see no sign, that is, that one culture's—"our" culture's—prevailing narratives of identity are in any way being contested by another's. Thus what I miss in Clifford's analysis (I can only slightly offer it in my own) is some developed awareness, if not a detailed description, of the very different narrative structures used by other cultures as explanatory emplotments and narratives of identity; *those*, I think, might provide examples that could more fully "contest the prevailing narratives of Western identity."

Consider, for example, the final chapter of *The Predicament of Culture*, "Identity in Mashpee." This lengthy essay treats the 1976 trial to decide a suit brought by the Mashpee Indians of Cape Cod for official recognition as an Indian *tribe*. The trial, Clifford writes,

> seemed to reveal people who were sometimes separate and "Indian," sometimes assimilated and "American." Their history

was a series of cultural and political transactions, not all-or-nothing conversions or resistances. (1988 342)

With his usual acumen, Clifford sees that the story of Mashpee identity cannot adequately be told as a tragic or comic story, however much "Stories of cultural contact and change have been structured by a pervasive dichotomy" (344). Of course, to the Mashpee's misfortune, the law requires choice between these dichotomous terms, "Indian" or "American," a tribe or not a tribe, "all-or-nothing." (It should be noted, however, that in 1978, for better or worse, the Bureau of Indian Affairs promulgated new administrative procedures for tribal "recognition." These *might* prescribe somewhat different narratives of identity. Although the Mashpee trial was in 1976, Clifford's write-up of it did not appear until 1988, ample time for him to make reference to the change—if only in parentheses like this one.) But for those of us not bound by legal convention, those who with Clifford can recognize that "all-or-nothing," tragic or comic stories will not do, is there then *no* single story appropriate to Mashpee transactional or relational identity? Can one do nothing but oscillate and veer *perpetually* to do justice, at least representationally, to the Mashpee?

While it is altogether likely that the Mashpee Clifford encountered at the trial in Boston were probably a good deal more familiar with the stories of Western literature and American popular culture than with traditional Wampanoag story forms, I would be very surprised if some among them had not internalized various modalities typical of those forms. The paradigmatic structures of Wampanoag narrative—or, for that matter, of Navajo, Iroquois, Apache, Okanagan, Osage, or Pomo narrative—need to be considered as a pole against which to test those of Western narrative. Clifford's "oscillations" between the tragic and comic poles of Western narrative structure can, as I have said, usefully dialogize Western tales of "cultural history," or identity, and that is all to the good. But they cannot, in my view, very well speak to the possible stories of "global cultural history" or to whatever concepts of identity exist among the present-day Mashpee.

Gerald Vizenor's insistence, for example, on a postmodern fluidity and "trickster"-like freedom for the individual is conjoined to a decidedly premodern allegiance to tribal identities as more nearly collectively constituted in terms of mutual responsibilities. Vizenor abhors the "tragic" and speaks, in general, for the "comic"; but it seems to me that the trickster narratives Vizenor recommends, and in his fiction produces, for all that they tend mostly toward (what I see as a recognizably Western) ironic structuration, still seem replete with possibilities that have yet to be explored fully.[6] *I* need to explore them more fully, at any rate, for an ethnocritical practice—and I think Clifford needs to explore them, or any practices at all like them, as well.

Otherwise, to amplify a point I made before, Clifford's practice can only continue Julia Kristeva's version of "feminist practice": it can, that is, "only be negative, at odds with what already exists so that we may say 'that's not it,' and 'that's still not it'" (in Alcoff 418). Thus, for Kristeva, in an essay called "*Oscillation* between Power and Denial" (my emphasis), anything like what Clifford raises as the "*political* issue of history as emergence" (1988 7, my emphasis), or indeed any politics, can only have a "negative function" (Alcoff 418). These are the problems with any

6. See, for example, *Earthdivers: Tribal Narratives on Mixed Descent*, and "Crossblood Survivance," Part I of *Crossbloods: Bone Courts, Bingo, and Other Reports*, as well as *Interior Landscapes: Autobiographical Myths and Metaphors*.

rigorously textualist position, poststructuralist or postmodernist, as I have remarked in the introduction; and those critics concerned to move to a politics outside the text will need to propose ways—as Nancy Hartsock, from whom I have earlier quoted, and Linda Alcoff do—to tell a more stable tale, even if it is only subjunctively constituted. One might, that is, in consideration of tribal narratives old or new, say: what if we told the story *this* way, or spoke conditionally of it *that* way, where these "ways" are neither tragic nor comic, not romantic or ironic, but, to adopt Gerald Vizenor's term, *mixedblood* narrative forms. From this perspective, the Mashpee "identities," so openly represented by Clifford, might, indeed, from a Western perspective, look like "a series of cultural and political transactions, not all-or-nothing conversions or resistances" (1988 342), but they might also, from an Indian perspective, look like—I don't know, perhaps some particular Wampanoag type that remains to be specified.

On the last page of "The Pure Products Go Crazy," the page on which he affirms that "modern ethnographic histories are perhaps condemned to oscillate between" (17) tragic and comic narrative structures, Clifford claims that his own book—certainly one of these "histories"—"surveys several hybrid and subversive forms of cultural representation, forms that prefigure an *inventive* future" (17, my emphasis). This seems to me an odd assertion: that hybrid forms are, indeed, potentially subversive forms is something I have most particularly learned from such writers as Gerald Vizenor, Gloria Anzaldúa, Guillermo Gómez-Peña, and, consistently, from Clifford himself. But if that is the case, how can these hybrid forms "prefigure" an exclusively "inventive future"? By the logic of everything that has come before, the future could not exclusively be "prefigured" as a story of invention, because any strictly comic narrative could never tell the whole story; it would need some form of the story of the future as tragic loss to—what? Dialogize, complicate, ironically subvert its claim to adequacy?

For Clifford has very strongly presented the case that—to take Edward Said's triad of world, text, and critic—whatever the world may be like, the critic in her text must tell its story inevitably as one of homogenization as well as invention, etc., himself perpetually veering and oscillating between these two perspectives. In regard to what, then, might we posit a purely "inventive future"? So far as I can tell, Clifford's permission of an apparently unqualified, comically inventive future here applies neither to the world, the text as product, nor to the critic as producer of the text, but, rather, to *writing* alone.

So far as this is true, I might note, too, that Clifford's admirable essay, "On Ethnographic Authority," both in its original version (1983) and in its slightly revised appearance in *The Predicament of Culture* (1988), also turned to *writing* as its ultimate horizon. In the final paragraph of that essay—I will quote its first and last sentences—a strictly inventive future for writing is endorsed, but, in this instance, nonetheless inevitably problematized. Clifford says,

> Experiential, interpretive, dialogical, and polyphonic processes are at work, discordantly, in any ethnography. . . . If ethnographic writing is alive, as I believe it is, it is struggling within and against these possibilities.(1983 142; 1988 54)

While it might be thought that some of the "processes . . . at work" in ethnographic writing could possibly be concordant with one another, as Clifford describes them they are

"struggling" discordantly. And so, here, at least, it is ultimately for writing as it is for the world, the text, and the
critic. The choice of verb here, "struggling," recalls the
choice of verbs to describe the condition of "modern ethnographic histories" and of the writer of those histories.
The histories were said to be ("perhaps") *condemned to
oscillate*" between two paradigmatic stories or "metanarratives," and, inasmuch as "modern ethnographic histories"
(17) don't actually write themselves—as, indeed, "writing"
doesn't quite write itself—the one who writes them must
also be *condemned* to oscillation or struggle—*"caught*," to
cite an earlier formulation, "between cultures" (9, my
emphasis).

If Clifford's ethnographic conjuncturalist "moving" between cultures (9) is, in his movement, "caught" between
cultures (9), "condemned" (11) to oscillate between cultures, then even his writing can't, for more than a moment,
be taken as exclusively comic and inventive. Writing, like
the world, the text, and the critic, must also be implicated
inevitably in a story of decline—a story which, to be sure,
like Clifford's ending to "The Pure Products Go Crazy," will
still swing back to an upbeat rhetoric of representational
aliveness and inventiveness, to the belief in strenuous yet
hopeful struggle, and to a whole world emergently "going
places."

The content of Clifford's form, the emplotment of his
story, is, then, as I have said, ironic through and through.
The predicament of culture is the same as the predicament
of the writer of culture, as it is, too, of cultural writing. No
one narrative will do; stories of homogenization and decline
must interact and intersect with stories of invention and
emergence, and equivalently for the world, the text, and

the critic. Still, as also noted, for writing, the impulse to ground an unsubverted comic inventiveness is allowed at least a momentary play.

In the same way, it seems to me that there is an impulse to see the predicament of the writer of culture—for all that this impulse is not indulged in any explicit way—in a distinctly tragic fashion. What I am laboring to say here is that I read Clifford's strongest leanings as oriented toward narrating cultural change in inventive, emergent, and politically progressive modes; for all that he regularly insists upon a radical relativization of these leanings, it nonetheless seems to me that he does, indeed, want to propose a "different" vision from that of William Carlos Williams, a comic vision. In regard to the situation of the writer of culture, however, I read Clifford as leaning strongly toward more nearly tragic descriptions (for all that, here, too, he regularly qualifies any description offered). Consider the following self-characterization. Clifford says,

> my topic is a pervasive condition of offcenteredness in a world of distinct meaning systems. . . . A modern "ethnography" of conjunctures, constantly moving *between* cultures, does not . . . aspire to survey the full range of human diversity or development. It is perpetually displaced. (9)

And notice that the practitioner of ethnographic conjuncturalism is not only "perpetually displaced," but—to cite more fully the words I quoted above—that "Intervening in an interconnected world, [he or she] is always, to varying degrees, 'inauthentic': caught between cultures" (11). Clifford risks, here, reinstantiating the oppositional categories or "pervasive dichotomy" (344) he has been at pains to deconstruct, for one can only be "offcenter" if "centeredness" is taken seriously as a meaningful, positive term; the quotation marks around "inauthentic," to be sure, qualify the invocation of the set authentic/inauthentic: but in relation to what other than a sense of authenticity would "inauthenticity" have semantic and affective force? It is the same with Clifford's use of the verb "displaced." Displacement, as the continuation of his sentence has it, means "both regionally focused and broadly comparative, a form both of dwelling and of travel in a world where the two experiences are less and less distinct" (9). Thus the ethnographic conjuncturalist today must be a dweller in culture and a traveler among cultures. This seems altogether unexceptional—for all that, as I have remarked above, Clifford's comparativity does not seem to me very broadly traveled outside the West. But I hardly see how the both/and of local/global, or regional/ "broadly comparative" need add up to a sense of being "perpetually *displaced*"—unless, to repeat, placement is something one believes in and only very painfully gives up.

This is to say that although Clifford's conclusion to his introduction promises a bright and inventive future for modern ethnographic writing, still, the language at this juncture suggests a decided nostalgia in regard to the critical writer, not for cultural "purity," but, rather, for that fuller empowerment, that greater "ethnographic authority," of an earlier generation. I am far from superior to such nostalgia: how many of us, after all—we academics who attempt to write culture and its history in one form or another—can honestly claim to be free of any longing for a time when one *might* actually have "aspire[d] to survey the full range of human diversity or development" (1988 9), to have done so with a clear conscience, and with the hope of telling the "whole" or "true" story?

With Clifford, I believe, of course, that *between* cultures is where critics must situate themselves, but I see that position as not *off* the center, but, instead, *on* the borders. The difference is that the border intellectual, or, in my specific terminology, the ethnocritic, ideally, and I trust, in actual material practice, is not engaged in writing or in acting out a tragic *or* a comic destiny or identity but, rather, with recognizing, accommodating, mediating, or, indeed, even bowing under the weight of sheer difference. This is not, of course, the way in which the metropolitan critic, securely draped in the mantle of full competence and authority, went about his business in the past. But surely those who write to produce—I return again to Said—noncoercive knowledge in the interest of social justice cannot mourn the passing of *that* type of authority; if *that* is what has been displaced, well, all to the good.

My guess, for what it may be worth, is that Clifford would not disagree. And yet he seems uncomfortable accepting even a provisionally stable commitment to a comically emplotted politics of emergence and invention, in the interest of what Allon White has called a cosmopolitan "unity-in-difference" (233), while trying bravely to speak up for what is nonetheless correctly named as displacement. Thus for all the upbeat conclusion to "The Pure Products Go Crazy," with its apparently unqualified endorsement of multiculturalism and "an inventive future"; with its distinct recognition "that Westerners are not the only ones going places in the modern world" (17); there is still the odd Foucauldian determinism constraining, condemning us to "oscillate" or "veer" to the pole of homogenization and loss, however much we may attempt to *choose* other forms of positionality.

Is it inappropriate to suggest that it is mostly for persons who had, in whatever degree consciously or unconsciously, expected to occupy positions of epistemological and discursive centrality, that an acknowledged loss of that centrality must be deeply disconcerting and productive of a sense of being displaced, offcenter, caught, or condemned? But—and I remind the reader here of the quotation from Nancy Hartsock earlier (p. 24)—for those persons who formerly never could expect to occupy such positions, the possibility the modern world opens is to perform in neither a tragic nor a comic plot, but, regardless of the form their story takes, simply to be visible and to be heard. Betweenness for them—I might offer bits of autobiography here in the interest of justifying the pronoun "us"—betweenness for those who have hitherto been marginalized for reasons of race, class, or gender first and foremost means nonperipherality: not centrality, nor an " 'alterity,' which understands itself as an internal exclusion" (Alcoff 418). Such people—and the historical probability is that they (here, I could not say "we") will for the most part be persons of color, and women, Elsie in New Jersey and globally—such people are not likely to think, speak, and write from a sense of lost authenticity or centrality. As they increasingly have the opportunity not necessarily to be "going places," but in whatever ways only to present themselves as not entirely Other nor yet the Same, they will not, I think, feel themselves caught, or describe their betweenness as a condemnation.

Let me cite the words of Gloria Anzaldúa in this regard. She writes, in the preface to her *Borderlands/La Frontera: The New Mestiza,*

> Living on borders and in margins, keeping intact one's shifting and multiple identity and integrity, is like trying to swim in a new element, an "alien" element. There is an exhilaration in

being a participant in the further evolution of humankind, in being "worked" on. I have the sense that certain "faculties"— not just in me but in every border resident, colored or noncolored—and dormant areas of consciousness are being activated, awakened.

It is along these lines that ethnocriticism wishes to constitute itself as a critical practice in no way condemned to ironic oscillations between Western narratives, but, rather, as freely choosing a commitment to the production of whatever narratives—and it is impossible to predict with any accuracy the forms these will take—may serve to tell the emerging story of culture change today and in the future. Anzaldúa's willingness to be "worked" on in the margins and on the borders is very different, I think, from Clifford's being caught between. And the difference makes a difference, for all that the "work" that must go forward needs both Clifford and Anzaldúa.

PART II

4. FIGURES AND THE LAW:

Rhetorical Readings of Congressional and Cherokee Texts

At this time 1890 we are too near the removal of the Cherokees for our young people to fully understand the enormity of the crime that was committed against a helpless race, truth is the facts are being concealed from the young people of today. School children of today do not know that we are living on lands that were taken from a helpless race at the bayonet point to satisfy the white man's greed for gold.

—U.S. ARMY PRIVATE JOHN G. BURNETT

This threat of being deprived of a great part of her domain by an alien and semi-barbarous people appeared intolerable and unthinkable to Georgia . . . [who] forbade the Indians to play with their make-believe government. . . . With the Indians out of the way, Georgia was for the first time in her existence master of her own territorial destiny.

—E. MERTON COULTER

In the second chapter of this book, I offered a rhetorical reading of one of anthropology's classic works, Franz Boas's *Race, Language, and Culture.* The intention was to examine the textual grounds for a number of contradictory generalizations about Boasian "science," and the various "conver-gences," as I have called them, of ethnography and litera-ture in the contexts of modernism and postmodernism. Boas's writing bears a signature, to take a term from Der-rida; it is author- and style-specific, in Clifford Geertz's sense;[1] thus my rhetorical critique of *Race, Language, and Culture* sought to give voice to what the text itself could not speak, what the individual author could not or would not say.

When one turns to the rhetorical analysis of those nearly anonymous texts called laws, however, the project of critical rhetorics—I mean by this term to offer a parallel to the recently developed field of critical legal studies[2]—in its at-tempt to speak what the text cannot or will not say becomes a critique of ideology. For laws, of course, are not merely public texts but publicly *sanctioned* texts. That is to say, their language does not merely express or represent but effectually permits, prohibits, or requires particular acts. Laws, then, are the specific outcome of successful rhetoric, public speaking oriented toward persuasion. Once that out-come has been written into law, however, these texts are no longer persuasive but coercive, and may be enforced with the full power of the state. Laws are fixed in letters; but the letter of the law remains open to acts of interpretation. These have traditionally been engaged in not by literary critics but by lawyers—although it is the case, of late, that the interests and concerns of some lawyers and some lit-erary people have also converged to a quite striking degree. If ethnography and literature are most readily seen to con-

---

1. See, for example, Derrida's "Otobiographies: The Teaching of Nietzsche and the Politics of the Proper Name," and Geertz's "Being There: Anthropology and the Scene of Writing," in *Works and Lives*.

2. For a recent overview, see Victoria Kahn, "Rhetoric and the Law."

verge in relation to *postmodernism*, law and literature, I believe, most readily converge in relation to *rhetoric*.

I will not attempt to give now (as I did not earlier) even a sketch of the historical development of rhetoric in the West from Plato to Aristotle; from the Romans to the Renaissance; thence until our own time. My particular concerns here, I believe, require only that I note my sense that rhetoric, in the Classical period where it began as a formal subject of detailed inquiry (and where, as Eric Cheyfitz has shown, it served as a pretechnological technology of control), concerned itself with analyzing the particular *figures* of speech appropriate to specific public *occasions* of speech, whether these were "deliberative" or "juridical" (Kahn 21). All the rare birds of rhetorical terminology—metalepsis and catalepsis, catachresis, oxymoron, antiphrasis, and so on—are subdivisions of the four "master tropes," metaphor, metonymy, synecdoche, and irony, and all are names for linguistic constructions, each one of which might be more or less effective in persuading an audience to a particular position, at a particular moment—whether justice (both legally and philosophically) or property were involved.

Rhetorical figures or tropes, then, provide charged images of their objects of concern; but these images, presented in any extended discourse, cannot help but imply a narrative, or, simply, tell a story. This is the case for contracts, laws, Supreme Court decisions, or formal histories quite as well as for the texts we conventionally refer to as "stories." As I have noted regularly throughout this book, in the West, these stories are intelligible as exemplars, variants, or combinations of the four plot structures—I am again following Northrop Frye and Hayden White—called romance, tragedy, comedy, or irony (satire, for White)— plot structures which may be discerned, as White has abundantly shown, in texts where the narrative is indeed implied rather than stated, and where the story told offers itself as "truth" rather than as "fiction," e.g., in history and historiography, and also, as I shall try to show, in law where it seeks to *make* history by *imposing* a story. My text is the Indian Removal Act of 1830.

I

The Indian Removal Act of 1830 presents a series of images rhetorically figured, and a story about the Indian, a particular narrative construction of Indian-white relations—both of which work together to make certain kinds of sense of the material they organize: the tropes in which images are presented, and the stories that presentation narrates, having, in a phrase of Hayden White's, explanatory force. Or, as Edward Said even more tellingly puts it, not merely explanatory force. In a brilliant discussion of what he calls "images of centrality," Said speaks of the power of these images to give "rise to semi-official narratives with the capacity to authorize and embody certain sequences of cause and effect, while at the same time preventing the emergence of counter-narratives" (1988 58). Finally, Said writes, "centrality is identity," determining "what *is* powerful, important and ours" (1988 57), and so, too, what, defined as "theirs," is precisely not important, is powerless. Said's "images of centrality" are, of course, cultural productions, of the "superstructure," as an older Marxism would say, and thus they can only be "semi-official" in their capacity to authorize. But the law of the land is most certainly official; and the "sequences of cause and effect" it authorizes, and the identities it recognizes as "powerful, important and ours," through the images it provides and the stories it tells, have predictive efficacity, for the law permits the state to compel compliance by means of force.

As is well known, the idea of "trans-lating" the eastern Indians westward so that an expanding Euramerican population might "improve" and more productively use Indian lands had already been considered by Jefferson and Monroe as a sort of permanent solution to America's Indian problem. This solution seems to have become an urgent national priority at the time of Jackson's presidency not only because (I am largely persuaded by Michael Rogin's arguments)[3] Jackson was obsessed with Indians; not only because it took until the latter 1820s for the white population's need or, as seems more substantially the case, *greed* for land to grow sufficiently to exert acute pressure upon Indian holdings; not only because gold was discovered in 1829 in Georgia at Dahlonega on the western boundary of the Cherokee nation; not only because even some clergy and laypersons sympathetic to the Indians became convinced they would do best beyond the corrupting influences of frontier whites. Important as all these factors were, there is also a narrative dimension to the history we are considering.

This is to say that Indian removal could finally be written into law and enforced in the 1830s because by that time, a certain *story* about America and about "civilization" had become sufficiently acceptable that it could be used as ideological justification for "certain sequences of causes and effects," for the policy of—to cite Berkhofer again— "expansion with honor" (145ff). This story, as numerous

---

3. See *Fathers and Children: Andrew Jackson and the Subjugation of the American Indian.*

commentators have remarked—and it is a story that has been reinvoked from the invasion of Massachusetts to the invasion of Panama and the recent war in the Gulf—organized images of the white man and the Indian in such a way as to satisfy Americans that they might not only have their way, but have it—in Alexis de Tocqueville's phrase, which I shall cite more fully below—in complete conformity and with "respect to the laws of humanity" (339), naked self-interest clothed with justice and sanctity.

The particular story to which I am referring has been told many times, by no one better than by Roy Harvey Pearce, who, more than thirty-five years ago, in *Savagism and Civilization: A Study of the Indian and the American Mind*, described the way in which "the history of American civilization would . . . be conceived of as three-dimensional, progressing from past to present, from east to west, from lower to higher" (49), with the acutely developing problem, therefore, as Pearce stated it, "of understanding the Indian, not as one to be civilized and to be lived with, but rather as one whose nature and whose way of life was an obstacle to civilized progress westward" (41). To achieve this "understanding" required, in Pearce's careful distinctions, a very particular "Idea, [a] Symbol, and [an] Image" (vi–vii). The idea was that of the savage and his savagism; the symbol was the Indian, as represented in a series of images whose functional purpose would be, on the level of culture, to reconcile our national interests with our national ideals. These *images*, I suggest, in order that they might represent the Indian *symbolically* in a manner consistent with the *idea* of his savagery, must be figured *ironically*, from a tropological perspective, and, from the perspective of narrative, must be emplotted, structured as a story *tragically*.

The story of Indian savagery must be structured as a tragedy because the story of Euramerican civilization—the Euramerican narrative of identity, in James Clifford's phrase—was structured as a comedy. Comedy is the name the West gives to stories that organize images in terms of a progress toward reconciliation and integration; in the Classical period, or in Shakespeare, for example, comic plots end with a dance, or a dinner, or both of these at a wedding. In general, the tale America seems to have told of itself, the story that gave the Euramerican self-images and an identity in the nineteenth century, was a narrative of the inexorable advance of civilization toward the fulfilment of its manifest destiny, the extension of the frontier ever westward, ever forward, to establish a continental arch from sea to shining sea.

The "civilized" protagonists of the American comedy, as in any comic story, encountered opposition and resistance, in this instance on the part of those they called Indian "savages." It is in the nature of comic plots that any regressive "blocking characters," in Northrop Frye's phrase (167), those who would stand as "an obstacle to civilized progress westward," in Pearce's phrase (1989 41), must be overcome—but the comic mood is such that no pain, no pity, or terror, is to be felt at their defeat. What I want to show is that the Indian Removal Act inscribes the narrative of the Indian as a tragedy, and that the tragedy of the Indian stands in relation to the comedy of the Euramerican as figures of the savage stand to figures of the civilized man.

If comedy is an integrative structure which cheerfully reconciles and unites its characters, tragedy is a dispersive structure which fearfully casts out and severs its characters from the places and persons they would be near. Terrible as such exile is, still, it is tragedy's insistence, it is just; the climactic moment of tragedy comes in the recognition of

the wisdom of resignation to the existing order of things—
an order that is presented as necessary and unalterable. To
tell a particular kind of story, comic or tragic, as White has
shown—as also to refuse to tell any *one* kind of story, as I
have tried to show—is always to offer a particular kind of
explanation of the world as experienced, or, to refer again
to Said, to authorize a particular sequence of historical
causes and effects (1988 7).

As it is on the macro-level of narrative structure or plot—
tragedy, comedy, and so on—so, too, is it at the micro-level
of sentence structure, or style. I return here to the subject
of the figures of language, which themselves present some
human beings as "in" and "us," other human beings as "out"
and "them." Ironic tropes such as antiphrasis or negation,
catachresis or misuse, oxymoron or paradox, and aporia or
doubt, all work at the level of style to deny and to disperse.
And these are the tropes, I suggest, which govern the representation of the Indian savage in the Indian Removal Act
as in much discourse of the period. (Such representations,
it should be noted, have particular effectivity in determining the *kind* of tragic emplotment in which they appear.)

2

The Removal Act is titled an "ACT TO PROVIDE FOR AN EX-
CHANGE OF LANDS WITH THE INDIANS RESIDING IN ANY OF
THE STATES OR TERRITORIES, AND FOR THEIR REMOVAL WEST
OF THE RIVER MISSISSIPPI."[4] Its first section asserts "that it

4. Because I quote extensively from the Act, and, because it is readily available
(e.g., in Washburn), I have not thought it necessary to reproduce it in its entirety.
As the reader will see, I *have* thought it necessary to reproduce the Cherokee
documents I discuss below because they are *not* readily available. Washburn, for
example, gives the text of the "Indian Removal Act," as he also gives the text of
the Supreme Court decision in Worcester v. Georgia of 1832. But he does not cite
the text of a single one of the "Cherokee Memorials to Congress," nor does he

shall and may be lawful for the President of the United States" to set aside specifically described and designated lands west of the Mississippi "for the reception of such tribes or nations of Indians as may choose to exchange the lands where they now reside, and remove there." As an act to *provide* for the exchange and removal of those Indians "*as may choose*" to exchange and remove, this legislation reproduces, in its very language, a number of paradoxes particular to the period, but, as well, paradoxes inherited from the broader context of Christian patriarchal culture.

Etymologically, that is, to provide is simply to see ahead, from Latin, *pro-videre*. The verb form makes its nominal appearance in the word *providence*, generally indicative of God's foreknowledge of events, with a strong implication of predestination. But this foreknowledge, in Christian doctrine, is also taken as compatible with free will, the human creature's ability to *choose*. As a pertinent literary example, consider John Milton's description of Adam and Eve, in *Paradise Lost*, as sufficient to stand yet free to fall. This is altogether paradoxical, in my view (although it may be a paradox that Milton exploits for antimonarchical effect). God knew, of course, that they *would* fall, but nonetheless—somehow—they were still sufficient to stand. Section I of the Removal Act both *provides* for an exchange, while it insists upon the free agency of the Indians. This paradoxical situation reproduces the paradox also central to pre-Christian classical tragedy where the protagonist cannot escape his fate yet nonetheless affirms his status as tragic

---

cite the text of the Cherokee petition to the Court that initiated Worcester v. Georgia. Peters's standard lawyers' edition of *Cases Argued and Decided in the Supreme Court of the United States*·(Book 8) summarizes this latter Cherokee document and quotes selectively from it, but no standard reference that I have been able to find offers a complete text.

(rather than, say, merely pathetic) by taking responsibility for his fate: it is as if he chose it. The Indian, to the framers of this bill, must not be mere victims of civilization's providence but free agents who can voluntarily "choose" to exchange and remove—for all that, in point of actual fact, as we shall see, there was not very much of a choice at all.

More particularly, these paradoxes reflect such things as the determination of Jefferson and Monroe that Indians must not be allowed to act against the best interest of the United States (although Monroe, who had to face the issue more acutely than Jefferson, was against the use of force), as this confronts the determination of another former president, John Quincy Adams, that the government keep its original promises to the Indians, regardless of American self-interest. Historically central to these paradoxes is what Brian Dippie has called the "embarrassment of 1802 when the federal government, in exchange for Georgia's western lands, bound itself by compact to extinguish existing Indian title in the state, despite the 'solemn guarantees' previously made to the indigenous tribes" (56–7). The problem facing the framers of the Removal Act was, in Robert Berkhofer's phrase, how to reconcile national interest with national honor.

In his First Message to Congress, President Jackson explicitly denied the right of independent governments or states (like that of the Cherokee) to exist within the United States (in particular, Georgia; cf. Guttmann and Halsey 37–8), and clearly affirmed his commitment to Cherokee removal. Yet even Jackson could not avoid the "providential" Christian paradox, as he asserted that Cherokee "emigration should be *voluntary*, for it would be as cruel and as unjust to compel the aborigines to abandon the graves of their fathers and seek a home in a distant land" (in Guttmann and Halsey 39, my emphasis). Jackson's inflexible determination that the Indians *choose* to remove encountered the Cherokees' inflexible determination not to choose to remove, and the impasse was resolved by the use of, first, subterfuge and intrigue, and, finally, state violence, which sent the Cherokee westward on the "Trail of Tears" in 1838.

Section II of the Removal Act states

> That it shall and may be lawful for the President to exchange any or all of such districts [newly created, in the west] . . . with any tribe or nation of Indians now residing within the limits of any of the states or territories, and with which the United States have existing treaties, for the whole or any part or portion of the territory claimed and occupied by such tribe or nation, within the bounds of any one or more of the states or territories, where the land claimed and occupied by the Indians, is owned by the United States, *or* the United States are bound to the state within which it lies to extinguish the Indian claim thereto. (My emphasis)

The language here, I believe, reflects Jackson's strong sense of the government's historical error in treating the Indians as sovereign nations in the past, offering, it appears (I am neither a lawyer nor a legal scholar), an interpretation of international and national law that would seek to remove the "embarrassment" of Article I, Section 4, of the Georgia Cession of April 24, 1802 (Guttmann and Halsey 10) simply by deciding the matter in Georgia's favor (e.g., "*or*," above). This section of the Act, that is, seems to assert that all land "claimed and occupied by the Indians" is in fact if not in deed "owned by the United States" and thus, that Indian occupancy is simply at the sufferance of the United States in the person of the President. This, to be sure, is the interpretation put forth by then Representative and, later, Governor of Georgia, Wilson Lumpkin in the House debate upon the subject, and it is consistent with the declaration of the Georgia Senate in 1827 "that the state might *properly* take possession of the Cherokee country by force, and *that it was owing to her moderation and forebearance that she did not thus take possession*" (1095 my emphasis). Here, the legal force of the federal government's past treaties with the tribes is simply abrogated in favor of the right of the states to regulate their internal affairs as they see fit, with Indians presenting no exception—something to which Chief Justice John Marshall would take exception in Worcester v. Georgia in 1832. Lumpkin's sense of the matter is that whatever Federal/Indian relations may be, Georgia/Indian relations are another matter altogether—with the effect, of course, that Indians be damned.

Although the Act has six more sections, we have already, by Section II, reached the climactic moment of our story, the tragic epiphany of the law which reveals a president in the position of god or fate, possessor in the name of the United States of all lands far and wide, who can remove or allow to be removed any Indians, as he sees fit, with the providence of this act—and this independent of those Indians' desire, for all the fact that they must be presumed to have a choice in the matter. What follows is largely denouement, the president and the United States offering financial payment or otherwise unspecified "aid and protection" to the forced exiles, as if to say, as typically with tragedy, that all is, if not well, at least as it should be: that the world represented here, however painful, is, nonetheless, just.

Thus Section III of the Act makes it "lawful for the President solemnly to assure" the Indians that "the United States will forever secure and guaranty to them, and their

heirs or successors" the new lands to which they have removed, a very curious assurance, even in regard to a
commander-in-chief with powers over the territories, inasmuch as the preceding section of the bill has just reneged
on all previous such assurances as guaranteed by treaty "forever." The Cherokee in their "Memorial" to Congress of
July, 1830 (I look at this again just below), were quite clear
that were they to remove and "make themselves comfortable in their new residence, they [would] have nothing to
expect hereafter but to be the victims of a future legalized
robbery!"[5] (Guttmann and Halsey 59)

Section IV announces "That if, upon any of the lands now
occupied by the Indians, and to be exchanged for, there
should be such improvements as add value to the land," the
president is to determine the value of these improvements
and pay for them—once more, an ironic provision in light
of the fact that capacity to improve the land had always been
a touchstone of civilization, the Indians now to be removed
for their inability to be civilized, yet paid for any improvements. One wonders at the spectacle of President Jackson,
who had said of Cherokee lands in his First Message to
Congress that these were "tracts of country on which they
have neither dwelt nor made *improvements*" (in Guttmann
and Halsey 39, my emphasis), charging the Treasury for just
these nonexistent improvements.

Section V specifically offers "the emigrants" such "aid and
assistance as may be necessary for their support and subsis-

5. A point made by de Tocqueville as well, e.g.,

the Indians readily perceive all that is provisional about the settlement proposed
for them. Who can guarantee that they will be able to remain in peace in their
new asylum? The United States pledges itself to maintain them there, but the
territory they now occupy was formerly secured to them by the most solemn
oaths. . . . No doubt within a few years that same white population which is
now pressing around them will again be on their tracks. (336)

tence for the first year after their removal." Section VI promises the exiles protection "at their new residence, against all interruption or disturbance from any other tribe or nation of Indians," and as well "from any other person or persons whatever." However sincere the government may have been in wishing to protect the removed Cherokee from further white encroachment and in preventing inter-tribal warfare (as, for example, with the Osage), its record in regard to the former was consistently abysmal, and its capacity in regard to the latter—considering that the Cherokee were being relocated to areas where there were already Chickasaw, Creek, Choctaw, and Osage—was modest at best. Thus I find a certain irony in this provision as well; and the Cherokee "Memorial" cited above once again may be consulted for the Indians' own understanding of the meaning of federal protection.

Section VII seems to me oddly placed and difficult to understand from the text alone; it would seem to respond, again, to the government's concern to prevent the setting up of sovereign states in the new territories to which Indians were removed, and, again, to prevent intertribal warfare. But the language is curious. Section VII states

> That it shall and may be lawful for the President to have the same superintendence and care over any tribe or nation in the country to which they may remove, . . . that he is now authorized to have over them at their present places of residence: *Provided*, that nothing in this act contained shall be construed as authorizing or directing the violation of any existing treaty between the United States and any of the Indian tribes.

Two matters especially strike me here. First, for all the blandly paternalistic benevolence of the phrasing, granting to the president the "same superintendence and care over"—the preposition seems telling (i.e., idiomatic usage would seem to permit "care *for*" as well as "care *over*")— the Indians he has had heretofore, there is something ominous in the assertion that there is no "world elsewhere," not "another country" in which the Indians, should they so choose, might escape presidential "superintendence and care." To read this phrase as ominous, let me say, is not a matter of a presentist perspective only; for many in the age of Jackson understood perfectly well the kind of "care" he would have "over" the Indians, the Indians included.

Second, since everything in this act is based upon a view that "existing treaties between the United States and . . . the tribes" misconstrued the claims of Indian title, the United States purchasing what might simply have been claimed by right of conquest, by eminent domain, or by the doctrine of *domicilium vacuum*, thereby rejecting the basis for all existing treaties between the United States and the tribes, it seems appropriate to read these words as offering an ironic sense of history—or else a deep hypocrisy.

Section VIII is the conventional appropriations section, concluding the matter by appropriating "the sum of five hundred thousand dollars" for "the purpose of giving effect to the provisions of this act." Thus, ironically or not, money has the last word.

The Removal Act was passed in the Senate by a vote of 28 to 20, and then, in the House, by a vote of 103 to 97. For want of four votes, in the words of Henry Storrs, Whig of New York, we might now "break up [the Indians'] society, dissolve their institutions, and drive them into the wilderness" (in Washburn 1057). Jackson signed the bill into law immediately, on May 28, 1830. As Alexis de Tocqueville summed up the matter:

The Spaniards by unparalleled atrocities which brand them with indelible shame, did not succeed in exterminating the Indian race and could not even prevent them from sharing their rights; the United States Americans have attained both these results with wonderful ease, quietly, legally, and philanthropically, without spilling blood and without violating a single one of the great principles of morality in the eyes of the world. It is impossible to destroy men with more respect to the laws of humanity. (339)

The "primary premise" of the imagery in which the Indian is depicted in the Removal Act, in Robert Berkhofer's phrase, "is the deficiency of the Indian as compared to the white" (113). As the published debate over the Removal Act makes clear, the bill denies to the Indian sovereignty over land and person; as "noble savage" the Indian is oxymoronically depicted; as "murderous savage," "embarrassment" (e.g., in the remarks of Wilson Lumpkin, Democrat of Georgia), encumbrance or nuisance, he is figured by catachresis (misuse, absurdity, anachronism, etc.) or antiphrasis, as negation of the civilized person, its antithesis or zero degree. Ultimately, inasmuch as it remains unclear at this time whether the Indian would indeed "civilize" himself or "vanish," no statement about him can quite have determinate meaning: the figure for such indeterminacy is the figure of aporia or doubt. The Indian Removal Act of 1830 set the terms of discussion for the "Indian Question" for more than half a century.

3

The full effects of the Removal Act were not felt by the Cherokee until 1838. First, in 1835, fewer "than one hundred Cherokees," of more than fifteen thousand eastern

Cherokee, in "alliance . . . with the Jackson-Georgia Removal Party" (Woodward 174–5) signed the Treaty of New Echota, agreeing to the cession of all the Cherokee's eastern lands to the federal government for a sum of five million dollars (*less* the cost for removing the Cherokee to the west, a cost which came to over one and a quarter million dollars). Then, in 1838, some twelve thousand remaining Cherokee were forced by federal troops under the command of General Winfield Scott to head westward on the infamous Trail of Tears. The kind protection of the government notwithstanding, fully one third, four thousand people, died en route.

But the Removal Act was only the first of several "documents of barbarism," in the recent phrase of one Native American legal scholar.[6] In the century and a half since its passage, a great many other Indian bills have been proposed and enacted to attempt to deal with America's ongoing "Indian problem." I will make reference only to those that seek to make general policy. First is the General Allotment or Dawes Act of 1887. The intention of Dawes was presumably to give the Indians a last chance at "civilization" by bringing them to a proper appreciation of the virtues of private property; the Act provided for the allotment in severalty of lands formerly tribally—communally, indeed "communistically"—held. Like the Removal Act, Dawes was supported both by those who genuinely wished to do what they thought best for Native people as well as by those who simply wanted another means of obtaining what land was left to the Indians. In 1934, under the Wheeler-Howard, or

6. See Robert A. Williams, Jr., "Documents of Barbarism: The Contemporary Legacy of European Racism and Colonialism in the Narrative Traditions of Federal Indian Law." I am grateful to Donald Bahr for bringing Williams's detailed essay to my attention.

Indian Reorganization Act, Indians were to be "reorganized," allowed, that is, to retain what remained of older, more traditional lifeways if they wished—their wishes, unfortunately, to be made known to the government by strictly parliamentary means that were unfamiliar at best, and, at worst, repugnant to many members of the tribes. In 1953, Indians were to be "terminated": according to the provisions of House Concurrent Resolution 108, the government announced its intention to terminate or sever its longstanding special relationship with the tribes. Only the Menominee and the Klamath, among the larger tribes, were actually "terminated" by the government (with predictably disastrous results) before this policy was amended and then abandoned. Nineteen sixty-eight brought the Indian Civil Rights Act, and 1975 the Indian Self-Determination Act, both of which, for all the positivity of their titles, brought very mixed blessings to Native peoples.[7]

The American "image" of the Indian, as presented seminally in Pearce's work and elaborated in the important studies of such scholars as Robert Berkhofer, Brian Dippie, Richard Drinnon, and Michael Rogin, appears "officially" as Indian "policy" in the "narratives" we call laws—where they have the most important material consequences. And it is, of course, possible to offer a narrative and figurative analysis of each of these major acts.

For example, the Dawes Act appears to be predicated on ironic images of an oxymoronic, or paradoxical, type that can be emplotted comically as a tale of acceptable citizenly integration into a turn-of-the-century society facing un-

7. For an overview see Michael Dorris's "The Grass Still Grows, the Rivers Still Flow: Contemporary Native Americans," and Williams, cited above. Excellent bibliographies of recent work can be found in W. R. Swagerty's *Scholars and the Indian Experience: Critical Reviews of Recent Writing in the Social Sciences.*

precedented immigration. The classic literary illustration here comes from Henry James's 1904 visit to Ellis Island (described in *The American Scene* of 1907), in which James recognizes the unanticipated necessity "to share the sanctity of his American consciousness, the intimacy of his American patriotism, with the inconceivable alien" (1968 85). In an age in which the "inconceivable alien" must somehow be conceived of as also an American, the Indian can become just another hyphenated citizen, no longer the American Indian but, oxymoronically, the Indian-American—an American who, like all his brother and sister hyphenate Americans, is to be melted in the great melting pot into a Christian capitalist.

This melting pot notion of monocultural purism or nativism was, apparently, particularly strong from 1915 or so to 1922 (cf. Matthews), for all that it was strongly opposed by movements for both cultural pluralism and liberal cosmopolitanism (cf. Hollinger). After the Great Depression, in the era of Franklin Roosevelt, cultural pluralism, cosmopolitanism, and, generally, a somewhat greater—if grudging—willingness on the part of the dominant culture to accept at least some degrees of difference as potentially "American" are more marked. In these years, to grant the fact that newly arrived Americans might choose to retain and display degrees of Italianness, or Jewishness (etc., etc.), no longer appears, at least to some, as quite such a profanation of the "sanctity of [the] American consciousness," nor a violation of "the intimacy of . . . American patriotism" as it did to James. In this context, the original inhabitants of this continent might also be permitted to retain traditional cultural forms, without—the irony here is all too apparent—seeming "un-American." The figure by which this view of the ethnic American is represented is metaphor, the figure based upon analogous substitutability; e.g., by analogy, *Chinese*-American or *Mexican*-American or *Native* American may be substituted for *American*. Non-WASP lifeways, in this view, need not be melted out or away, but, instead, they may become distinctive threads in the uniquely American coat of many colors. This alternative image of America has its counterpart today in the image—call it residual or emerging—of American society as a rainbow or mosaic. In any case, the Wheeler-Howard or Indian Reorganization Act of 1934 would seem to image the Indian metaphorically while (still) emplotting his story comically.

The "termination" policy, according to which the federal government announced its intention to sever special relationships with (and responsibilities to) the tribes, images the Indian in more or less ironic tropes of a catachrestic type, and projects, for the story of the "terminated" Native, radically ironic emplotments. Indians are once again figured as anomalous and antithetical persons, and so they may be cast adrift to manage as they can. Stories about these drifters and outsiders will be cast in the ironically absurd narrative mode known in the West from Kafka, on to—I here name artists whose influence is roughly contemporaneous with the institution of the termination policy—Beckett, Ionesco, Antonioni, and Edward Albee. Finally, it may be said that the Indian Civil Rights Act and the Self-Determination Act, heir to the reformational and reintegrative hopes of the sixties, recapitulates Wheeler-Howard's imagery and structure: metaphor, figuratively; comedy, narratively. Once again Indians are to be allowed to manage their own affairs—so long as they do so, as John Collier himself wrote, "with the aid of modern organization methods" (in Dorris 52).

These remarks take their subject matter at what is obviously a very high level of generalization. But, as I hope I have shown in my analysis of the Indian Removal Act, particularization of a rhetorical, narratological, and historical nature would certainly be possible. Rather than attempt this, however, I want to turn to the sort of analysis urged most strongly by my ethnocritical perspective, and examine an "official" Cherokee response to the threat of removal. Thus, to take a phrase from Roy Harvey Pearce, I want to try "to do for the Red side of the story what [I] did for the White" (1973 90).

But there are a great many problems in the way of any attempt "to do for the Red side of the story" what is fairly easily done "for the White."

4

The most "advanced" of the "five civilized tribes," the Cherokee were able, by 1830, to write their own language in the syllabary devised by the mixedblood Sequoyah (George Guess) in 1821. In the estimate of one of their number, John Ridge, by 1826 approximately a third of the eastern Cherokee were competent in the writing of English.[8] As early as 1808, the Cherokee had adopted their earliest known written law, and in 1827, amid much fanfare,

---

8. See Ridge's "Essay on Cherokee Civilization," in which he writes, "I suppose that there are one third of our people who are able to read & write in the English Language. In the Cherokee Language, there is a large majority who read and write in George Guess' syllabic character" (736). But in the "Resolution and Statement of the Missionaries" resident in the Cherokee Nation at the end of 1830, the missionaries note that they "have before [them] the names of 200 Cherokee men and youths who are believed to have obtained an English education sufficient for the transaction of ordinary business" (Guttmann and Halsey 68), obviously a far, far smaller figure than Ridge's earlier estimate. The missionaries would seem to agree, however, that "a majority [of the Cherokee] . . . can read with greater or lesser facility" in "their own language in Guess's [Sequoyah's] alphabet" (69).

they had drafted and adopted a constitution modeled
closely upon that of the United States—both of these documents written in English. Thus the Cherokee were well
positioned, when the pressures upon them of Georgia and
of Jackson to remove intensified, to fight for their rights by
a variety of textual means, among them letters, petitions,
and "Memorials"[9] to the courts, the Congress, and the various officers of the federal government, and also by means
of articles and editorials in *The Cherokee Phoenix*, a newspaper founded in 1828 by Elias Boudinot and edited by him
until 1832 (it ceased publication in 1834). *"The Cherokee
Phoenix,"* according to Rennard Strickland, "contains the
most articulate presentation of the Cherokee position" (67n)
on removal. Speaking for what seems to have been an overwhelming Cherokee consensus in opposition to removal,
the *Phoenix* was apparently "sent to the four corners of the
United States," inspiring "white newspaper editors in New
Orleans, New York, Washington City, Philadelphia, Boston,
and Baltimore to recopy its editorials citing Jackson's and
Georgia's oppression" (Woodward 168). These editorials (in
English and in the Sequoyah syllabary) no doubt provide
"semi-official" narrative responses to the removal threat—
for all that much of what appeared in the *Phoenix* was often
supposed to be the work of—or, at the least, carefully over-
seen by—the Rev. Samuel Worcester, longtime Congrega-
tional Minister to the Cherokee.[10]

9. So far as I have been able to determine, a "Memorial," in the nineteenth
century, seems to be what we might call a memorandum. The Cherokee Memorials could thus be described as memos petitioning to Congress; they are not—I
can say this much with relative certainty—memorializing texts, i.e., they do not
exclusively (although they sometimes do in part) seek to recall the memory of
persons or times gone by.

10. But see the volume compiled by J. F. and A. G. Kilpatrick, called *New
Echota Letters: Contributions of Samuel A. Worcester to the Cherokee "Phoenix,"*
for Elias Boudinot's confirmation of Worcester's rejection of that charge, pp. 93ff.

But what of an "official" document, one to parallel the Indian Removal Act? I believe that there can be no such Cherokee text, strictly speaking, because the Cherokee in 1830 could only produce laws—not merely persuasive but coercive texts—to regulate their internal affairs. They had not the power—nor, I believe, the tradition or inclination—to "provide" for the behavior of others outside the Cherokee Nation. While Georgia and the United States could and did pass legislation determining what the Cherokee might and might not do, the Cherokee could not and did not pass legislation to determine what Georgia and the United States might and might not do. Instead, as I have said, they wrote and distributed editorials in the private sector of their own Nation and in the United States generally, and sent petitions and "Memorials" dated, passed, and signed by members of the General Council of the Cherokee Nation (Principal Chief, Assistant Principal Chief, Executive Counsellors, etc.) to the federal government. It is to these latter documents, I believe, that one must look for a text at all approximating to the discursive order of the Indian Removal Act.

Correctly anticipating that President Jackson's First Annual Message to Congress (I have referred to it above) would strongly support their removal from the east, the General Council of the Cherokee Nation met in November of 1829 to draft a "Memorial" to both Houses of Congress petitioning for their right to remain. This Memorial is the nearest thing I know to a Cherokee parallel to the Indian Removal Act.[11]

Bills for the removal of the Cherokee having been introduced into both Houses early in 1830, and debate on the

11. Closest in *time*, as well as closest in discursive order to the Removal Act. There are, to be sure, "Cherokee Memorials to the Congress" of an earlier date, as there are also memorials that follow the passage of the Removal Act.

Removal Act having begun in the House on February 24, this "official" document of the Cherokee Council, along with twelve other memorials "from the native citizens of the nation themselves, and adopted throughout the country, and to which are appended upwards of three thousand names" (H. R. 311 1), was "Committed to the Committee of the Whole House on the State of the Union to which is committed the bill No. 287, to provide for the removal of the Indian tribes in any of the States and Territories West of the river Mississippi, and for their permanent location" (1). It was "Presented, and laid on the table, March 15, 1830."

I will offer some analysis of this "official" Cherokee Memorial shortly, supplementing my account (in the notes, for the most part) with reference to the first of the individual petitions from the "native citizens of the nation." This latter text has been widely known to the world, let me note, as a consequence of its inclusion, *in condensed paraphrase*, in the tenth and last section of Volume I of de Tocqueville's *Democracy in America.*[12] But before proceeding, it seems necessary to ask what sort of analysis would be appropriate to a document like this.

12. I reproduce it in full in Appendix B to this chapter. It should be noted that de Tocqueville's citation of this Memorial, although it is given inside quotation marks, is *not*, as his most recent editor, J. P. Mayer, states, a "slightly summarize[d]" version (cf. 338) of the full text. Prior to the 1880s or thereabouts, the conventions of citation were very different from what we take them presently to be. Thus, in spite of the quotation marks, what de Tocqueville offers is an abbreviated paraphrase. Inasmuch as he quotes only four of a full seven paragraphs of the Cherokee text, his account, I think, is hardly "slightly summarize[d]." I won't take the space here to compare de Tocqueville's version with the original—for all that that might be a fruitful exercise—but will only remark that de Tocqueville's version represents, to my view, a text midway between the highly formal Euramerican manner of the "Memorial of the Cherokee Council" and the somewhat more traditional manner of the "Memorial from the Citizens of the Cherokee Nation."

This is to say that inasmuch as we have before us texts in English—and texts, it appears, originally composed in English rather than, as so much so-called "Indian oratory,"[13] translated from Indian to English—which are specifically addressed to a Euramerican audience, it might seem proper to perform upon them just the sort of rhetorical analysis one might perform upon any text in English. And yet, surely it is also worthwhile at least to raise the question (for all that, as I note just below, I can't very well answer it) whether such texts might not owe something to traditional Cherokee oratorical practices, so that the imposition upon them of a purely Western analytic grid would badly distort them. As the first Memorial from the individual Cherokee citizens puts it, "we address you according to usage adopted by *our* forefathers, and the great and good men who have successfully directed the Councils of the nation *you* represent" (7 my emphases). This, it seems to me, means according to the "usage[s]" of Western rhetorical practice, and also to those of traditional Cherokee oratorical practices.

But traditional Cherokee oratorical practices, like those of most of the indigenous people of the Americas, are very little known.[14] Most of what there is to work from in textual form are, to reorient a phrase from Donald Bahr, "foreign policy" speeches in English translation of (one may reason-

13. See, for example, the collections by Armstrong, Nabokov, Sanders and Peek, and Vanderwerth.

14. Studies of traditional oratorical practice are currently having something of a renascence among anthropologists, historians, and linguists. Among the studies of which I am aware, see those by Donald Bahr, Nora and Richard Dauenhauer, and Michael Foster, among others. In regard to Cherokee documents of the Removal experience, as Raymond Fogelson has pointed out, very few exist. I am grateful to Professor Fogelson for suggesting a number of sources that have aided my understanding of these matters.

ably assume) varying accuracy—although there do not exist transcriptions of Native language originals against which to compare them. In this regard, the oratorical speeches translated into English by Euramericans obviously differ from the Cherokee documents composed in English by Cherokee. And yet the translated speeches *and* the Cherokee Memorials alike result from what are artificial, or, at the least, nontraditional occasions. For the speeches, the occasion for rhetorical performance is an encounter between delegations of whites and Indians for the purpose, in the vast majority of cases, of negotiating Indian land cessions. On these occasions, it should be noted, neither party could proceed in a manner entirely familiar to their culture, although this similarity does not suggest an equality: however necessary innovations of eloquence were to both Native and non-Native peoples, the latter always held the balance of power.

This is to say that Euramericans, on these imperial occasions, had to engage in a measure of formal improvisation, while the Native Americans, as colonial subjects, had to improvise in regard to content, a much more radical step. The whites, whose power depended upon such things as fixing boundaries and property lines, making deeds, arranging payments for land, and so on, speak of these matters to the Natives in a kinship language they had not for centuries used among themselves or with any other Western nation, a language—to take a term from Michael Paul Rogin—of "fathers and children": e.g., The Great White Father in Washington reminds his Red Children, etc. Meanwhile, the Indians seem to have spoken in much the same language they had always used among themselves and with other Indians (e.g., often beginning with formulas that had cosmological reference, indicating the distinctiveness and long duration of their own culture or "way," etc.) but found themselves in the position of trying to make this traditional formulaic language speak of things it never had spoken of (permanent boundaries, deeds, payments for land, annuities, etc.), in Eric Wolf's terms, to make a kin-ordered language convey capitalist concerns. To press the matter no further, I will only say that while I am far from prepared to attempt, here, any reconstruction of the principles of traditional Cherokee oratory, it yet seems reasonable to assume that traditional Cherokee public speech would inevitably have been based upon the cultural "postulates," in Rennard Strickland's phrase, "commonly accepted by the traditional Cherokee" (21), and that they would reflect the epistemological, ethical, and psychological views of Cherokee people.

5

And yet, having said this much (or little), I must nonetheless confess that in the "official" Memorial of the General Council of the Cherokee Nation to Congress, I don't find anything of substance that I might refer to traditional Cherokee oratorical practices. The majority—twenty-two of the thirty-seven signatories—of the "Memorial" affix an "x mark" rather than a "proper" signature in alphabetic script or in the Sequoyah syllabary to this document, and thus announce themselves as people who do not write. But the "President of Committee," Lewis Ross, the "Clerk of Council," John Ridge, the Principal Chief, Assistant Principal Chief, and two of the three "Executive Counsellors" signing approval of the document do affix their names in script. And these are very likely the men responsible for composing the actual text—one which, as I have said, seems to be in close conformity to American (Western, textual, legal) practice.

To repeat, I find little or nothing in it that would seem to be dependent upon traditional (oral, unlettered) Cherokee practice,[15] but it has not been readily available for study, and I have reproduced it in its entirety in an appendix to this chapter so that any sharper eye or ear than mine may discover what I may have missed. Let me add here that the distance of the Cherokee Memorial from traditional Cherokee oratory, as it seems to me, has—as Eric Cheyfitz has shown in discussions of "Frederick Douglass" in his narrative, and of Caliban in *The Tempest*—both alienating and liberating potentialities. On the one hand, to accede to the "master's" language, in the Cherokee case, to adopt the prevailing legalistic mode, is to abandon one's own language; on the other hand, to take possession of the master's "books" is to obtain some important part of the master's power— which then, to be sure, may be turned to one's own purposes.

The Memorial of the Cherokee Council opens with what I take to be deliberate although unstated reference to the Declaration of Independence. Jackson had cited the Declaration, in an opinion presented to the Cherokee by the Secretary of War in 1829, as impugning Cherokee rights to their aboriginal homelands, and the Memorial does indeed offer a counterargument to Jackson's on this point later on

15. This is not the case with the first Memorial from the native citizens of the Nation which employs kinship language—initially that of children speaking to their elders and father(s), then, speaking to "Brothers" (7). There is also in the narrative structure of this document a (mythic?) sense of cycles, it seems to me: of a movement from a height to a low point with the distinctive possibility, phoenix-like, of a rise-again, as the Cherokee memorialists describe their former loftiness in regard to the whites, their subsequent and present lowliness, and their hopes to follow the whites—and here, I would say, the structuring principle shifts—in a progress to civilization and salvation, a progress that would not be likely cyclically to reverse itself.

in the text. But by opening with language that parallels the Declaration's own well-known language, the Cherokee, I believe, seek to substitute metaphorical figures for the ironic, antiphrastic figures (e.g., as noted above, the Indian as opposite and negative of the white man, etc.) regularly employed for the representation of Native people by Jackson, Georgia, and the proponents of removal. The opening words of the Cherokee Memorial, I mean to say, by echoing the language of the Declaration of Independence assert the legitimacy, at least, of political equivalences between the Cherokee and the American colonists. As two peoples who each had, formerly and in the present, to fight for their right to independence, Cherokee and Euramerican may be metaphorically *compared* rather than antiphrastically *contrasted*, analogical comparability being the essence of metaphorical figurations.[16]

Addressed, as I have said, "To the Honorable Senate and House of Representatives of the United States of America in Congress assembled" (2), the Cherokee Memorial of 1830 begins:

We, the representatives of the people of the Cherokee nation, in general council convened, compelled by a sense of duty which we owe to ourselves and nation, and confiding in the justice of your honorable bodies, address and make known to you the grievances which disturb the quiet repose and

16. Both the "Memorial of the Cherokee Council" and that of the native citizens insist upon a history of political equivalence. Both reject the notion that the Cherokee were ever mere tenants at will on their ancestral lands, citing the indisputable fact that both Great Britain and the American government regularly made treaties with them as one sovereign nation with another. The "Memorial of the Cherokee Citizens" also asserts the metaphorical comparability of Cherokee and Euramericans in its notation of the fact that both peoples have known the conditions of largeness and smallness, power and powerlessness.

harmony of our citizens, and the dangers by which we are surrounded. (2)

The Declaration of Independence does not *begin* this way, of course, for it initially narrates the wrongs done to the colonists by King George. But it then moves to the following words:

> We, therefore, the representatives of the United States of America in General Congress assembled, appealing to the supreme judge of the world for the rectitude of our intentions . . .

Where the Declaration *first* establishes the "long train of abuses and usurpations" for which the British King George III is responsible, the Cherokee Memorial only *later* establishes some of the abuses not of George but of his namesake state, Georgia. Where the colonists were no longer *petitioning* George, their principal oppressor, but presenting a "Declaration" to all the world to judge the justice of their case, the Cherokee are decidedly petitioning—not Georgia, their principal oppressor, nor the president, Georgia's staunch supporter, but, rather, petitioning the Congress of the United States, just that body that had adopted the Declaration. (Cf. Thomas Jefferson, "Congress proceeded the same day to consider the Declaration of Independence, which had been reported and lain on the table the Friday preceding, and on Monday referred to a Committee of the whole" [639]—exactly the referee of the Cherokee Memorial.)

Yet in spite of the similarity I have remarked, there is a crucial difference to note as well. For unlike the American colonists who found themselves compelled "in the course of human events" to *declare* their independence, the Cherokee find themselves compelled, rather, to *affirm* theirs. And the Cherokee, I believe, are aware of and mean strategically to exploit the irony that the central, virtually sacred document that had proclaimed the sovereignty of the United States Americans should now be instantiated as the document—so Jackson had claimed—serving to undermine the sovereignty of the indigenous Americans. For "It remains to be proved," the Cherokee Council asserts with a turn to the specifically logical rather than the rhetorical dimension of the issue, "how our right to self-government was affected and destroyed by the Declaration of Independence, which never noticed the subject of Cherokee sovereignty" (3).

Whatever the metaphorical equivalence of Cherokee Indians and American colonists, there is, again, a difference. For, as the Cherokee memorialists write, "It is a subject of vast importance to know whether the power of self-government abided in the Cherokee nation at the discovery of America . . . and whether it was in any manner affected or destroyed by the charters of European potentates" (2–3). And the bulk of the Cherokee Memorial rehearses a history in which both the British colonialists and the American colonists become sovereign (and so free to be imperialists in their turn), consistently treated with those in original possession of the land as independent and (themselves) sovereign nations. That is to say, from the "discovery" of America until the present moment, the representatives of European powers and of the United States treated with the Cherokee *metaphorically* from a legal and political perspective.

Thus the Cherokee anticipate Jackson's charge in his First Message to Congress that it is intolerable and unconstitutional for any state to allow an Indian tribe "to *erect* an independent government" (Guttmann and Halsey 38 my emphasis) within its borders. It is the insistence of the Cherokee, supported with a very great deal of (to my mind persuasive) evidence, that they have always been, and have been treated as, an "independent government," a nation sovereign on its own territory. Here again the Cherokee seem fully aware of the irony inherent in the fact that, having recently taken for themselves the specific forms of the American government—having, as they put it, exercised their "right to *improve* our Government" (4 my emphasis)—they should find that government perceived as an invention, newly erected, rather than as merely a version of what has always been.

In addition to these local, or thematic, ironies, I would suggest that the "official" Cherokee Memorial, from the point of view of emplotment, attempts to replace America's "official" tragic narrative of Indian decline with either an ironic or a comic counternarrative.[17] In figurative terms, to repeat, the Cherokee seek to undo an ironic tropology and to put in its place a metaphorical one; in narrative terms, however, the Cherokee offer to the Congress not the tragic tale it is used to, but instead, a tale that in the light of past

17. The "Memorial of the Native Citizens" accepts that their story thus far seems to have taken the outline of a Christian tragedy, i.e., that "By the will of our Father in Heaven, the Governor of the whole world, the red man in America has become small, and the white man great and renowned" (7). But they make it quite clear, in the same way as the "Memorial from the Cherokee Council" does, that if they, "who are remnants"—the language, is, as frequently throughout the text, reminiscent of the Old Testament—are to "share the same fate" (7) as the many tribes "now nearly extinct" (7), their story will be marked by injustice and unrighteousness, a cruelly ironic tale. The native citizens, like the Council, conclude with fervent hopes that this will not be their story, although they do not develop the comic prospects in the detail that the Council does, as I note below.

history and present circumstances can only be emplotted ironically or comically.

For the Cherokee Memorial insists that if, indeed, the Cherokee people must remove, they will do so entirely against their will, *not* voluntarily or by free choice, for "our attachment to the soil of our ancestors is too strong to be shaken" (H. R. 311 5). Thus the Cherokee refuse to accede to the central condition of tragedy, as it is understood by Sophocles or, indeed, by Jackson in his First Message to Congress, refusing a voluntary resignation to their fate. "The power of a State," the Cherokee fully recognize, "may put our national existence under its feet, and coerce us into her jurisdiction; but it would be contrary to legal right, and the plighted faith of the United States' Government" (4). Cherokee removal, *as emplotted by the Cherokee,* is not the tragic story the whites would tell of the sad-but-just punishment meted out by God, fate, or even the progress of history; instead, the Cherokee insist, the story of their expulsion can be nothing but the story of ironic victimization; should they be removed from their homeland, theirs would be no tragic tale, but rather, the merely pathetic story of people in the wrong place at the wrong time who, despite all their efforts to save themselves, were nonetheless crushed not by right but by might alone. The Cherokee memorialists will not allow their dispossession to be seen, as savagist ideology would have it, as inevitable or necessary, neither God's will, nor Nature's law. Rather, should they be "translated" west of the Mississippi, such an outcome would be the result of no more than the force of American imperial power.

But, of course, the purpose of the Cherokee Memorial in substituting such a bitterly ironic story for the comfortable tragedy familiar to American savagist thought is precisely to enlist the aid of Congress in preventing that story from taking place. Having announced their firm adherence "to what is right and agreeable to [themselves]," and their strong attachment "to the soil of [their] ancestors" (5), the Cherokee shift to a sketch of a happier outcome than that of removal. Noting that they have "been invited to a retrospective view of the past history of Indians who have melted away before the light of civilization, and the mountains of difficulties that have opposed [their] race in their advancement in civilized life," they yet "rejoice that [their] nation stands and grows a lasting monument of God's mercy, and a durable contradiction to the misconceived opinion that the aborigines are incapable of civilization" (5). As the preceding quotation may already indicate, the Cherokee, as they move toward the conclusion of their Memorial, offer a narrative of identity in which they describe themselves not only as politically analogous to Americans in regard to independence and sovereignty, but as like them in sharing a morally, religiously, and socially progressive future.

The Cherokee delegation writes,

> The opposing mountains that cast fearful shadows in the road of Cherokee improvement, have dispersed into vernal clouds; and our people stand adorned with the flowers of achievement flourishing around them, and are encouraged to secure the attainment of all that is useful in science and Christian knowledge. (5)

The florid imagery continues as the Cherokee look to a continuance of "the fostering care of the United States" under which they have "prospered" (5); the latter phrase is repeated as they appeal, in conclusion, "for justice and humanity to the United States, under whose kind and fostering care [they] have been led to the present degree of civilization, and the enjoyment of its consequent blessings" (6). With "patience" the Cherokee await the "final issue of [Congress's] wise deliberations" (6), and, rhetorically at least, propose a comic future in common with the dominant Euramerican society, as each progresses, at its own pace, toward the heights of Christian civilization.

The Cherokee Memorial, as I hope the reader will agree, is a very powerfully persuasive document. Nonetheless, it did not sufficiently persuade the Congress, where, finally, in the House, for want of four votes, as I have already noted, the Indian Removal Act was passed, and the Cherokee committed by law to the ironic destruction they had clearly foreseen and fought to avoid. Subsequent Memorials to Congress did not prevent the extension of Georgia law over the Cherokee in June of 1830, nor their forced removal westward in 1838.

MEMORIALS

OF

THE CHEROKEE INDIANS,

Signed by their representatives, and by 3,085 individuals of the Nation.

———

FEBRUARY 15, 1830.

Presented, and laid on the table.

MARCH 15, 1830.

Committed to the Committee of the Whole House on the State of the Union to which is committed the bill No. 287, to provide for the removal of the Indian tribes in any of the States and Territories West of the river Mississippi, and for their permanent location.

———

Copy of a note addressed to the Speaker of the House of Representatives by the Cherokee Delegation, submitting memorials in behalf of their Nation.

BROWN'S HOTEL, WASHINGTON CITY,
15th February, 1830.

Hon. SPEAKER *of the House of Representatives:*

SIR: The accompanying memorials you will please lay before the House over which you preside; the one from the late General Council of our nation, and signed by all the members of that body, and principal chief, in behalf of the Cherokee nation, relative to the present unpleasant state of affairs in consequence of certain causes therein stated; the others, twelve in number, are from the native citizens of the nation themselves, and adopted throughout the country, and to which are appended upwards of three thousand names. They have been forwarded to us by mail, to be laid before Congress. Their object, as will appear, is to prove to that honorable body, that the many reports of late circulated by officers of the Government, that a greater portion of the Cherokees are favorably disposed to a removal Westward, and are only restrained by the threats and tyranny of their chiefs, are erroneous, and entirely unfounded. They wish to speak of their wishes and determination in that respect themselves, and to be heard by the representatives of the United States; they wish them to be convinced, that, to know their feelings and interests, is to know that they ardently desire to remain in peace and quietude upon their ancient territory, and to enjoy the comforts and advantages of civilization; that the great mass of our citizens are opposed to removal, (as has been plainly demonstrated by the offers and inducements lately held out to them) and that it is not the fear of chiefs that

has forced upon them this determination to remain; but that it has been produced by causes no less than convincing evidence, that their only and best
hopes of preservation and advancement in moral and civil improvement is
to remain where their Great Father alone placed them. There they wish
to pursue agriculture, and to educate their sons and daughters in the sciences
and knowledge of things which pertain to their future happiness. With
these remarks, we submit the memorials for the consideration of Congress,
humbly hoping that the grievances of our nation will be heard, and duly
considered.

   With sentiments of regard and esteem,
    We have the honor to be,
      Very respectfully,
       Your ob't serv't,
        GEORGE LOWREY,
      As't Prin. Chief Cher. Nation.

    LEWIS ROSS,
    WILLIAM HICKS,
    RICHARD TAYLOR,   Cherokee De-
    JOSEPH VANN,   legation.
    WILLIAM S. COODEY,

———————

*To the Honorable Senate and House of Representatives of the United
States of America in Congress assembled.*

We, the representatives of the people of the Cherokee nation, in general
council convened, compelled by a sense of duty we owe to ourselves and
nation, and confiding in the justice of your honorable bodies, address and
make known to you the grievances which disturb the quiet repose and harmony of our citizens, and the dangers by which we are surrounded. Extraordinary as this course may appear to you, the circumstances that have
imposed upon us this duty we deem sufficient to justify the measure; and
our safety as individuals, and as a nation, require that we should be heard by
the immediate representatives of the people of the United States, whose humanity and magnanimity, by permission and will of Heaven, may yet preserve us from ruin and extinction.

The authorities of Georgia have recently and unexpectedly assumed a
doctrine, horrid in its aspect, and fatal in its consequences to us, and utterly at variance with the laws of nations, of the United States, and the subsisting treaties between us, and the known history of said State, of this nation, and of the United States. She claims the exercise of sovereignty over
this nation, and has threatened and decreed the extension of her jurisdictional
limits over our people. The Executive of the United States, through the
Secretary of War, in a letter to our delegation of the 18th April last, has
recognised this right to be abiding in, and possessed by, the State of Georgia; by the Declaration of Independence, and the treaty of peace concluded
between the United States and Great Britain in 1783; and which it is urged
vested in her all the rights of sovereignty pertaining to Great Britain, and
which, in time previously, she claimed and exercised, within the limits of
what constituted the " thirteen United States." It is a subject of vast importance to know whether the power of self-government abided in the
Cherokee nation at the discovery of America, three hundred and thirty-

seven years ago; and whether it was in any manner affected or destroyed by the charters of European potentates. It is evident from facts deducible from known history, that the Indians were found here by the white man, in the enjoyment of plenty and peace, and all the rights of soil and domain, inherited from their ancestors from time immemorial, well furnished with kings, chiefs, and warriors, the bulwarks of liberty, and the pride of their race. Great Britain established with them relationships of friendship and alliance, and at no time did she treat them as subjects, and as tenants at will, to her power. In war she fought them as a separate people, and they resisted her as a nation. In peace, she spoke the language of friendship, and they replied in the voice of independence, and frequently assisted her as allies, at their choice to fight her enemies in their own way and discipline, subject to the control of their own chiefs, and unaccountable to European officers and military law. Such was the connexion of this nation to Great Britain, to wit, that of friendship, and not allegiance, to the period of the declaration of Independence by the United States, and during the Revolutionary contest, down to the treaty of peace between the United States and Great Britain, forty-six years ago, when she abandoned all hopes of conquest, and at the same time abandoned her Cherokee allies to the difficulties in which they had been involved, either to continue the war, or procure peace on the best terms they could, and close the scenes of carnage and blood, that had so long been witnessed and experienced by both parties. Peace was at last concluded at Hopewell, in '85, under the administration of Washington, by " the Commissioners, Plenipotentiaries of the United States in Congress assembled:" and the Cherokees were received " into the favor and protection of the United States of America." It remains to be proved, under a view of all these circumstances, and the knowledge we have of history, how our right to self-government was affected and destroyed by the Declaration of Independence, which never noticed the subject of Cherokee sovereignty; and the treaty of peace, in '83, between Great Britain and the United States, to which the Cherokees were not a party; but maintained hostilities on their part to the treaty of Hopewell, afterwards concluded. If, as it is stated by the Hon. Secretary of War, that the Cherokees were mere tenants at will, and only permitted to enjoy possession of the soil to pursue game; and if the States of North Carolina and Georgia were sovereigns in truth and in right over us; why did President Washington send " Commissioners Plenipotentiaries" to treat with the subjects of those States? Why did they permit the chiefs and warriors to enter into treaty, when, if they were subjects, they had grossly rebelled and revolted from their allegiance? And why did not those sovereigns make their lives pay the forfeit of their guilt, agreeably to the laws of said States? The answer must be plain—they were not subjects, but a distinct nation, and in that light viewed by Washington, and by all the people of the Union, at that period. In the first and second articles of the Hopewell treaty, and the third article of the Holston treaty, the United States and the Cherokee nation were bound to a mutual exchange of prisoners taken during the war; which incontrovertibly proves the possession of sovereignty by *both* contracting parties. It ought to be remembered too, in the conclusions of the treaties to which we have referred, and most of the treaties subsisting between the United States and this nation, that the phraseology, composition, &c. was always written by the Commissioners, on the part of the United States, for obvious reasons: as the Cherokees were unacquainted with letters.　Again, in the Holston treaty, eleventh article, the following remarkable evidence is contained that our nation is not under the jurisdiction of any State: " If any citizen or inhabitant of the United States, or of either of the territorial districts of the United States, shall go into any town, settlement, or territory, belonging to the Cherokees, and shall there commit any crime upon, or trespass against, the person or property of any peaceable and friendly Indian or Indians, which, *if committed within the jurisdiction of any State, or within the jurisdiction of either of the said districts*, against a citizen or any white inhabitant thereof, would be punishable by the laws of such State or district, such offender or offenders shall be proceeded against in the same manner as if the offence had been committed *within the jurisdiction of the State or district* to which he or they may belong, against a citizen or white inhabitant thereof."　The power of a State may put our national existence under its feet, and coerce us into her jurisdiction; but it would be contrary to legal right, and the plighted faith of the United States' Government.　It is said by Georgia and the Honorable Secretary of War, that one sovereignty cannot exist within another, and, therefore, we must yield to the stronger power; but is not this doctrine favorable to our Government, which does not interfere with that of any other?　Our sovereignty and right of enforcing legal enactments, extend no further than our territorial limits, and that of Georgia is, and has always terminated at, her limits.　The constitution of the United States (article 6) contains these words: " All treaties made under the authority of the United States shall be the supreme law of the land, and the judges in every State shall be bound thereby, any thing in the laws or constitution of any State to the contrary notwithstanding."　The sacredness of treaties, made under the authority of the United States, is paramount and supreme, stronger than the laws and constitution of any State.　The jurisdiction, then, of our nation over its soil is settled by the laws, treaties, and constitution of the United States, and has been exercised from time out of memory.

Georgia has objected to the adoption, on our part, of a constitutional form of government, and which has in no wise violated the intercourse and connexion which bind us to the United States, its constitution, and the treaties thereupon founded, and in existence between us.　As a distinct nation, notwithstanding any unpleasant feelings it might have created to a neighboring State, we had a right to improve our Government, suitable to the moral, civil, and intellectual advancement of our people; and had we anticipated any notice of it, it was the voice of encouragement by an approving world. We would, also, while on this subject, refer your attention to the memorial and protest submitted before your honorable bodies, during the last session of Congress, by our delegation then at Washington.

Permit us, also, to make known to you the aggrieved and unpleasant situation under which we are placed by the claim which Georgia has set up to a large portion of our territory, under the treaty of the Indian Springs, concluded with the late General M'Intosh and his party; and which was declared void, and of no effect, by a subsequent treaty between the Creek Nation and the United States, at Washington City.　The President of the United States, through the Secretary of War, assured our delegation, that, so far as he understood the Cherokees had rights, protection should be afforded; and, respecting the intrusions on our lands, he had been advised, " and instructions had been forwarded to the agent of the Cherokees, directing him to cause their removal; and earnestly hoped, that, on this matter,

all cause for future complaint would cease, and the order prove effectual."
In consequence of the agent's neglecting to comply with the instructions,
and a suspension of the order made by the Secretary afterwards, our border
citizens are at this time placed under the most unfortunate circumstances,
by the intrusions of citizens of the United States, and which are almost
daily increasing, in consequence of the suspension of the once contemplated
"effectual order." Many of our people are experiencing all the evils of
personal insult, and, in some instances, expulsion from their homes, and loss
of property, from the unrestrained intruders let loose upon us, and the encouragement they are allowed to enjoy, under the last order to the agent for
this nation, which amounts to a suspension of the force of treaties, and the
wholesome operation of the intercourse laws of the United States. The
reason alleged by the War Department for this suspension is, that it had
been requested so to do, until the claim the State of Georgia has made to a
portion of the Cherokee country be determined; and the intruders are to
remain unmolested within the border limits of this nation. We beg leave
to protest against this unprecedented procedure. If the State of Georgia
has a claim to any portion of our lands, and is entitled by law and justice to
them, let her seek through a legal channel to establish it; and we do hope
that the United States will not suffer her to take possession of them forcibly,
and investigate her claim afterwards.

Arguments to effect the emigration of our people, and to escape the
troubles and disquietudes incident to a residence contiguous to the whites,
have been urged upon us, and the arm of protection has been withheld, that
we may experience still deeper and ampler proofs of the correctness of the
doctrine; but we still adhere to what is right and agreeable to ourselves;
and our attachment to the soil of our ancestors is too strong to be shaken.
We have been invited to a retrospective view of the past history of Indians,
who have melted away before the light of civilization, and the mountains of
difficulties that have opposed our race in their advancement in civilized life.
We have done so; and, while we deplore the fate of thousands of our com-
plexion and kind, we rejoice that our nation stands and grows a lasting
monument of God's mercy, and a durable contradiction to the misconceived
opinion that the aborigines are incapable of civilization. The opposing
mountains, that cast fearful shadows in the road of Cherokee improvement,
have dispersed into vernal clouds; and our people stand adorned with the
flowers of achievement flourishing around them, and are encouraged to secure
the attainment of all that is useful in science and Christian knowledge.

Under the fostering care of the United States we have thus prospered; and
shall we expect approbation, or shall we sink under the displeasure and
rebukes of our enemies?

We now look with earnest expectation to your honorable bodies for
redress, and that our national existence may not be extinguished before a
prompt and effectual interposition is afforded in our behalf. The faith of
your Government is solemnly pledged for our protection against all illegal
oppressions, so long as we remain firm to our treaties; and that we have,
for a long series of years, proved to be true and loyal friends, the known
history of past events abundantly proves. Your Chief Magistrate himself
has borne testimony of our devotedness in supporting the cause of the United States, during their late conflict with a foreign foe. It is with reluctant
and painful feelings that circumstances have at length compelled us to seek
from you the promised protection, for the preservation of our rights and

privileges. This resort to us is a last one, and nothing short of the threatening evils and dangers that beset us could have forced it upon the nation; but it is a right we surely have, and in which we cannot be mistaken—that of appealing for justice and humanity to the United States, under whose kind and fostering care we have been led to the present degree of civilization, and the enjoyment of its consequent blessings. Having said thus much, with patience we shall await the final issue of your wise deliberations.

With sentiments of the highest regard and esteem,

We have the honor to be, very respectfully,

Your obedient servants.

LEWIS ROSS,
President of Committee.

ECHOTA, CHEROKEE NATION, *Nov.* 5, 1829.

Joseph Vann.
David Vann,
James Daniel.
W. M. Boling,
Thomas Foreman.
Edward Guntee,
Daniel Griffin.
Samuel Ward,
Samuel Downing.
James Hamilton,
M. Baldridge,
George Saunders,
John Timson,
Alexander M'Daniel,
R. Taylor,
William S. Coodey,
    Clerk National Committee,
Going Snake,   his x mark.
        Speaker of Council,
Charles Reece,   his x mark.
Sleeping Rabbit, his x mark.

Choo Nungkee,   his x mark.
Archy Campbell,   his x mark.
Laugh at Musk,   his x mark.
Bark,   his x mark.
Chulio,   his x mark.
Soft Shell Turtle,   his x mark.
Walking Stick,   his x mark.
Moses Parris,
John R. Daniel,
Woman Killer,   his x mark.
James Bigby,   his x mark.
Deer in the Water,   his x mark.
Situaka,   his x mark.
Tecah-le-loo-ca,   his x mark.
Robin,   his x mark.
Choo-wa-loo-ca,   his x mark.
Cricket,   his x mark.
Nah-hoo-lar,   his x mark.
White Path,   his x mark.
Ne-cawee,   his x mark.
Tor-yes-kee,   his x mark.

JOHN RIDGE,
    Clerk of Council.

Approved:

JOHN ROSS,
    Principal Chief.

GEORGE LOWREY,
    Assistant Prin. Chief.

GEO. M. WATERS,
WILLIAM HICKS,
MAJOR RIDGE, his x mark.
    Executive Counsellors.

MEMORIAL OF THE CHEROKEES.

To the Honorable the Senate and House of Representatives of the United States of America in Congress assembled:

The undersigned memorialists humbly make known to your honorable bodies, that they are free citizens of the Cherokee nation. Circumstances of late occurrence have troubled our hearts, and induced us at this time to appeal to you, knowing that you are generous and just. As weak and poor children are accustomed to look to their guardians and patrons for protection, so we would come and make our grievances known. Will you listen to us? Will you have pity upon us? You are great and renowned—the nation which you represent is like a mighty man who stands in his strength. But we are small—our name is not renowned. You are wealthy, and have need of nothing; but we are poor in life, and have not the arm and power of the rich.

By the will of our Father in Heaven, the Governor of the whole world, the red man of America has become small, and the white man great and renowned. When the ancestors of the people of these United States first came to the shores of America, they found the red man strong—though he was ignorant and savage, yet he received them kindly, and gave them dry land to rest their weary feet. They met in peace, and shook hands in token of friendship. Whatever the white man wanted and asked of the Indian, the latter willingly gave. At that time the Indian was the lord, and the white man the suppliant. But now the scene has changed. The strength of the red man has become weakness. As his neighbors increased in numbers, his power became less and less, and now, of the many and powerful tribes who once covered these United States, only a few are to be seen—a few whom a sweeping pestilence has left. The Northern tribes, who were once so numerous and powerful, are now nearly extinct. Thus it has happened to the red man of America. Shall we, who are remnants, share the same fate?

Brothers—we address you according to usage adopted by our forefathers, and the great and good men who have successfully directed the Councils of the nation you represent. We now make known to you our grievances. We are troubled by some of your own people. Our neighbor, the State of Georgia, is pressing hard upon us, and urging us to relinquish our possessions for her benefit. We are told, if we do not leave the country which we dearly love, and betake ourselves to the Western wilds, the laws of the State will be extended over us, and the time, 1st of June, 1830, is appointed for the execution of the edict. When we first heard of this, we were grieved, and appealed to our father the President, and begged that protection might be extended over us. But we were doubly grieved when we understood from a letter of the Secretary of War to our Delegation, dated March of the present year, that our father the President had refused us protection, and that he had decided in favor of the extension of the laws of the State over us. This decision induces us to appeal to the immediate Representatives of the American people. We love, we dearly love our country, and it is due to your honorable bodies, as well as to us, to make known why we think the country is ours, and why we wish to remain in peace where we are.

The land on which we stand we have received as an inheritance from our fathers, who possessed it from time immemorial, as a gift from our common Father in Heaven. We have already said, that, when the white man came to the shores of America, our ancestors were found in peaceable possession of this very land. They bequeathed it to us as their children, and we have sacredly kept it, as containing the remains of our beloved men. This right of inheritance we have *never ceded*, nor ever *forfeited*. Permit us to ask, what better right can the people have to a country, than the right of *inheritance* and *immemorial peaceable possession?* We know it is said of late by the State of Georgia, and by the Executive of the United States, that we have forfeited this right—but we think this is said gratuitously. At what time have we made the forfeit? What great crime have we committed, whereby we must forever be divested of our country and rights? Was it when we were hostile to the United States, and took part with the King of Great Britain, during the struggle for Independence? If so, why was not this forfeiture declared in the first treaty of peace between the United States and our beloved men? Why was not such an article as the following inserted in the treaty: "The United States give peace to the Cherokees, but, for the part they took in the late war, declare them to be but tenants at will, to be removed, when the convenience of the States within whose chartered limits they live, shall require it." That was the proper time to assume such a possession. But it was not thought of, nor would our forefathers have agreed to any treaty, whose tendency was to deprive them of their rights and their country. All that they have conceded and relinquished are inserted in the treaties, open to the investigation of all people. We would repeat, then, the right of inheritance and peaceable possession which we claim, we have never ceded nor forfeited.

In addition to that first of all rights, the right of inheritance and peaceable possession, we have the faith and pledge of the United States, repeated over and over again, in treaties made at various times. By these treaties, our rights as a separate people are distinctly acknowledged, and guaranties given that they shall be secured and protected. So we have always understood the trea' es. The conduct of the Government towards us from its organization until very lately, the talks given to our beloved men by the Presidents of the United States, and the speeches of the Agents and Commissioners, all concur to show that we are not mistaken in our interpretation. Some of our beloved men who signed the treaties are still living, and their testimony tends to the same conclusion. We have always supposed that this understanding of the treaties was in concordance with the views of the Government, nor have we ever imagined that any body would interpret them otherwise. In what light shall we view the conduct of the United States and Georgia, in their intercourse with us, in urging us to enter into treaties, and cede lands? If we were but tenants at will, why was it necessary that our consent must first be obtained, before these Governments could take lawful possession of our lands? The answer is obvious. These Governments perfectly understood our rights—our right to the country, and our right to self Government. Our understanding of the treaties is further supported by the intercourse law of the United States, which prohibits all encroachments upon our territory. The undersigned memorialists humbly represent, that if their interpretation of the treaties has been different from that of the Government, then they have ever been deceived as to how the Government regarded them, and what she has asked and promised. Moreover, they have uniformly misunderstood their own acts.

In view of the strong ground upon which their rights are founded, your memorialists solemnly protest against being considered as tenants at will, or as mere occupants of the soil, without possessing the sovereignty. We have already stated to your honorable bodies, that our forefathers were found in possession of this soil in full sovereignty, by the first European settlers; and as we have never ceded nor forfeited the occupancy of the soil, and the sovereignty over it, we do solemnly protest against being forced to leave it, either by direct or indirect measures. To the land, of which we are now in possession, we are attached. It is our fathers' gift; it contains their ashes; it is the land of our nativity, and the land of our intellectual birth. We cannot consent to abandon it for another *far inferior*, and which holds out to us no inducements. We do moreover protest against the arbitrary measures of our neighbor, the State of Georgia, in her attempt to extend her laws over us, in surveying our lands without our consent, and in direct opposition to the treaties and the intercourse law of the United States, and interfering with our municipal regulations in such a manner as to derange the regular operation of our own laws. To deliver and protect them from all these and every encroachment upon their rights, the undersigned memorialists do most earnestly pray your honorable bodies. Their existence and future happiness are at stake. Divest them of their liberty and country, and you sink them in degradation, and put a check, if not a final stop, to their present progress in the arts of civilized life, and in the knowledge of the Christian religion. Your memorialists humbly conceive, that such an act would be in the highest degree oppressive. From the people of these United States, who, perhaps, of all men under heaven, are the most religious and free, it cannot be expected. Your memorialists, therefore, cannot anticipate such a result. You represent a virtuous, intelligent, and Christian nation. To you they willingly submit their cause for your righteous decision.

CHEROKEE NATION, *December* 18. 1829.

5. LITERARY "CRITICISM" / NATIVE AMERICAN "LITERATURE"

> *I embrace the world. I am the world. The white man has never understood this magic substitution. The white man wants the world; he wants it for himself alone. . . . He enslaves it. An acquisitive relation is established between the world and him. But there exist other values that fit only my forms.*
>
> —FRANTZ FANON

> *The nearer a study comes to live performances (the orator's breath, the speed at which he talks, where he raises his voice), the finer becomes the distinction between being a student and becoming an orator. In studying a religious art, where breath has overtones of "strength" and "spirit," this ground must be traversed cautiously.*
>
> —DONALD BAHR

> *In order for criticism to be responsible, it must always be addressed to someone who can contest it.*
>
> —TALAL ASAD

The criticism of Western literatures, as is well known, is more than two milennia old, extending at least from Plato to the present. Criticism of Native American literatures, however, is at best little more than two centuries old. This is to say that although as early as 1612 William Strachey produced a rough transcription and a paraphrase of what he called a "kind of angry song against us" (78–9) by the Powhatans, it was not until the European "Romantic" period (1760s or so) that the conditions of possibility existed for the recognition that Native American people did in fact produce and circulate something like what Westerners call literature, something that might be worthy of critical attention.

Having discussed this matter on a number of occasions,[1] I will only briefly recall to the reader, here, that the indigenous people of the present-day United States, inasmuch as they did not rely upon alphabetic writing as a means of information storage and transmission, initially seemed, in the eyes of the European invaders, barred from possessing a *littera-ture*, defined as the culture of letters (*littera*, letter). But in the second half of the nineteenth century, the meaning of *literature* shifted away from an emphasis on the form of presentation (writing) toward an emphasis on the content of the presentation (imaginative and affective material). By the time, for example, Bishop Percy's collection of Scottish ballads appeared (1765) to impress such as William Wordsworth with the expressive powers of illiterate, rustic men who, as Wordsworth put it in the preface to *Lyrical Ballads*, "convey their feelings and notions in simple and unelaborate expressions" (446), it increasingly became possible to speak of an "oral literature" as something other than a contradiction in terms.

Although as late as 1823, according to Victor Barnouw,

---

1. E.g., chapter 1, above; and for a fuller discussion, see "Native American Literature and the Canon," in *The Voice in the Margin*, pp. 96–131.

Lewis Cass, Governor of the Michigan Territory, "sent a questionnaire about Indian customs to traders, military men and Indian agents under his jurisdiction," which included the question, "Do [the Indians] relate stories, or indulge in any work of the imagination?" (Barnouw in Norman in press), his curiosity in this particular area seems to have been somewhat retrograde. For by the time Cass sent out his questionnaire, it had not only been noted that the Indians did, indeed, produce *literature*, but it was as well the case that this indigenous literature was increasingly becoming available for *criticism*. By 1823, that is to say, there were already some few *texts* of Native stories, songs, or other "work[s] of the imagination," *translations* into English of one sort or another.

What I am trying to say is simply that the first condition of possibility for a Western literary criticism of Native American literatures is the recognition that Native Americans do, indeed, produce discourse that might be called literature; and that the second condition of possibility for a Western literary criticism of Native American literature is the availability of *texts* of that literature. The relation between a criticism that is absolutely and unequivocally textual in orientation, and a literature that is oral (and so entirely independent of, indifferent to, and both historically and in the present frequently resistant to all forms of textualization) is, of course, highly problematic—to the degree that any possible "relation" between Western criticism, even ethnocriticism, and Native American literatures may be wishful and naive. I will return to this complex and difficult matter. For the moment I will only repeat that Western literary criticism has been and—so long as it remains Western literary criticism—will continue to be text-based (regardless of the existence of audio and videotapes, etc.), while reminding the reader that Native literatures are and continue to be oral and performative.

To produce the texts of an Indian literature requires the work of transcribers (because Indian literary performances are oral performances) and of translators (because it has always been, and, unfortunately, remains the case—with, to be sure, significant exceptions—that a majority of the literary critics of Indian literatures, myself included, have little or no competence in Indian languages). The first full textualization and translation of a Native American performance I know in the present-day United States is that of Lt. Henry Timberlake in the eighteenth century. Here are a few lines of Timberlake's "Translation of the WAR-SONG, *Caw waw noo dee, &c*":

> Where'er the earth's enlightened by the sun,
> Moon shines by night, grass grows, or waters run,
> Be't known that we are going, like men, afar,
> In hostile fields to wage destructive war;
> Like men we go, to meet our country's foes,
> Who, women-like, shall fly our dreaded blows. (81)

Timberlake's verse translation—a typical instance of a new matter ("primitive" war songs) initially appearing in an older manner (heroic couplets)—are bound to strike the contemporary reader as inevitably very distant from what any eighteenth-century Cherokee warriors might actually have sung.

Nor is it at all clear how much of the Cherokee language Lt. Henry Timberlake knew. His *Memoirs* (1767), in which this "translation" appears, suggest that he had spent enough time among the Cherokee to achieve some linguistic competence in their language. Still, it is altogether likely that Timberlake, working from the Cherokee (and working, probably, with an Indian who knew some English; working, as well, either from memory or from whatever rough notation of the original he or another had made), had not the linguistic "control" of the original language, in Dell Hymes's term,[2] that we assume, say, a Pope or a Johnson, translating in roughly that same period from the Greek or Latin, would have had of those tongues. And Timberlake did not have (he could not have had, as I have noted) a fixed or authoritative text of the original upon which to base his translation.

Thus, in retrospect, at least, we may see Timberlake as presenting a founding instance of what would become the paradigmatic situation for subsequent translators of Native American literatures, a situation that finds them somewhere between the typical position of translators from Indo-European languages able to work from a given/fixed/authoritative text, and that of anthropological translator-investigators who encounter, as Talal Asad puts it, not society/culture as texts but, rather, "people who speak" (155)—which "speaking," of course, is eventually textualized in ethnographic discourse.

Although Native languages were already being studied in the seventeenth century (so that the Bible might be translated into Indian), and no less than George Washington and Thomas Jefferson collected Indian wordlists for learned societies in the eighteenth century, detailed comprehension of Native languages seems to have reached a first plateau of relative sophistication only after the middle of the nine-

2. For this see Hymes's "Some North Pacific Coast Poems: A Problem in Anthropological Philology," first published in 1965, in *In Vain I Tried to Tell You* (1981).

teenth century. Samuel Worcester's earlier labors among the Cherokee, to be sure, included work on the Cherokee language, and later clerics like Bishop Riggs in the Dakotas, and H. R. Voth among the Hopi, or ethnographic workers like Washington Matthews and Frank Hamilton Cushing in the southwest, and Horatio Hale in the northeast, among others, provided a base—syllabaries, dictionaries, grammars, and the like—which was built upon "scientifically" in the twentieth century by the academic, anthropological linguistics largely founded by Franz Boas. Systematic study of the indigenous languages of the Americas continues to develop today, and there remains a very good deal of work to be done (as well as a good deal of work that can never be done, because there are no more speakers of a number of Indian languages). Thus, if *texts* are needed for the Western *criticism* of Native American literatures, and if most of those who have written criticism of Native American literatures have needed texts in English, then the trustworthiness of the available translations is, as Dell Hymes has pointed out in detail, a matter of considerable importance. I agree with Hymes and others that the accuracy of translations is a matter of major concern, although I would suggest that it may be possible to judge at least some few English texts of Native American literatures "bad" translations while yet judging them to be at least potentially "good" criticism. This distinction first requires one to take a position as to what "good" translation is (I have been throughout trying to take a position as to what "good" criticism is), and I will reserve this matter, too, for further discussion.

For a Western criticism of Native American literatures to develop, I have said, there must first be the recognition that there is such a thing as indigenous literature, and, second, there must be a minimal control of the languages in which these literatures are expressed for their textualization in various forms of translation. Yet one more condition for criticism must be met, and that is a knowledge of the cultures whose concerns Native American literatures—like any literatures the world over—address and express. This may perhaps most easily be illustrated by citing an anecdote presented by the anthropologist Laura Bohannon in an essay called "Shakespeare in the Bush." In it, Bohannon recounts her attempt to offer a plot summary of *Hamlet* to the Tiv people of West Africa when, Bohannon having often asked them to tell their stories, they asked her to tell them one of hers. At every point in Bohannon's summary, the Tiv interrupted to assure her that she must be getting the story wrong—for no son would act as Hamlet did toward his mother, no young person speak as Hamlet did to an elder, no spirit behave as she said Hamlet's father's ghost did, and so on. However "timeless" and "universal" we might think Shakespeare to be, *Hamlet* as he wrote it made little sense to the Tiv.

In just the same way, we may well recognize that Native American stories that include instances of mother-in-law avoidance may make the wrong kind of sense to Westerners, as mother-in-law jokes may confuse or disturb many Indian audiences: all narratives that involve kinship relations are sure to be somewhat baffling if one does not know how a given culture expects kin to behave toward one another (and most Native narratives deal substantially with kinship relations). Frequent patternings of fours and fives in Plains and Northwest Coast stories will seem odd to people whose own pattern numbers are three or seven. Those used to looking others in the eye, vigorously shaking their hand, and inquiring casually of their health will not readily understand why such behavior causes laughter or consternation among the Hopi and other Indian people. To develop any critical approach whatever to Native American literatures that deal with such matters—and all songs and stories, all literatures everywhere, deal with such matters—one needs an understanding of that people's cultural assumptions.

While no one disputes this in an absolute way, nonetheless, a certain rejection of the need for detailed, culture-specific information has arisen recently from two different versions of a perspective I will call "esthetic universalism." Both versions, in their strong forms, are obstacles in the way of any approximation to an ethnocriticism.

The first type of esthetic universalism holds that for all the differences in cultural custom all over the world, art is, nonetheless, essentially the same everywhere. Thus Karl Kroeber writes that

> even an inexperienced reader can rewardingly apply to traditional Indian narratives the kind of critical attitude he brings to other literatures. When one does this, the primary discovery one makes is that *diversity* of interpretation is possible because the narrative truly is a work of art. (1981 8)

"A majority of Indian stories," Kroeber continues,

> appeal to enough common features in human nature to allow us at least entrance to their pleasures—if only we can relax sufficiently to enjoy them. (1981 9)

Kroeber here replicates the worst aspects of Lévi-Straussian idealism as in such comments as the following:

> The mythical value of the myth is preserved through the worst translation. *Whatever our ignorance of the language and cul-*

ture [!] of the people where it originated, a myth is still felt as a myth by any reader anywhere in the world. (Lévi-Strauss in Berman Ms. 1)

As Judith Berman has shown in a careful reading of one of Boas's translations from the Kwakiutl, even Boas, who most certainly was not ignorant "of [Kwakiutl] language and culture," could produce a text that leaves us "wondering how much of the 'mythical value' of a myth really does emerge in a bad translation" (ms. 1).

In the same idealistic vein as Lévi-Strauss and Kroeber, we have Jarold Ramsey's citation of the Nez Percé translator, Archie Phinney, to the effect that

Any substantial appreciation of these [Nez Perce] tales must come . . . from vivid feelings within oneself, feeling as a moving current [of?] all the figures and the relationships that belong to the whole myth-body. (Ramsey 1983 xxi)

Ramsey rhetorically asks, "Doesn't Phinney's formula ring true for us, too, literature being what it is, and our imaginations of life being what they are?" (xxi). The difficulty, of course, is that just what literature "is," as I have noted, not to say what "our imaginations of life" in different languages and modes of presentation "are," may not be so clear or universal as Ramsey assumes. As a participant in Nez Percé culture, a speaker of the language, and a fully prepared auditor of mythic stories, Phinney may well judge the effectiveness of any given telling as it does or does not produce "vivid feelings" in him. For Ramsey to appropriate Phinney's criteria as so easily available to the Western reader is naive at best, and even then a naivete perpetuating the worst imperial arrogance.

Even Kroeber's ideally "relaxed" reader, for all that she may spot "common features in human nature" in Indian literatures and permit herself the very greatest "*diversity* of interpretation," may find her readings either banal or simply mistaken. A reading of Indian literature that discovers in it, for example, the observations that people age and die, or that spring brings renewal to nature, would produce the identity of Indian literature to all other literatures by ignoring the particular, different, and other manner—the culturally-specific modes and codes—by and in which such observations are presented. And such a reading may simply be misinterpreting particular cultural details, taking them in ways that would be quite appropriate to Western literary art but which are not at all appropriate to Native American literary art. "Diversity" of interpretation is certainly possible for any rich literature, but it is not the case that anything goes; egregiously mistaken interpretations are the most usual consequence of an "inexperienced" reader applying "the kind of critical attitude he brings to other literatures" to the literatures of a very different culture. This is one more instance of—to take a well-known phrase from William Bevis—assuming "we" will get Indian literature as cheaply as we got Manhattan.[3]

The second type of objection to an insistence on the importance of ethnographic information in the understanding of Native American literatures is more recent, and more complex in its implications. This objection derives its force from the context of postmodernism. Gerald Vizenor, the Anishinabe (Chippewa) poet, novelist, and critic is the foremost proponent of an anti-social-scientific, postmodernist approach to Native American literatures. Vizenor's sense,

3. See Bevis, "American Indian Verse Translations."

more or less similar to that of postmodernist anthropologists like Stephen Tyler, as I have noted above, is that social-scientific "knowledge" is predominantly knowledge of its own rules, codes, and concepts for making sense of culture, not of culture itself. Human linguistic behavior—"literature"—like human behavior generally, for Vizenor is best exemplified by the figure of the trickster, whose shape-changing, limit-transgressing antics provide the best guide—it is inherent in the nature of the trickster *not* to provide a *model*—to who and what we are, and, as well, to how we ought to read.

Although there are a good number of Native American narrative types that neither deal with tricksters nor court their style and mode, for Vizenor the trickster is everywhere: "The trickster is a communal sign in a comic narrative: the comic *holotrope* (the whole figuration) is a consonance in tribal discourse" (1989a 9). Whatever is "evoked" (I make reference again to Tyler, whom Vizenor approvingly quotes) by the sentence above, there is also the following to consider: "The instrumental language of the social sciences," Vizenor writes, "are [sic] tragic or *hypotragic* modes that withhold communal discourse" (1989a 9). A couple of pages later in the same essay, however, Vizenor remarks that

> social science studies reproduced new theories and contributed not so much to the doom of tragedies, but to a new insolence in tribal literature, an outbreak of *hypotragedies.* (1989a 11)

Grammatically, the "new insolence in tribal literatures" would seem to stand in apposition to—to be virtually synonymous with—"an outbreak of *hypotragedies.*" *If* that is the case, then it becomes difficult to understand how "hy-

potragedies," typical of the social sciences, are actually in-
imical to that "communal discourse," which surely marks
"tribal literatures." It may be that Vizenor means *"hypotragedies"* to be in apposition to "new theories" in "social science studies." In any case, the passage quoted above continues, "The trickster, a semiotic sign in a third-person
narrative, is never tragic or hypotragic, never the whole
truth or even part truth" (1989a 11). The terms hypotragic
and hypotragedy come up again and again, not only in Vizenor's preface and introduction to *Narrative Chance,* and
in his "Trickster Discourse: Comic Holotropes," the essay
which concludes the book, but as well in his later "Trickster
Discourse," in which the hypotragic is tied to monologue,
the unpardonable sin of the social sciences. Most recently,
tricksters are explicitly tied to the postmodern: "Crossbloods hear the bears that roam in trickster stories, and the
cranes that trim the seasons close to the ear. Crossbloods
are a postmodern bloodline" (1990 vii), Vizenor writes.
What is valorized here is the "comic and communal, rather
than [the] tragic and sacrificial; [for] comedies and trickster
signatures are liberations" (1990 viii).

Vizenor's sense of postmodern/trickster/comic "liberations," if I have at all gotten the point, insists upon the
absolute difference of all linguistic acts and all texts one
from another, a form of radical epistemological relativism
that, in its own way, can lead to another type of esthetic
universalism, in this case, one that would emphasize the
absolute irreducible distinctiveness of all phenomena, one
from another, rather than their ultimate sameness—an es-
thetics, as I think, in the ironic mode. Like Stephen Tyler's
postmodern ethnography, which *"describes* no knowledge
and *produces* no action," transcending both "by *evoking*
what cannot be known discursively or performed perfectly,"

something "beyond truth and immune to the judgment of performance" (123), Vizenor's critical remarks resist semantic clarity in the interest not of logical but, rather, of rhetorical and evocative force, his prose offering itself as the concrete embodiment and illustration of any doctrine it would at once uphold and subvert. What I believe it cannot claim is to offer a superior, a "better" account (according to any criteria whatsoever) of Indian literatures ("tribal narratives," trickster narratives, "communal discourses," and so forth) than social-scientific accounts. Nonetheless, as I have already suggested in chapter 3—and this is a matter to which I shall return soon—I believe Vizenor's critical writing may well be adapted for the development of an ethnocriticism of Native American literatures.

Western criticism, I have said, must constitute itself by work on texts rather than on actual performances and this, as I have also said, is a problem of major proportions for someone like myself who is interested not only in Western critical approaches to Indian literatures but in the development of an *ethnocritical* approach. Ethnocriticism, as I have been trying to define it and, in whatever degree, to practice it, cannot strictly be just a further development of Western critical practice. Rather, it must be a practice which seeks, to cite Jana Sequoya's formulation, a "convergence—which does not, however, comprise an identity—of indigenous and Western epistemes" (3); in Talal Asad's sense, it must be no less than an attempt, in language, at "learning to live another form of life" (149).

The problem is how to achieve this "convergence" or "learning" when the ethnocritical encounter is one between "competing ways of having stories," ways in which capitalist/individualist "ways" confront Indian sacred or "communitarian ways" (Sequoya 14), or, to refer again to Asad, of "different uses (practices), as opposed merely to different writings and readings" (160) of the work in question.

To take these matters into account is to question not only the possibility of a criticism of Native American literatures, but as well of an ethnocriticism, inasmuch as—in Sequoya's development of her argument, one to which Asad's commentary has particular relevance—indigenous literatures in the postcontact period must actively seek to distance themselves from Western (textual) critical practice in order to maintain their value and integrity. For all that ethnocriticism wishes to engage on an equal footing with Native literary practice, it cannot help but do so in a context of vastly unequal power relations. Thus, for all that the ethnocritic may decently and sincerely attempt to inquire into and learn from the Otherness of ongoing Indian literary performances, the sociopolitical context being what it is, she or he cannot help but threaten to swallow, submerge, or obliterate these performances. This is not to say that nothing can be done; but good-will or even great talent alone cannot undo the current differential power relations between dominant and subaltern cultural production.

Sequoya's comments come in a penetrating critique of Leslie Marmon Silko's highly acclaimed novel, *Ceremony*. And, indeed, it is likely that what most readers will know of Indian literary production today is the poetry and fiction of what may justifiably be called—the phrase is Kenneth Lincoln's—the recent "Native American Renaissance." This is work *written* in English for publication, and even though a very good deal of it appears under the imprint of small presses with limited means for advertisement and distribution, it nonetheless has a circulation far greater than the performances of contemporary-traditional (this adjectival phrase must *not* be taken as oxymoronic) Native singers and storytellers. These latter, as is inevitably the case for oral literature, even in an "age of mechanical reproduction" far more complicated than any Walter Benjamin imagined, do not circulate very far beyond the community of their intended (and culturally prepared) auditors. I do not know whether the singing and storytelling in which a fair number of Native people are, today, actively engaged is sufficiently abundant to justify speaking, in this regard, too, of some sort of "Renaissance." (But there is the whole question of the very specific Western implications of that term, in any case, implications which, obviously enough, imply analogies to the rediscovery of "lost" "classical" traditions which tend to distort the history of Native literary production. Lincoln, it seems to me, intends the term in a vaguely honorific sense, and it is in *that* sense, and that sense only, that I have invoked and found it acceptable.) I think I do know that any indigenous criticism *of* this work will mostly appear *in* this work, so that it, too, will not circulate much beyond the storytelling communities.

I mean to say that contemporary singing and storytelling goes on in communities that use those performances as means of affirming and validating their identities as communities—communities, which, insofar as they are traditionally oriented, do not separate those stories from their performers, audiences, and occasions, and so have no reason to develop any distinctive category of "criticism" about them. This is not in the least to say that Indian people have no ideas or thoughts about the "literature" they perform or participate in; it is to say that they have no need to produce a body of knowledge *about* it that is separate and apart *from* it. As a point of fact and an illustration of that point, let me note that my pronominal uses of "it" in regard to Native peoples' understanding of their literature is a Western convention that probably accords very badly with what I understand to be the actual ways Indians think about these things: for there is no abstract category like "literature" or "knowledge" that might be the antecedent of such an "it." (This is *not*, I should say, an instance of Spivak's catachrestical criticism: rather it is a fairly common problem of cross-cultural criticism.)

In the West, there is a more or less (the issue is currently much contested) distinctive category of discourse that can be referred to as "literature," and *its* knowledge, indeed, knowledge *it*self, exists as a reified object, a commodity, an "it." The Western literary critic tries to know literature and to obtain knowledge about *it*, which he or she then has—in the best of cases, to teach *it*, and share *it*, and pass *it* democratically on to others. But in any event, a virtual thing is involved, one that is alienated from *its* lived experience precisely to become alienable, i.e., transferrable or translatable (and, again, for ostensibly "good," disinterested, even transcendentally Kantian purposes, as well as for "bad," and economically interested ones). This is, to repeat, not the case for traditional Indian people both today and in the past.

It may be helpful here to mention, by way of illustration, the work of Harry Robinson, a contemporary Okanagan storyteller.[4] Because so few in the Similkameen Valley in Southern British Columbia where he lives speak Okanagan any more, Robinson, who learned his stories in his native language, nonetheless tells them today in English. Wendy Wickwire, who has published some of Robinson's stories, notes that

---

4. I am grateful to Professor Anthony Mattina for bringing Robinson's work to my attention.

in speaking English Harry uses pronouns indiscriminately. "He," "she," "it," and "they" are interchangeable, no matter what the antecedent. In most cases, Harry uses the plural neuter "they," rather than the singular "he," "she," or "it." (Wickwire 15)

Wickwire adds, "This is common in the speech of native elders" (15), and this may or may not be related to the few remarks I have offered about Indian ways of "having" stories. (I would not want to engage the problematics of any Whorfian linguistic determinism; but, again, see Asad's discussion of uses/practices.)

Wickwire sums up a good deal of what I have been trying to say when she writes of her decision not to edit out of Harry Robinson's "traditional" stories some " 'modern contaminants.' " I will quote her at some length:

The purist might edit some or all of the "modern contaminants" out of Harry's stor[ies], believing these to be tarnished post-contact influences on an otherwise traditional body of knowledge. This is typical of the scientific tendency to crystallize living, evolving oral culture—to transform myth into a static artifact, an "urtext" which contains the purest essence of what, to the Western mind, a native North American culture *is* (was). To do so is to miss the point entirely. In an oral tradition such as Harry's, where nothing is fundamentally new, and where creation is not some moment in the past, but remains present as the wellspring of every act and every experience in the world, the body of what is known is an integral part of creation. (23)

Thus "to crystallize Harry's stories, either on tape or in book form," as Wickwire is fully aware, is to "fix . . . these living stories in time. They will now no longer evolve as they have for hundreds of generations," and so her "book might be criticized for Homerizing Harry." By "criticized," of course, Wickwire means blamed, disapproved of. But it is only by "Homerizing Harry" that her book—and, most particularly, his stories—may indeed be criticized: by which *I* mean that his stories may be turned into subject/objects of a Western criticism of Native American literature. So far as Harry Robinson's stories do live and evolve, their evolution would contain *within* them any "criticism" *of* them, revisions, and variously selected "contaminants" serving as implicit commentary, and serving as an integral part of—to return to Sequoya's discussion—the "particular relationships with the conditions which produce them and specifically position the audience with respect to those [conditions]" (Sequoya). It would seem, then, that what is necessary for Native American oral literatures to become subject/objects of criticism is, to put the matter baldly, that they die.

To the extent that this is, however unfortunately, true, it bears upon the prospects for a properly ethnocritical account of Native American oral literatures, calling into question, as I have fully tried to acknowledge, the practice of the project I have been defining in theory. For it may well be the case that the Western view of history, for example, as compared or contrasted with the historical view of High Plains (and, I suspect, other Indian) people (see p. 16), like the Western view of literature and of criticism as compared or contrasted with the view of traditional people, cannot "converge" or satisfactorily be mediated—or, as I shall take the matter up, "translated." It may be that unless one is quite willing "to murder to dissect," the differences are irreconcilable. Short of reaching such a conclusion—but also, I admit, quite short of the specific outline of a practice—I can only offer the following speculations. And, in Eric Cheyfitz's phrase, "Only the other has the right to decide if these figures touch his or her facts" (xix).

Although I have been critical of Gerald Vizenor's trickster criticism just above, a criticism located explicitly by Vizenor within the Western postmodern episteme (postmodern, over the past several years has, indeed, become one of Vizenor's favorite words), there may—again, as I have noted above and in chapter 3—be ways in which Vizenor's "loosening the bounds" of Western discursive categories could be reoriented for ethnocritical purposes. I would once more cite the extremely fascinating conjunction of Vizenor's commitment to postmodern "trickster" fluidities with their ostensibly comic, infinite openness, and his commitment to what I have called premodern tribal identities, with their strong sense of natural rights and responsibilities—and as well to a view of the natural world utterly and entirely different from the postmodern alienation of late capitalism. Vizenor, at any rate, is at the height of his powers, and his very special work is clearly worth watching in its ongoing development.

It also seems to me—I admit to tentativeness and unsureness here—that there may be possibilities for the development of a nonviolent, anti-imperial ethnocritical practice for Native American song and story, not directly but indirectly—I will discuss another indirect route in detail just below—through the study of Native American oratory. Oratorical performances, like narrative or lyric performances, are always ritualistic, in varying degrees sacred—if, as I think, one can indeed speak of degrees of the sacred—and, like the songs and stories, committed to defining, affirming, and sustaining the communal life. But oratorical performances are those developed for specifically public occasions, and some of these, in post-contact times, increasingly have had to be adapted, far more than the songs and stories, to the pressures of nontraditional—which is, of course, to say Western, pressures. The Cherokee Memorials responding to the Indian Removal Bill, which I have attempted to analyze as rhetorical *writing*, had, as they continue to have, oral analogues. In the present, Native oratory ranges from the ritual oratory of the Pima and Papago (Tohon O'odham) analyzed by Donald Bahr, to that of the Iroquois longhouse ceremonies analyzed by Michael Foster, to oratory for the dedication of fish hatcheries analyzed by Anthony Mattina and his student, Donovan Lytle, to the Tlingit speech acts studied by Richard and Nora Dauenhauer.[5] I am admittedly offering no more than general intuitions here, but it seems to me that in the current revival of interest in Native American oratory there are possibilities for the development of an ethnocritical practice that may in time be adjusted to produce, as well, an ethnocriticism of Native American song and story.

Bahr's broadly suggestive (and rather overlooked) study of 1975 (one of the epigraphs to this chapter comes from this text) may offer some important possibilities in these regards, contending, as it does, "that the original collections of ritual oratory should be returned to the Pimans in written form and in a manner that will facilitate their use" (1975 3); that the "methodological eminence [Bahr] assigned to the written Piman version is a lonely eminence . . . because no reader of the next pages will be able to relate to it in a familiar manner" (28); and, thus, that his "written text is a

5. I have already cited Bahr's study of Pima and Papago ritual oratory. See Works Cited for the unpublished manuscripts by Mattina and Lytle. I also there give references for the important recent studies of oratory by Nora and Richard Dauenhauer, Miguel León-Portilla, and Joel Sherzer.

product without a public at the present time, pure schol-
arship" (28). Moreover, Bahr writes that its methodological
base or "theory was 'made up' by [him] and is not the product of any orator" (30). "No Piman orator," Bahr affirms, "is
presently known to be interested in the problem of writing
and very little is known about how orators think or theorize
about their oral art" (30). But perhaps out of these aware-
nesses something further can come—especially if it should
turn out, as Bahr tentatively dares hope, that Pimans might,
indeed, become interested in the "returns" he and others
have made. Nonetheless, as Sequoya has once again pointed
out (personal communication), any specifically ethnocritical
approach to Native American oral literary practice, even to
oratory, will have to take into account the enormously different visibilities and powers of the dominant culture and
the Native American minority, Asad's specification of what
he calls "unequal languages" (156).

To the extent that any sort of critical practice consistent
with ethnocritical aims already has some actual if incipient
existence, I would suggest it may be found not in the formal
discourses of Western criticism, but, rather, as one might
perhaps guess from the discussion thus far, in the practice
of *translation* from Native American literatures into English. It should be clear that I am not thinking, here, of
Henry Timberlake's procedures or of their later analogues.
Instead, I am thinking of those moments in the history of
translation when the intentions of poet-translators from the
dominant culture more nearly seemed to approach the intentions of Indian performers than anything Timberlake
could have imagined. I think these might be examined for
another indirect route toward an ethnocriticism of Native
American literatures.

By way of illustration, let me only mention the translation

versions of Indian songs done by Mary Austin in the twenties and thirties of this century, before turning to the translation *versions* of Jerome Rothenberg from the sixties to the present. It has been said by some that so far as these two consider themselves actually to be doing translation, they do "bad" translation, and I believe there may be a measure of justice in that judgment.[6] I would like to argue, however, that "bad" as these texts may be as translations, they nonetheless may be quite "good"—at least useful—as criticism. (In this I differ from Talal Asad insofar as he differentiates clearly between *translation* and *criticism*.) Further, the fact that translation-as-criticism to some extent mirrors the Native American way of doing "criticism"—critical practice, that is, only as internal to an evolving literary practice— it may do somewhat less violence to the literatures it "criticizes."

Before going on to develop this point, I suppose I must say something about how I understand the distinction between "good" and "bad" translation—and I continue to print these two words within quotation marks for obvious reasons—although even to approximate an adequate account of this matter would take us far out of our way. Because my critical orientation is more nearly cultural-materialist than idealist, I am largely in agreement with Bahr's view (although I don't mean at all to suggest that he shares my critical orientation) of "good" translation. I agree, that is, with his "simple but somewhat extreme position that English translations of non-English poetries ought to reflect the style of the original even at the expense of looking or

6. Bevis, in the essay cited in note 3, early made a case against Rothenberg's translations (and Austin's as well), and more recently, William Clements has published a useful if, in my view, somewhat extreme critique in "Faking the Pumpkin: On Jerome Rothenberg's Literary Offenses."

sounding odd in English" (1975 2). Consistent with this is Robert Brightman's recent observation that "By common consensus," there are "two necessary requirements" for translators. First is "some control of the original language from which the English translation is rendered," and second is the "explicit specification of the syntactic, semantic, lexical, prosodic, or other parallelisms that are used to delimit the text into lines and/or more inclusive units of poetic measure" (179). This sort of view would exclude Mary Austin entirely and Jerome Rothenberg at least partly as potentially "good" *translators*, as it also seems to exclude Howard Norman, a study of whose *The Wishing Bone Cycle* provides the occasion for Brightman's remarks.

Of course, there have been radically different views of "good" translation, ones that privilege the translator's ability to rise above fidelity to the letter of the original's style in the interest of capturing its "essence" or "spirit." Somewhat less usual are the views of Rudolf Pannwitz, Walter Benjamin, and Maurice Blanchot (I shall turn to them soon), attempting, in Benjamin's words, to make "both the original and the translation recognizable as fragments of a greater language, just as fragments are part of a vessel" (78). The standards according to which one may judge the degree to which any given translation may or may not have fulfilled this task remain mysterious to me, although Asad's instantiation of Benjamin's commitment to the *"intentio"* of the original demystifies the matter to a great extent.

One of the reasons Jerome Rothenberg's work is so interesting is that—and the reader has already many times encountered my attraction to this sort of endeavor—he importantly *mediates* idealist and materialist concerns, paying at least some measure of attention to "syntactic, semantic, lexical, prosodic" (Brightman 179) elements of the original, while feeling quite unconstrained to cut loose from those elements in search of the essentially (perhaps he would say "universally") "poetic" dimension of the original (Asad's/ Benjamin's "*intentio*"). In a recent essay, called " 'We Explain Nothing, We Believe Nothing': American Indian Poetry & the Problematics of Translation" (1991), Rothenberg not only defends his translation practices (in a tone and manner that are not at all defensive), but demonstrates his awareness of the ways in which translation is inevitably criticism. The particular kind of criticism Rothenberg's "ethnopoetic" translations perform is about the nearest approximation to anything I know of an ethnocritical practice for Native American literature already in place.

Rothenberg begins with an epigraph from an essay of Maurice Blanchot. Blanchot writes:

> Likeness, as [Walter] Benjamin rightly says, is not at issue here: if one requires that the translated work resemble the work to be translated, no translation is possible. What is involved, rather, is an identity that takes off from an alterity: the same work in two languages foreign to each other, and this mutual foreignness thus making visible the movement by which this work always becomes *other*, the very motion from which must be drawn the light which will transparently illuminate the translation. (84)

Without endorsing Blanchot's commentary as a whole (I balk, for example, at the notion of any form of transparent illumination, as well as, in the context of imperialism— which does not seem to concern Blanchot—the notion of "*mutual* foreignness"), still there is much that is useful here. Blanchot has in mind a famous passage in Benjamin's essay, "The Task of the Translator," in which Benjamin cites ("as the best comment on the theory of translation that has been published in Germany" [Benjamin 80]) some remarks of Rudolf Pannwitz. Pannwitz is quoted as follows:

> Our translations, even the best ones, proceed from a wrong premise. They want to turn Hindi, Greek, English into German *instead of turning German into Hindi, Greek, English.* Our translators have far greater reverence for the usage of their own language than for the spirit of the foreign works. . . . The basic error of the translator is that he preserves the state in which his own language happens to be instead of allowing his language to be powerfully affected by the foreign tongue. (In Benjamin 80–1, my emphasis)[7]

Now Benjamin, like Blanchot, isn't in the least interested in the imperial relations between European metropolitan powers and others; his project, the mystico-theological side of Benjamin which some (not I) admire, is a kind of impossible imagining of a totalized and unitary language, what must have been before the Tower of Babel; what God would speak or think. Eric Cheyfitz, in his study of the relations between translation and imperialism, also cites Pannwitz/ Benjamin, and does so for purposes much closer to my own, as, with significant differences, does Talal Asad. (See also David Murray.)

7. Inasmuch as it is translation I am talking about, it should be noted that the translation of Pannwitz's German into English is that of Harry Zohn. Blanchot's citation of Pannwitz is probably—I haven't been able, I regretfully admit, to check this—from the French translation of Pannwitz-in-Benjamin. This appears in the English translation of Blanchot by Richard Sieburth rather differently than in Zohn, as follows:

> Our translations even the finest ones proceed from a false premise they want to germanize sanskrit greek english instead of sanskritizing hellenizing anglicizing german . . . , etc. (Blanchot 85)

This is very effective—but I suspect quite "free" in its translation of Pannwitz!

This is to say that so far as translation may be imagined as a *critical* practice that seeks to undo its largely imperial history—its claim to speak for those who have no eloquent language of their own, its domination of the foreign figure of speech (Aristotle's definition of metaphor) by domesticating it, siting-by-citing it within one's own discourse, and so on—Pannwitz's is an exemplary conceptualization. According to Cheyfitz, Montaigne, in his essay on the cannibals, attempts "to displace the univocal opposition between the proper and the figurative with an equivocal, or kin-based relationship, where mastery [based in such an opposition] is impossible" (Cheyfitz 155). In much the same way, Rothenberg affirms the view that

> translation . . . involves . . . a discourse on its own problematics. . . . [I]t functions as a commentary on the other and itself and on the differences between them. It is much more a kind of question than a summing up. (1991 2)

Inasmuch as translation from Native American literatures raises questions "that center on orality, . . . on the sacred, and . . . on the question of imperial displacement" (1991 3), Rothenberg claims "that translation as a process is a principal means by which [these questions] can be explored" (3).

As Montaigne, in Cheyfitz's analysis, "uncannily imagines the language of the cannibals so he can alienate his own language in it" (Cheyfitz 163), as Asad insists that translation must be "learning to live another form of life" (149), so, too, does Rothenberg cite the Brechtian term *"Verfremdung"* to speak of his "own urge" in what he has called " 'total translation' " (14), "as much to cultivate the mystery [of otherness, difference, alterity] as to dispel it" (14), or to take that "mystery" into his own language. If, to return once more to Cheyfitz's discussion of Montaigne, the project of anti-imperial translation—this might, indeed, better be called *sublation*—is "to blur the frontier between the proper ['literal'] and figurative meanings of essential ethnological vocabulary" (Cheyfitz 155), this project, in Rothenberg's practice, seeks inevitably to challenge "the dominant assumptions" in the West "about the form and function of the poetic act" (11), in Asad's account, to cause the translator critically to examine "the normal state of his or her own language" (157). Thus translation can become "a calling into question of dominant attitudes in the colonizing culture" (31), and perhaps "help foster [in the dominant culture] the conditions for a new, even a newly *sacred* sense of poetry and of life" (31)—a sense that might, in fact, learn a good deal from traditional Indian peoples.

Of great importance to Rothenberg's view of translation is his determination, as he has said again and again, to get as far away as he can from *writing* (1968; 1991). Just as his former colleague and fellow translator Dennis Tedlock has committed his translation procedures to the production of what Tedlock calls a "performable translation" (13), so, too, does Rothenberg also—often at least, if not always—produce performable translations, translations, indeed, which he has on many occasions performed. (And, I might note, my own response to his performances, a response that seems to be consistent with what I have heard from others who have heard him, finds them to have great power.) This is not to say, unfortunately, that I believe the translations from Native American literatures Rothenberg has done fully achieve the goals he has stated. On the page, for example, Rothenberg privileges the visual in ways that do not, in my opinion, provide parallels for the aural. There is also a thoroughly Western subjectivistic individualism—e.g., as he admits, he does things frequently as they *feel* right to *him*—to his work that is probably all but inescapable but which nonetheless obtrudes upon any close approach to the cultural bases of tribal performances. And, as Sequoya has pointed out in a comment on Rothenberg's essay (personal communication), there remains in the forefront of his project the desire for self-transformation which (without denying the integrity of Rothenberg's commitment to social transformation as well) is quite alien to traditional performers. All of this notwithstanding, I would still say (or perhaps merely repeat) that Rothenberg's translations may nonetheless have possibilities, tentative though they may be, for the material practice of an ethnocriticism—so far as this may be possible for Native American literatures.

6. NATIVE AMERICAN AUTOBIOGRAPHY AND THE SYNECDOCHIC SELF

Although studies of Native American autobiography have become more numerous of late, no one of these has yet taken as its central focus the matter that has perhaps more than anything else occupied students of Western autobiography, that is, the nature of the "self" presented in these texts. This is not to indicate an error or omission; to the contrary, inasmuch as the centrality of the self to Western autobiography has no close parallel in Native American autobiography, any immediate orientation toward the self would inevitably have seemed ethnocentric, at the least premature. But to say that the Western understanding of the self, in its various historical representations, is neither prioritized nor valorized in Native American autobiography is not at all to say that subjectivity is, therefore, absent or unimportant in these texts. Whether or not Paul Heelas is correct in his generalization (and I think he probably is not) that "the autonomous self is universal" (48), it is very likely the case that some sense of self—perhaps Amélie Rorty's "reflective, conscious subject of experience, a subject that is not identical with any set of its experiences, memories or traits, but is that which *has* all of them" (11)—is indeed to be found universally, and so, to be sure, among Native American people.

The problem is that every term in Rorty's (or in any other) description is culture-specific, inflected in its meaning by the particular cultural codes according to which we differentially "have," as historically and geographically situated men and women, our similar "experiences" as human beings.[1] What, after all, does it mean for the Hopi to be "reflective," for the Yaqui to be "conscious," for the Chippewa to be a "subject," for the Ojibwa to "have" experiences? Humans are or do all of these things, and we are or do them in the same ways—differently. Considerations of this sort have animated work in the ethnography of the self, from its rudimentary and initially "anti-psychological"[2] be-

1. If not another "problem," another consideration is that while *some* sense of self may be universal, it is not the case that that sense of self, whatever it may be, receives cultural validation. As we shall see, not selfhood, hallmark of "individualist" society so much as personhood, hallmark of the "holist" society (Dumont passim) is what is found among most of the world's people.

2. Clyde Kluckhohn, quoted by A. I. Hallowell (387n). I would not be quite so certain as Marsella, DeVos, and Hsu, writing at the meridian of Reaganism, that "The Self has returned!" nor so unequivocally cheered if that were indeed the case. Nevertheless, it does seem to be true that psychological anthropology, for better or worse, is currently on an upswing and that its focus of study is whatever name we choose to give to the unitary male's or female's own sense of himself or herself as a unit entity. Almost by definition, a strictly conceived *psychological* anthropology tends to privilege the individual perception of self, projecting a Western bourgeois bias. For a tough, ideologically inflected account of the early culture and personality movement, see Harris 1968. Although culture-and-personality studies may be dated from as early as 1910, their influence, through Benedict, Mead, Sapir, and others (cf. n. 7, below), is more nearly a matter of the thirties. Hsu is particularly hostile to "personality" as the reference term for this type of study, which may account for the title of his co-edited text, *Culture and Self*. Thomas Williams lists over a hundred and twenty references that permit the interested reader to trace the historical trajectory from culture and personality to psychological anthropology in his "The Development of Psychological Anthro-

ginnings in the form of "culture and personality" studies from about 1910 on, to its current existence in the form of a decidedly "psychological anthropology." Yet for all of this work, we are still far from any conceptual and terminological consensus about how to speak of the self, the individual, or the ego, the "I," or "me," the "modal personality," the "model of identity"—or, indeed, the "subject," where each of these terms signals not only a personal preference, a research interest or emphasis, but as well, as Paul Smith has recently shown, a disciplinary affiliation (subjects coming more or less from philosophy, individuals and selves from the humanities, egos and modal personalities from the social sciences, etc.).[3] Even to the extent we do know how these terms apply to the West, we know less well how they apply (or don't apply) to the rest, whose thought on such matters is reduced (or elevated) to the level of "indigenous psychologies."[4]

To be sure, these studies are barely a century old, so that it would be premature to abandon, as a certain postmodernist strain of thought would urge, further efforts in the direction of some greater accuracy of description and explanation. Yet it is necessary to acknowledge, here, a practical rather than a theoretical problem certain to beset ad-

pology," the introduction to a collection of essays on the subject. For the "continuities" between the two orientations, see also the study by Philip K. Bock. Victor Barnouw's textbook, in its fourth edition as of 1985, still adheres to the older nomenclature for its title. The introduction by John Kirkpatrick and Geoffrey M. White to their *Person, Self, and Experience: Exploring Pacific Ethnopsychologies* offers a particularly sophisticated and thoughtful account of these matters. The journal, *Ethos*, published by the American Society for Psychological Anthropology was founded in 1973.

3. See *Discerning the Subject*.

4. See, for example, Paul Heelas and Andrew Lock, eds., *Indigenous Psychologies: The Anthropology of the Self*.

vances along these lines, one akin to that Freud posited for the general prospects of psychoanalysis.[5] I refer to the fact that while it is a fairly simple matter to convince people that their eating or greeting habits are cultural rather than natural, it is considerably more difficult to convince them that the ways in which they think and deeply feel about themselves are also more nearly culturally than biologically determined. And modern Western concepts of the self are so thoroughly committed to notions of interiority and individualism that even anthropologically sophisticated Westerners have a tendency to construct their accounts of the varieties of selfhood as an evolutionary narrative, telling a story of a progression from the social and public orientation of ancient or "primitive" self-conception (the self as social "person") to the modern, Western, "civilized," egocentric/individualist sense of self.[6]

This tendency may be responsible for what I take as the essentially comic plot of Marcel Mauss's 1938 essay, most recently translated as "A category of the human mind: the notion of person; the notion of self." Mauss's seminal study tells a story which has as its happy ending the emergence of the "*moi*," the Western post-romantic self as veritably "sacred," a construction that surpasses what Mauss calls the *personnage* models of the Native Americans, Mauss's chief illustrative example, and the *personnalité* models of ancient and/or non-Western peoples generally. For Mauss, Native American self-consciousness was minimal, or, better, de-

5. Sigmund Freud, "One of the Difficulties of Psychoanalysis."

6. Paul Heelas, who develops practical applications of Andrew Lock's distinction between concepts of the self as "in control" or "under control," according to what he calls "idealist" or "*passiones*" models (39ff), quotes Edward Tylor, Lucien Lévy-Bruhl, and C. Hallpike in ways that would seem to indicate their attachment to a Western view for all their (rudimentary, in Tylor's case) commitment to versions of cultural relativism.

fined by the etymology of the word person (*personne, personnage*), from Latin *persona, per sonare*, as this referred to the mask through which the actor spoke his role in public. Not an individual with rights and responsibilities before the law (this must await the Roman addition of the right to a personal *praenomen* or "forename," and the Christian invention of "the moral person"), the Indian was rather the representative of his ancestor or his clan, an actor who merely performed his appointed character. As Mauss would have it, the Indian knew little or nothing of that consciousness which is properly and proudly a *self*-consciousness, "an act of the 'self,' " and which, from Fichte on, saw "the revolution in mentalities . . . accomplished" (22). Mauss drew some of these conclusions from the investigations of Boasian anthropologists, and he offers particular data from the Hopi. In this regard, as Peter Whiteley has recently shown, Mauss either ignored or was quite simply wrong in his understanding of the complexities of Hopi naming practices (Whiteley 1988). For all that Hopis do, indeed, identify with clan and sodality roles, Whiteley's carefully gathered data show that Hopis also take great pleasure in the distinctive, "poetic," and, indeed, quite individualistic qualities of some of the names they formerly and continuously bestow and appreciate (Whiteley 1991). These comments are intended to suggest a complexity to the "red side" of the story greater than most commentators have thus far allowed; this is *not* to say that Native American and Eurmerican conceptions of the self *are*, after all, more nearly alike than Mauss claimed.

For, there is little or nothing in the indigenous cultures of the Americas to parallel what I will offer here as an illustration of the apogee of the "modern" Western *moi*, what we find in a text like Gerard Manley Hopkins's "As kingfishers catch fire, dragonflies draw flame," in which the inward self appears both as actor in "God's eye," and sublimely unique romantic consciousness.

For Hopkins,

> Each mortal thing does one thing and the same:
> Deals out that being indoors each one dwells;
> Selves—goes itself; *myself* it speaks and spells,
> Crying *What I do is me: for that I came.* (53)

But this lovely indoor self, in Mauss's tale, unfortunately was never present to the poor outdoor Indian.

In his ultimate celebration of the inward self, Mauss, as a number of commentators have noted, seems to renege on his initial promise to "leave aside everything which relates to the 'self' (*moi*), the conscious personality as such," and to focus instead on the "social history" (3) of the person, the category of prime concern to Mauss's uncle and *maître*, Emile Durkheim, as it was to that major but—at least in literary circles—currently somewhat obscure figure, George Herbert Mead. Mead's "social theory of the self," as Stephen Lukes has remarked, sought "to explain how it can be, in all societies and cultures, that" in Mead's words,

> all selves are constituted by or in terms of the social process, and are individual reflections of it [yet] every individual self has its own peculiar individuality, its own unique pattern. (Lukes 287)

In this regard, any attempt to privilege the sacred inviolability of the self by setting it in opposition to society or culture, standard Western bourgeois practice at least since Fichte, involves, to return to Lukes, "a significant loss of understanding" of everything beyond the local/Western. To avoid such a loss, we get in the forties and fifties a re-description of the Native American sense of self by such writers as Dorothy Lee and George Devereux, among others, in ways that relativize the matter in the interest, to invoke again the phrase of Fischer and Marcus, of anthropology as cultural critique. Whatever Indian sense of self—and this is no more monolithic than any "Western" sense of self—one may describe now seems less "primitive" and retrograde than, indeed, more "advanced," wiser than what prevails in the West in its superior comprehension of the dynamic interaction, not the opposition, between any self and any society. Oddly, or not so oddly, we have, in this period, a comic narrative of identity once more—only the protagonist is different![7]

7. But there is a complicated history here, which, although it is beyond the scope of this chapter, is very well worth detailing. The background involves Ruth Benedict's prescriptive "descriptions" of Native American personality clusters (1934); Margaret Mead's Pacific excursus (1928); and Erik Erikson's intervention culminating in detailed accounts of *correlations* (Erikson being quite careful to deny any claim to statements of a directly causal nature) between Yurok and Sioux childrearing practices and adult character structures. The work of Anthony Wallace with the Tuscarora and A. I. Hallowell with the Ojibwa also deserves mention, as does that of George Spindler and the "Rorschachists." George Devereux's important invention, as it were, of ethnopsychoanalysis commences with the practical demonstration of his *Reality and Dream: Psychotherapy of a Plains Indian*, and achieves full theoretical statement in *From Anxiety to Method*. Current work along a variety of these lines, as I have noted above, is abundant. Still, the conclusion of Richard Shweder's recent three-part essay, "Rethinking Culture and Personality Theory," is that "Most of the postulates of the culture and personality school . . . worked out in the 1940s and 1950s . . . do not weather well under empirical and conceptual scrutiny" (I 255–6). Shweder's own positions are "worked out" in his "Does the concept of the person vary cross-culturally?" (co-authored with Edmund J. Bourne).

Before developing this point just a bit further, it seems to me useful to speak of the point Carter Revard has so shrewdly raised in regard to any narratives of Indian identity. Revard, I mean to say, has raised the important issue of demographic or topic-al influences on generic geneses. For one thing, as he writes,

> I wonder how much mere demographics has to do with the differences between Native American and Western literature. I take a major fact to be that in a small, relatively classless society where everyone knows everyone else, it is redundant for anyone to offer an autobiography. I take as another major fact that cities are meant to hide lives, to make sure nobody knows what one has been doing, to try and prevent circumstances of family and parentage from constraining a person's claims on society or claims for herself. I take it that in a society where there are many people and most of them have never met or meet only for brief moments, where "privacy" means one can hide everything in the past from anyone else, THERE it is possible to offer autobiography. (Personal communication)

Any Indian sense of self we may derive from Native American autobiography must, I believe, take these considerations into account. And these considerations, as I shall have occasion to note shortly, bear on the matter of voice and text in Native American self-presentation.

To return to the particular history of the thirties and forties, however, it was Devereux's opinion that for Native Americans "maximum individuation and maximum socialization go hand in hand" (291), while Lee concluded that Lakota cultures demonstrate "autonomy and community in transaction" (1986 41). Of the Wintu self, Lee noted (her generalizations supported by impressionistically selective "ethnoscientific" citations from Wintu grammar and diction), that it is

> not clearly opposed to the other, neither is it clearly identical
> with or incorporated in the other. On most occasions it partic-
> ipates to some extent in the other, and is of equal status to the
> other. (1959 137)

Wintu know "society" more readily than the "self," the reverse of our Western knowledge; but most of all, Wintu
seem to have found a way to reconcile what often appears
to Euramericans as an opposition between self and society.[8]

In any event, insofar as we would attempt to generalize
about the Native American self from the available studies,
that self would seem to be less attracted to introspection,
expansion, or fulfillment than the Western self appears to
be. It would seem relatively uninterested in such things as
the "I-am-me" experience,[9] and a sense of uniqueness or
individuality. More positively, one might perhaps instantiate an "I-am-we" experience as descriptive of the Native

8. To the extent this is true, it might then be said that some Native American
cultures seem to have reconciled the apparently antithetical implications of the
English words *subject* and *individual*, for all that these are often used as syn-
onyms. As Raymond Williams has usefully pointed out, the etymology of the first,
from the Latin *sub-* and *jactum* (p.p.), to be thrown under or beneath, persists in
the senses of being subject to, the subject of, subjected, and so forth (e.g., Lock's
self "under control"). The etymology of individual, however, continues to carry
with it the original sense of indivisible, as if one were fully present to oneself and
uniquely empowered as causal agent (e.g., Lock's self "in control"). This sense of
the individual, espoused historically by a certain vulgar humanism in the fifties,
called forth an equivalently vulgar anti-humanism in the sixties and after (as, e.g.,
in much of Foucault), with no place whatsoever for the active force of human
agency. For a fine account of these matters see Kate Soper's *Humanism and Anti-
Humanism*.

9. For the "I-am-me" experience, see Herbert Spiegelberg's discussion in
Eakin, pp. 217–9.

sense of self, where such a phrase indicates that I understand myself as a self only in relation to the coherent and bounded whole of which I am a part (e.g., the quotation from Lee above). Here, Jane Fajans's distinction between the "*person* as a bounded entity invested with specific patterns of social behavior, normative powers, and restraints, and the *individual* as an entity with interiorized conscience, feelings, goals, motivations, and aspirations" (370 my emphasis) is useful. Native Americans (along with most of the world's people, it would seem) tend to construct themselves not as individuals but as persons. As Carter Revard had shown over ten years ago, in his comments on the autobiographies of Geronimo and others, and as David Brumble, from a somewhat different perspective has convincingly affirmed (1981, 1989), for Native American persons, "the notions of cosmos, country, self, and home are inseparable" (Revard 1980 86).

At this point it would be possible to proceed with readings of several Native American autobiographies in order to determine whether their authors do or do not seem to conceive themselves in the ways suggested by the available anthropological and psychological literature. The danger here is that such readings tend not to be actual "readings" at all, but, instead, tautological exercises in the "discovery" of literary "evidence" for psychological or anthropological "truths" already established elsewhere, as if autobiography were no more than a museum for the self where one could peer through language as through the transparent glass of a case.

Concerned to avoid such vulgar reductionism, it is tempting to adopt the militantly formalist position of a Paul de Man, which insists that autobiography is no more than a figure of reading, an effect of language, and thus can provide no reliable information about selves—or about any-thing else outside the orders of language.[10] This position denies that we can ever know another self in autobiogra-phy—affirming (what for the deconstructionist is apparently abundant recompense) that what we can know is simply the infinite play of linguistic signification.

How, then, to navigate between the Scylla of a purely realistic/referential reading and the Charybdis of a purely linguistic/figural reading? How to satisfy a thoroughly rep-utable interest in the subject of autobiography as biograph-ical existent, and as cultural and historical agent, while cen-tering one's commentary on what autobiographical texts present linguistically, the actual words from which any sense of self must be inferred? For, to speak, now, only of Native American autobiographies, one finds little or no ex-plicit mention of who-I-am, little or no mention at all of the self as the object of conscious and developed concern.

Let me propose as one avenue of approach—and so an attempt at mediating the two positions—that we appropri-ate terms for the figures of language as applicable to some facts of life. With all due apologies to the reader for elabo-rating what may well be obvious, I want to state as clearly as I can here the potential contribution the discussion to follow hopes to make; this is also, I am well aware, to specify the grounds for that discussion's limitations and weaknesses. I mean to suggest that the West's traditional fourfold rhe-torical division of *elocutio* and *poeisis* into metaphor, me-tonymy, synecdoche, and irony, a division invented to name linguistic relations, may be taken (metaphorically) as nam-ing relations of an actual/"realistic" type between the per-

10. See "Autobiography as De-Facement." The figure specified by de Man is prosopopeia. For an excellent brief discussion see Eakin, pp. 184–91, whose own view is rather different. Paul Smith comments on de Man's essay as well, pp. 105ff.

son/individual and others (or society) and so may provide terms for a theory of self-conception and self-situation *as these appear in the texts we call autobiographies.*

If it is indeed the case, for example, that there are peoples who actually do conceive of themselves as in some very real sense interchangeable with their ancestors and their posterity (the Balinese, in Clifford Geertz's account, perhaps?[11]), then we might expect any stories they tell about themselves to show a *metaphorical* conception of the self, one that constructs identity paradigmatically, along the vertical axis of analogical selection. Metonymy and synecdoche I take as terms that name relations of a part-to-part and a part-to-whole type. Thus, where personal accounts are strongly marked by the individual's sense of herself predominantly as different and separate from other distinct individuals, one might speak of a *metonymic* sense of self. Where any narration of personal history is more nearly marked by the individual's sense of himself in relation to collective social units or groupings, one might speak of a *synecdochic* sense of self, both metonymy and synecdoche constructing identity syntagmatically, along the horizontal axis of contiguity and combination.

While I am ignorant of specific instances of an *ironic* sense of self elsewhere in the world, I would suggest that some of what might be called "modernist" senses of self in the West may be usefully categorized as ironic. The exemplary texts here (I cite novelistic examples for the purer types fiction can construct; autobiographical nearequivalents may readily enough be found) are, at the earliest, Melville's uncanny imagination of the "confidence

11. For a sketch of the Balinese "self" as well as some others, see Geertz's " 'From the Native's Point of View': On the Nature of Anthropological Understanding."

man," and Dostoyevsky's story of the "underground man," these followed by a whole library, as it were, of ironic modern "characters": T. S. Eliot's fragmented voices out of "the waste land," Robert Musil's "man without qualities," Kafka's "arrested" and metamorphosed men, Virginia Woolf's disembodied monologists in *The Waves*, right on to Samuel Beckett's portrayals of the self as contingent to the point of virtual dissolution. In these texts there is neither the metaphorical sense of the cosmic interchangeability of persons; nor the metonymic sense of the specific uniqueness of otherwise comparable individuals; nor the synecdochic sense of personal representation of a collective entity. Rather, there is only the sense of self-identity as fact-with-no-meaning: I-am-I, but so what. Or, in the specifically antiphrastic form, I am not like him, not like her, certainly not like them, that's not me, nor that, nor am I much like anything at all.[12]

From the perspective of a rhetorical hardliner like de Man, the procedure I have outlined represents no more than a categorical error: one cannot cross the line from language to life inasmuch as it is the very essence of figures to signify *only* linguistically and *not* realistically. That is to say, if one takes the standard illustration of synecdoche, "fifty sail" for "fifty ships," it is obvious that the figure makes no sense realistically:[13] although one *can*, of course, visualize fifty *sails* coming across the water, the image itself is un-

---

12. The typical affective response to such a sense of self in modernist literature is the feeling of alienation and anxiety. The postmodern self, it should be said, is also constructed ironically and rhetorically presented by the figure of *catachresis*, "abusive" or absurd usage. Its affective response I see as what Fredric Jameson has referred to as schizophrenic "euphoria." See Jameson's "Postmodernism, or the Cultural Logic of Late Capitalism." For *catachresis*, see chapter 2.

13. Granted, it makes *surrealistic* sense, but surrealistic sense I take as a textual effect. Surrealistic *speech* by definition could not have ordinary or normative force.

likely to refer to anything one might actually see. Literally, it makes no sense. The same is true for "he is all heart," e.g., visualizing "him" as an assemblage of arteries, auricles, ventricles, etc. Nonetheless, I am making the assumption that the part-to-whole relation named by the term synecdoche and the part-to-part relation named by the term metonymy, along with the relations termed metaphoric and ironic as these are posited in language, can usefully be applied to relations we experience in life, particularly, here, the relation of the individual self, or subject to other individuals selves, or subjects, and to collectively constituted groups.

I am assuming, to put it in the phrase of George Lakoff and Mark Johnson, that there are, indeed, "metaphors we live by" (q.v.); and that, as M. Brewster Smith has written, "the metaphorical texture of our views of self is part and parcel of our metaphorical construction of the world" (74). I tend to believe that there is not a radical epistemological break between the use of metaphor in life, as in Lakoff and Johnson's sense that metaphor quite unself-consciously and unambiguously involves "*understanding and experiencing one kind of thing in terms of another*" (5 my emphasis), and the use of metaphor in texts, as in Gerard Genette's sense of the figure precisely as "a sense of figure, . . . [whose] existence depends completely on the awareness that the reader has, or does not have of the ambiguity of the discourse that is being offered him" (54). For all that the former emphasizes the sense-constructing possibilities of figures, while the latter asserts the sense-deconstructing possibilities of figures, I take the difference as a matter of emphasis rather than one of opposition.[14] Thus I will suggest that the

14. Lakoff and Johnson rather casually take the figure of metaphor as a master trope (all other figures are taken as kinds of metaphors) and assume that what is understood and experienced in the natural-language and ordinary-usage examples

theory of tropes has value for a theory of self-conception, and that its usefulness resides most particularly in its giving us a way of speaking of the self as it is actually presented textually, in autobiography. I shall further suggest that cultural techniques of information transmission—oral as differentiated from written techniques—also correlate with particular figural preferences and particular conceptions of self.

In a provocative article, Stephen Tyler has attempted to place the "Standard Average European"[15] preference for seeing as a way of knowing and for writing as a way of conveying what is known against the backdrop of an ignored or undervalued non-Western preference for doing and speaking. Evading the formalist-structuralist distinction between metaphor and metonymy that, at least since Roman Jakobson's famous essay on "Linguistics and Poetics," has become a virtual staple of poetics—"the irreplaceable bookends of our own modern rhetoric," in Gerard Genette's phrase (107)—Tyler focuses on a distinction between metonymy and synecdoche, not so much as parallel terms concerned

---

on which they exclusively base their argument (they are totally unconcerned with metaphors in writing) is always clear and unambiguous. There is a kind of extraordinary complacence in asserting categorically, as they do, for example, that "UNKNOWN IS UP," and "KNOWN IS DOWN" (137), without (say) taking into account the "metaphor" of "consciousness raising." To have one's consciousness raised, whatever this may indicate in terms of "understanding and experiencing," would seem to move up toward knowing. But even if I am wrong, if, that is, a "better" interpretation of the "metaphor" bears out the unknown/up, known/down interpretation, clearly there is at least the possibility of a certain ambiguity. In the same way, for all that a Genette, a de Man, or a Derrida can always show the persistence in any apparently plain statement of some further possibility of signification and so the possibility of some further ambiguation, that does not prevent us from "understanding and experiencing" some relatively clear meaning. I offer these remarks in support of my contention that the textual and ordinary uses of metaphor are different versions of the same.

15. "Standard Average European" is a category Tyler takes from Benjamin Whorf, whose work he specifically praises in some polemical notes.

with relations of contiguity, contact, or correspondence (syntagmatic relations as opposed to the paradigmatic relations of substitution definitive of metaphor, or the antiphrastic relations of negation definitive of irony), but as terms differentiable by the *kinds* of relation with which they are concerned. For Tyler—and I have already accepted his account of these matters in my remarks above—metonymy is concerned with part-part relations while synecdoche is concerned with part-whole relations. Here I want to propose that while modern Western autobiography has been essentially metonymic in orientation, Native American autobiography has been and continues to be persistently synecdochic, and that the preference for synecdochic models of the self has relations to the oral techniques of information transmission typical of Native American cultures. Let us (briefly) take this second matter first.

Traditionally, the autobiographical forms (such as they were) that existed among Native American peoples—the *coup* story on the Plains foremost; accounts of dreams or mystic experiences[16]—were communicated orally, Indians of the present-day United States not having developed alphabetic writing, and (therefore) publicly as well. One did not tell of one's war honors in private, to one's wives or best friends, but to assembled members of the tribe, an audience that included eyewitnesses to the events narrated who were dutybound to object to or deny any false claims. In the same way, we know that the most powerful visions (e.g., the celebrated visions of Black Elk at ages five and nine)[17] were often enacted tribally, dramatically performed in public so that their full effect, which is to say their collective

16. See, for example, the study of Lynne Woods O'Brien.
17. See *Black Elk Speaks*.

effect, might be experienced ("done," as Tyler might say). I win honors, then, not only for me (most assuredly for me, however, particularly on the Plains, but elsewhere as well) but for us, the tribe; I am granted a vision, but the vision is not just for me, nor is any of it usable or functional until it is spoken, even performed publicly. This sense of personal eventfulness and this manner of communicating the personal orally, dramatically, performatively, in public, to the extent that they inform any written text of an Indian is very clearly more likely to privilege the synecdochic relation of part-to-whole than the metonymic relation of part-to-part. Speech always assumes a present listener as opposed to writing, where the audience is absent to the author, the author absent to the audience.[18]

It is the part-to-part relation, however, that seems to mark Western autobiography—itself marked by writing.

As evidential shorthand, consider that *locus classicus* of modern autobiography, Rousseau's *Confessions*. "I understand my own heart," Rousseau writes, "and understand my fellow man. But I am made like no one in the whole world. I may be no better, but at least I am different" (17). The units compared are precisely that: units, one-to-one, man-

18. The link between metonymic self-conception and the primacy of textual communication is affirmed by Rousseau when he writes,

I know nothing of myself til I was five or six. I do not know how I learnt to read. I only remember my first books and their effect upon me; *it is from my earliest reading that I date the unbroken consciousness of my own existence.* (19, my emphasis)

Scenes of reading and/or writing, as I have noted elsewhere (1981), are central to the eastern American tradition of autobiography and even before Thoreau. It remains to add what recent feminist criticism has solidly established, that orality— speech, the voice, and the *mother* tongue—and textuality—writing and the *father's* pen(is)—are, indeed, perceived as gender-related in the West, where men tend toward metonymic presentations of self, and women—in this like Indians and tribal peoples generally—tend toward synecdochic presentations of self.

to-man, part-to-part. Rousseau does not see himself as an aberration, one who cannot accurately be classed among the genus, Man; rather, he is specifically different from other individual men, from each and every one of them, one-by-one. For all that any full understanding of Rousseau must take into account his deeply social and "communitarian" commitment—it may, indeed, reasonably be claimed that any autobiography, however "individualistic," also implies a theory of society—still, the figures of his self-representation in the *Confessions* tend toward the metonymic.

If we turn to Thoreau, writing half a century after Rousseau, we find much the same sort of thing. Addressing his "neighbors," in the headnote to *Walden*,[19] Thoreau promises (or threatens) to "wake" them up; addressing his "readers" in the book's second paragraph, he promises to answer their questions "concerning [his] mode of life." In every case, "the *I* or first person . . . will be retained" in his book, for it is "always the first person that is speaking" in writing. What Thoreau would provide is what he himself

> require[s] of every writer . . . a simple and sincere account
> of his own life, and not merely what he has heard of other men's
> lives; some such account as he would send to his kindred from
> a distant land; for if he has lived sincerely, it must have been
> in a distant land to me. (1)

"Perhaps," Thoreau continues,

> these pages are more particularly addressed to poor students.
> As for the rest of my readers, they will accept such portions as

19. That *Walden is* an autobiography is assuredly open to question. Given the current sense of the broadness of the autobiographical genre, I will simply take it as such without further comment.

apply to them. I trust that none will stretch the seams in putting on the coat, for it may do good service to him whom it fits. (1–2)

It seems reasonable to read these remarks metonymically: Thoreau's model of proper speech-in-writing images the individual man addressing other individual men (there remains the problem of what women were to do with these constructions), who, while they certainly make up the generalized categories of "neighbors," or "readers," or "writers," or "students," must finally read as he writes, in the "first person," each individually "putting on the coat" to assess its fit. This metonymic construal of the individual autobiographer asserting his or her individuality against or with the individuality of others persists into the twentieth century—when, as I have noted, it begins to dissolve. "I am I because my little dog knows me" (64), Gertrude Stein wrote—but in a book she ironically called *Everybody's Autobiography.*

When we turn to Native American autobiography the situation is rather different. Native American autobiography, a post-contact phenomenon in its written forms, exists in two types which I have elsewhere called the Indian autobiography and the autobiography by an Indian.[20] The first of these is constituted as a genre of writing by its original, bicultural, composite composition, the product of a collaboration between the Native American subject of the autobiography who provides its "content" and its Euramerican editor who ultimately provides its "form" by fixing the text in writing. Autobiographies by Indians, however, are indeed self-written lives; there is no compositeness to their

20. See my *For Those Who Come After.*

composition, although inasmuch as their subject, in order to *write* a life, must have become "civilized" (in many cases Christianized as well), there remains the element of biculturalism. In both sorts of texts, let me claim, we find a privileging of the synecdochic relation of part-to-whole over the metonymic relation of part-to-part.

At this point, the reader may well expect some illustrative demonstration of a synecdochic nature to make its entrance, a detailed reading of a single text being offered as representative of a larger body of autobiographical work. I will not fail to conform to such expectation. I have chosen to consider an autobiography by an Indian rather than an Indian autobiography for two reasons. First, it is the case that every aspect of the Indian autobiography, including the particular sense of self conveyed, is at least theoretically ascribable to its non-Native editor as much as to its Native subject. This fact raises questions it would be too cumbersome to deal with just here. More importantly, to work with the autobiographies of traditional, tribal persons—and Indian autobiographies are almost exclusively focused on this sort of person—and then to show that they are indeed traditionally tribal, relationally synecdochic, courts even a greater circularity than what is inevitable to such exercises. As noted above, Indians who write their own life stories must first have learned to write and at least to that extent been influenced by the dominant Euramerican culture. To see whether their autobiographical presentations of self therefore have also been influenced by the dominant culture—whether they have, in my terms, tended to move from synecdochic to metonymic senses of the self—seems the more interesting tack to take. I proceed now to consider the autobiographical work of the Reverend William Apes (1798–1837?).

One of the very first autobiographies by an Indian is *A Son of the Forest* (1829) by the mixedblood Pequot and Methodist preacher, the Reverend William Apes.[21] This text was followed in 1833 by Apes's *The Experiences of Five Christian Indians*, the first chapter of which, the "Experience of the Missionary," offers a second brief autobiography by Apes ("the Missionary"). This makes no reference to *A Son of the Forest* but instead promises a further autobiographical volume, "a book of 300 pages, 18mo. in size; and there, the reader will find particulars respecting my life" (4). Apes was never to write such a book, although his further publications—*Indian Nullification of the Unconstitutional Laws of Massachusetts, Relative to the Marshpee Tribe . . .* (1835), in part an account of political work on behalf of the Mashpees, which landed him in prison, and *Eulogy on King Philip, as Pronounced at the Odeon in Federal Street, Boston . . .* (1836), a fierce attack on the Puritan origins of American racism—are both intensely personal. All of his writing, I would suggest, may fruitfully be read as pieces of an extended autobiography.

By 1798, the year of William Apes's birth, Pequot cultural integrity was at a low point. This is to say that aboriginal lands had been usurped or heavily encroached upon by

21. Apes was preceded as an autobiographer by the Reverend Samson Occom, a Mohegan, who wrote a brief account of his life in 1762, and by Hendrick Aupaumut, generally referred to as a Mahican, who produced a text in 1792 that at least contained a good deal of autobiographical material. The *Memoir of Catherine Brown, a Christian Indian of the Cherokee Nation* as edited by the missionary Rufus Anderson appeared in 1824. The very brief life history of Paul Cuffe, like Apes, a Pequot, appeared in 1839. By that time the first Indian autobiography, J. B. Patterson's *Life of Black Hawk* (1833), had been published. For further references, see the indispensable annotated bibliography by David Brumble (1981) and its "Supplement" (1982), as well as Brumble's recent full-length study, *American Indian Autobiography* (1988). My own book (1985), as well as the introduction to Swann and Krupat (1987a), may also prove helpful.

whites so that traditional ecological economies and cultural practices were severely disrupted where they were not entirely destroyed. Disease, alcoholism, and Christianity served as further agents undermining tribal coherence and cultural competence, with predictable effects on Native self-conception—although Apes came to view Christianity as part of the solution, rather than part of the problem. Apes did not live long with his parents who tended to move about considerably. Placed with his grandparents, Apes was so cruelly treated—at the age of four, his arm was broken in three places (ASOF 12) as the result of a drunken beating administered by his grandmother—that he eventually was sent to live "among good Christian people" (13). Their goodness did not prevent them from "selling" (31) him to a judge who worked him and "sold" (35) him to someone else. I will not detail Apes's life-adventures further;[22] suffice it to say that he eventually became a convert to evangelical Methodism, attaining to the position of licensed Methodist "exhorter" (111), although the license to preach, which he desired, was still, at the conclusion of *A Son of the Forest*, withheld from him.

At this point in his life, Apes seems to see himself as something like Mauss's Christian " 'moral person'," virtually "a metaphysical entity" (19). Although Mauss reads the Christian stage of Western self-conception as a step on the

22. A further account of Apes's life and work, most particularly in relation to the Bakhtinian concern with the plural elements of "individual" speech appears in my "Monologue and Dialogue in Native American Autobiography." Barry O'Connell's forthcoming edition of Apes's complete works offers, in its introduction, the best and most complete account to date. O'Connell also makes a case for spelling (and pronouncing) this writer's name as Apess. For all that I am now fairly well persuaded that Apes is better spelled and pronounced Apess, I retain the earlier form for this chapter which was completed long before I had the benefit of O'Connell's very fine work. See also David Murray on Apes.

way toward (these are, of course, my terms, not those of Mauss) metonymic construals of self, it needs to be said that this is by no means the only reading possible. Christian tradition gives us abundant instances of solitary individuals seeking relation foremost with God (e.g., the early desert fathers, medieval mystics, Louis Dumont's "outworldly" Christian individuals), but it also gives us abundant images of individuals defined foremost by a sense of commonality and community (Dumont's post-Calvinist "inworldly" Christians). For every "I" focussed exclusively on "Thou," for everyone trying to love her particularized neighbor, there are also those who are committed to doing unto *all* others as they would have done unto themselves; those committed to what William Bradford called "the church or commonwealth" (39), made up of persons who believe that—I return to Dumont—"we should embody that other world in our determined action upon this one" (116).

It is this latter sense of Christian self-definition that is important to Apes, who does not fail to grasp its political implications. Toward the close of *A Son of the Forest*, Apes writes:

> I feel a great deal happier in the *new* [Methodist Society] than I did in the *old* [Methodist Episcopal] church—the government of the first is founded on *republican*, while that of the latter is founded on *monarchial* principles. (115)

And Apes "rejoice[s] sincerely in the spread of the principles of civil and religious liberty—may they ever be found 'hand in hand' " (115). He believes that

> If these blessed principles prevail . . . the image of God in his members will be a sufficient passport to all Christian priv-

ileges; and all the followers of the most high will unite together in singing the song of praise, *Glory to God in the highest, &c.* (115)

In this way Apes seeks to replace the lost paradise of the Pequots—what he called in the first paragraph of his auto-biography "the goodly heritage occupied by this once peaceable and happy tribe" (7)—with the paradise regained in Christ. The tribe to which he would now belong, defining himself by his membership, is that of "the followers of the most high." Obviously enough, "*all* the followers of the most high" (my emphasis) must include Indians—at least those Native "members" of the saved in whom "the image of God" is to "be a sufficient passport to all Christian priv-ileges." "Look brethren," Apes exhorts in his penultimate paragraph,

> at the natives of the forest—they come, notwithstanding you call them "*savage*," from the "east and from the west, the north and the south," and will occupy [because the last shall be first?] seats in the kingdom of heaven before you. (116)

Yet for all that Christian Indians will share equally with Christian whites a heavenly heritage in the future, those same Indians, now, in the present, are abused and discrim-inated against by whites. Nor is it Indians only, as Apes came increasingly to understand, but blacks and all people of color[23] who suffer from American race prejudice. Here, the incompatibility of Christianity and racism emerges as a major theme of William Apes's subsequent writing (as it would, of course, become a theme of Frederick Douglass

23. This includes the Jews, who, as Apes writes in *The Indian's Looking Glass,* "are a colored people, especially those living in the East, where Christ was born" (60)!

and the abolitionists). I shall try to say in a moment how this bears on the question of his synecdochic self-definition.

Consider, in these regards, Apes's second brief autobiography, "The Experience of the Missionary." Addressed to the "youth," "those poor children of the forest, who have had taken from them their once delightful plains, and homes of their peaceable habitations" (3), Apes's account of his life here places a particular emphasis on those aspects of his suffering that occurred because of race prejudice. In a text of only seventeen pages, Apes's increased awareness of the problem of color in America is indicated by such phrases and sentences as "Had my skin been white" (8), "Now, if my face had been white" (9), "I would ask the white man, if he thinks that he can be justified in making just such a being as I am . . . unhappy . . . because God has made us thus" (17), "I was already a hissing-stock, and a by-word in the world, merely because I was a child of the forest" (19), and so on.

In these regards, consider also that the cover of the first edition of *The Experience . . .* gives its full title as *The Experiences of Five Christian Indians: Or the Indian's Looking Glass for the White Man.* But *The Indian's Looking Glass . . .* is not merely an alternate title for the collection of autobiographies, but the title of a pamphlet or sermon that appears after the fifth "Experience," at the end of the book. This is a brilliant and violent attack on racism. I will quote its first two sentences; they indicate, I believe, a new strength and stylistic assurance.[24] Apes begins:

24. The grammar, to be sure, is questionable, the two sentences properly constituting but a single sentence. But it should be remembered that Apes's written style is very much the transcription of an oral manner. Whatever he may or may not have known and remembered of aboriginal orality, his commitment to a Christian tradition of "exhorting" and "preaching" provides a continuity with Native modes of communication. It is fitting, therefore, that his final work is "only" the text of what was orally "pronounced at the Odeon."

Having a desire to place a few things before my fellow crea-
tures who are travelling with me to the grave, and to that God
who is the maker and preserver both of the white man and the
Indian, whose abilities are the same, and who are to be judged
by one God, who will show no favor to outward appearances,
but will judge righteousness. Now I ask if degradation has not
been heaped long enough upon the Indians? (53)

If this book of "Experiences" is to be taken—as the "or"
rather than "and" on the cover would seem to urge—as
providing a "looking glass" for the white man, then what
that looking glass reflects above all are the "national crimes"
(56) of white Americans. Here is the extraordinary passage
in which this phrase occurs; I believe it is worth quoting at
length:

Assemble all nations together in your imagination, and then let
the whites be seated amongst them, and then let us look for
the whites, and I doubt not it would be hard finding them; for
to the rest of the nations, they are still but a handful. Now
suppose these skins were put together, and each skin had its
national crimes written upon it[25]—which skin do you think
would have the greatest? I will ask one question more. Can you
charge the Indians with robbing a nation almost of their whole
Continent, and murdering their women and children, and then
depriving the remainder of their lawful rights, that nature and
God require them to have? And to cap the climax, rob another
nation to till their grounds, and welter out their days under the
lash with hunger and fatigue under the scorching rays of a burn-
ing sun? I should look at all the skins, and I know that when I

25. I find it difficult not to think of Kafka's "In the Penal Colony" just here.
Apes's image of corporeal criminal inscription resonates with a good deal of contemporary theoretical work.

cast my eye upon that white skin, and if I saw those crimes written upon it, I should enter my protest against it immediately, and cleave to that which is more honorable. And I can tell you that I am satisfied with the manner of my creation, fully—whether others are or not. (56)

Apes's next work (the *Indian Nullification . . .*) continues to be concerned with racism, announcing it explicitly as central to his life. Writing in the third person, Apes states in his introduction that the author "wishes to say in the first place"

that the causes of the prevalent prejudice against his race have been his study from his childhood upwards. That their colour should be a reason to treat one portion of the human race with insult and abuse has always seemed to him strange; believing that God has given to all men an equal right to possess and occupy the earth, and to enjoy the fruits thereof, without any such distinction. (10)

Apes now sees himself quite self-consciously as the prophet of colorblind Christianity, and this bears upon the question of self-definition inasmuch as it would seem he can be fully himself only as an Indian member of the tribe of the non-racist saved. It is the part-to-whole relation in which the self as such is validated only in its social-collective (Christian) personhood that is important to Apes. But let us come finally to William Apes's last known text, the *Eulogy on King Philip*.

Apes's turn to King Philip is rather a return, for the initial sentence of his first work, *A Son of the Forest*, had described its author as "a native of the American soil, and a descendant of one of the principal chiefs of the Pequot

tribe, so well known in that part of American history called
King Philip's Wars" (ASOF 7). It was Philip's defeat in war
which initiated the Pequots' loss "of the[ir] goodly heritage," and so it may come as no surprise to discover that a
vindication of Philip, the narrative reconstitution of his
"defeat" as a victory, now becomes for Apes the necessary
condition for any recuperation of that "goodly heritage."
The *Eulogy* proclaims Philip "the greatest man that was
ever in America" (EKP 55–6), providing a revisionist history of the Pilgrim invasion: "the seed of iniquity and prejudice was sown in that day" (21), when the Pilgrims invaded
these shores, Apes writes. Speaking to the descendants of
the Pilgrims and Puritans in Boston, Apes would yet say:

> Let the children of the pilgrims blush, while the son of the
> forest drops a tear, and groans over the fate of his murdered
> and departed fathers. He would say to the sons of the pilgrims,
> (as Job said about his birth day,) let the day be dark, the 22d of
> December, 1622; let it be forgotten in your celebration, in your
> speeches, and by the burying of the Rock that your fathers first
> put their foot upon. For be it remembered, although the gospel
> is said to be glad tidings to all people, yet we poor Indians
> never have found those who brought it as messengers of mercy,
> but contrawise. We say therefore, let every man of color wrap
> himself in mourning, for the 22d of December and the 4th of
> July are days of mourning and not of joy. (20)

And so, Apes continues, "while you ask yourselves, what do
they, the Indians, want? you have only to look at the unjust
laws made for them, and say they want what I want," which
is that "all men must operate under one general law" (59).
That law is to be, as Apes had earlier written, both "civil
and religious" (ASOF 115), for it is the worldly implication

of Christianity as Apes understands it that the "image of God in his members" be the "sufficient passport to all Christian privileges" (ASOF 115), not only in heaven but here on earth as well—and, as he says, "first, in New England" (EKP 59).

Curiously—amazingly?—Apes's *Eulogy* was sufficiently popular to warrant a second edition in 1837, after which year, as I have noted, no more is known of the Reverend William Apes. So far as his writings may be taken as formally and informally autobiographical, it seems reasonable to suggest that they show him engaged in a very particular form of synecdochic self-definition. Recalling from the first a lost tribal identity and a "goodly heritage" in which all share together, he attempts with increasing self-consciousness to reconstitute and redefine his "tribe" and its "heritage" in Christian terms as a means of constituting and defining himself—this latter process, in typical Native American fashion, hardly self-conscious at all. The tribe to which Apes will ultimately belong must finally be made up not so much of Pequots or Puritans, not even only of Christians, "but [of] men" (EKP 59). In the end, as I have said, Apes is simply an Indian member of the colorblind saved, one of those nonracist Christians who, like most Indians traditionally, are usually more interested in their integration within a principled community rather than in their unique or "sacred" individuality.

Apes's synecdochic presentation of self finds parallels in a great many autobiographies by Indians. I would instance first, Sarah Winnemucca Hopkins's *Life Among the Piutes: Their Wrongs and Claims* (1883), whose very title proclaims her individual life as comprehensible foremost in relation to the collective experience of her tribe. Then there is

Charles Alexander Eastman's *From the Deep Woods to Civilization: Chapters in the Autobiography of an Indian* (1916) with its conclusion, "I am an Indian. . . . I am an American" (195). Approaching the present, there is Leslie Marmon Silko's *Storyteller* (1981) which, as I have described it elsewhere,[26] conceives of individual identity only in functional relation to the tribe. Silko, as a contemporary Laguna "storyteller," takes her place in a line of "storytellers as far back as memory goes" (Dedication); she is what she does to sustain her community. Finally, we may look to the ongoing autobiographical projects of the Minnesota Chippewa novelist and critic, Gerald Vizenor, who, in a number of recent autobiographical texts, as I have earlier noted, invokes the "mixedblood," or "crossblood," the trickster, and the author as categories in relation to which he may define himself. Inasmuch as, in Vizenor's view, "mixedbloods loosen the seams in the shrouds of identity" (1987 101), they have a ready relation to tricksters—those jokers, shape-changers, and limit-challengers—and to writers of fiction, poetry, or criticism who are all, if true to their vocation, focused on the powers of the imagination. And Vizenor defines himself in relation to these "tribal heirs to a wild baronage" (to take the subtitle of his *The Trickster of Liberty*); for all that these each take self-definition as a loose and impermanent thing, yet they have a certain collective sense of responsibility as identity.

For all of this, I would not want to be understood as claiming that all autobiographies by Indians must necessarily be unimpressed by varieties of individualism, nor that all autobiographies by Native people must take synecdoche as their defining figure. The autobiographies by the much-

26. See "Monologue and Dialogue. . . ."

acclaimed N. Scott Momaday, a Kiowa, seem to me as met-onymic in their orientation as Rousseau's, for example.[27] In the same way, Western autobiography is hardly constrained to metonymic strategies. A good deal of autobiographical writing by Western women, it seems, and certain forms of Christian autobiography, as I have noted, are quite likely to adopt synecdochic types of self-identification, as are the autobiographies of writers whose deep commitment to political egalitarianism works to structure their self-conception in a part-to-whole manner: I think here, for ex-ample, of Prince Peter Kropotkin, Emma Goldman, and, more recently, Assata Shakur.[28] So far as one may general-ize, however, it does seem to be the case that Native Amer-ican autobiography is marked by the figure of synecdoche in its presentation of the self.

27. See *The Way to Rainy Mountain* and *The Names*, and my discussion in the study cited above.

28. See *Memoirs of a Revolutionist, Living My Life*, and *Assata*. Shakur's use of lower case "i" within sentences (she capitalizes "I" at the beginning of sen-tences, where all letters equivalently get to appear in upper case) seems a gesture in the interest of bringing the individual ego back to proper scale as simply an existent among others.

CONCLUSION:

For Multiculturalism

In a late volume of verse called *May-Day and Other Pieces* (1867), Ralph Waldo Emerson published a long poem titled "The Adirondacs." The poem details a hiking trip to New York that Emerson had made in 1858 with a group of Boston friends. As they tramp through the wilderness, Emerson and his friends, as Gay Wilson Allen, his biographer, writes, "meet a traveler with a newspaper announcing that the [trans]Atlantic cable has been completed and is operating" (636). "Emerson exults," says Wilson Allen, who quotes, as illustrative of Emersonian exultation, a few lines from "The Adirondacs."[1] Emerson writes:

> Thought's new-found path
> Shall supplement henceforth all trodden ways,
> Match God's equator with a zone of art.

Emerson goes on in this inflationary vein with some lines from "The Adirondacs" that Wilson Allen does not quote, lines that are particularly interesting to me. For Emerson continues:

> It is not Iroquois or cannibals,
> But ever the free race with front sublime,

1. I want to thank Willard Gingerich for bringing these lines of Emerson to my attention.

And these instructed by their wisest too,
Who do the feat, and lift humanity.

• • •

We flee away from cities, but we bring
The best of cities with us, these learned classifiers,
Men knowing what they seek, armed eyes of experts.
We praise the guide, we praise the forest life:
But will we sacrifice our dear-bought lore
Of books and arts and trained experiment,
Or count the Sioux a match for Agassiz?
O no, not we! (193)

Louis Agassiz, Professor of Natural History at Harvard, Emerson's alma mater, was, whatever his other achievements, a convert to the so-called "American School" of ethnology, which taught the theory of polygenesis—multiple creations—as an explanation of what were, in the nineteenth century, usually taken to be innate racial differences. And, in 1850, Agassiz had pronounced himself on the biologically determined characteristics of African Americans and Native Americans, distinguishing between "the submissive, obsequious negro" and the "indomitable, courageous, proud Indian" (in Dippie 92). Proud, but obviously no match, culturally, for the white "learned classifier" and his armed vision. Another of the hikers on Emerson's tramp through the Adirondacks was the famed jurist Oliver Wendell Holmes, Sr., who, in what must surely be an *ex cathedra* opinion, according to Brian Dippie, "likened the Indian to a red crayon sketch" (84), only the roughest version of the white man, who, no doubt, represented the highest form of Man in full oil portrait.

"[C]ount the Sioux a match for Agassiz?" No, Emerson

proclaims, "no, not we." Emerson's "no" to the Sioux, the Iroquois, and any other presumptive "cannibals" or "savages" has been reiterated recently in regard to non-Western cultural production generally by the National Endowment for the Humanities report of October, 1989, called "50 Hours: A Core Curriculum for College Students." In it, Lynne Cheney, head of the Endowment, reaffirms the Western supremicism of the Endowment's former head, the egregious William Bennett, and thus offers official government support for the positions of such champions of the West's "dear-bought lore/ Of books and arts and trained experiment" as Allan Bloom, Walter Jackson Bate, and others.

Emerson's worry that anyone *might* think to "count the Sioux a match for Agassiz" finds a minor contemporary equivalent in such things as a 1988 column in the New York *Tribune* in which I am specifically chided (among others more notable than I) for "starting [my] American literature students with parallel readings in the Book of Genesis and Iroquois Indian creation stories. The list," writes the *Tribune* columnist with apparent disgust, "goes on and on." On and on to the point where Christopher Clausen, in a piece in *The Chronicle of Higher Education*, "bets" that Alice Walker's *"The Color Purple* is taught in more English courses today than all of Shakespeare's plays combined" (6).

But Clausen, like Emerson before him, is overreacting. I have no statistics for college English courses, but the *New York Times* for June 23, 1989, under the headline "School Reading Lists Shun Women and Black Authors," affirms that

> Required reading lists in the nation's high schools continue to emphasize the works of Shakespeare but largely ignore the lit-

erary contributions of women and members of minorities, a new survey says. (21)

And Arthur Applebee's monograph, *A Study of Book-length Works Taught in High School English Courses*, published the same year as the *Times* article appeared, finds that not Alice Walker, but, rather, John Steinbeck, Charles Dickens, and Mark Twain are, in fact, the most generally assigned American novelists. This is the case, as Henry Louis Gates, Jr., points out, "even in public schools with the highest proportion of minority students" (1990 13). No doubt there may be some study I have missed, but my guess is that the teaching of Sioux or Iroquois—Native American—literatures in American high school and college courses generally occurs so infrequently and irregularly that the statistics are hardly even worth compiling.

So Professor Clausen is safe, at least for the moment—for all that one *could*, of course, make the case that high school students might actually learn more from a careful reading of Walker's novel (not my favorite book by an African American writer) than from *Romeo and Juliet*—which, according to the survey reported in the *Times*, tops the list of Shakespeare plays assigned. And, so far as American literature is concerned, one could also make the case that any number of African American, Native American, and Latino/a writers might be studied with at least as much pleasure and profit as Cooper, Longfellow, Whittier, William Cullen Bryant, or some of the other elite, WASP males who have traditionally been offered as among the best and brightest of American literary production.[2]

Given the social and political demands of American

2. This little list obviously does not include the major canonical figures whose canonical status seems, for now, justifiably secure.

women and minorities of late, given the demands of colonized peoples from Africa to Armenia, to be heard, I can understand why Cheney and Bennett and Clausen feel threatened on the cultural front. I don't, however, know any particular reason why Emerson's pride in the achievement of transcontinental communication should need to affirm itself by means of a direct contrast to the presumed absence of artistic and scientific achievement among the Iroquois or D/Lakota (the Sioux). The obvious general reason for calumniating the Indians in order to praise Euramericans is, of course, the one Roy Harvey Pearce documented more than thirty-five years ago in his seminal *Savagism and Civilization*. There, Pearce showed how, from the first days of settlement, Americans regularly tended to define their own particular brand of "civilization" in direct opposition to a fantasized, or ideologically constructed Indian "savagery." In a simplified formulation, to be an American was no longer to be a European without yet becoming an Indian.

What is curious to note is that by 1860 or so, when Emerson wrote these lines, the need to praise white "civilization" by opposing it to red "savagism" was—in Emerson's Massachusetts, at least, if not in the Dakotas or New Mexico— already an anachronism. It is even more of an anachronism today—if, that is, one agrees, as I do, with James Clifford, that the "future is not (only) monoculture" (1988 16). Indeed, I believe the multicultural "future" is already here; nonetheless, inasmuch as monocultural supremacy is still promoted at the highest institutional levels, those of us who would speak for multiculturalism must continue to argue on its behalf.

As I said in the introduction, I understand the term multiculturalism to refer to that conceptualization and organization of cultural studies in the university which engages the other in such a way as to provoke an interrogation of and a challenge to what we take as ours. In a certain sense, indeed, the term multiculturalism is redundant if, as I have suggested, culture is best conceived in a manner analogous to Bakhtin's conception of language as a socially plural construct in which our own speech is never entirely and exclusively our own, but always heteroglossic and polyvocal, formed always in relation to the speech of others. As Bakhtin says, "language lies on the borderline between oneself and the other. The word in language is half someone else's" (in Clifford 1988 41)—as culture is always, if not "half someone else's," at least never all one's own. No more than language as a medium of actual communication could culture *in historical time* ever be pure; only as the projection of an idealized logic could one posit either a strictly pure speech or culture.

A multicultural approach to the teaching of literature thus is consistent with the project of anti-imperialist translation, as I have tried to outline it in chapter 5, where I appropriated Benjamin's citation of Pannwitz's remarks as an encouragement to permit one's "own" language or culture to be powerfully affected by the language or culture of the foreigner, by values and attitudes "we" had defined as Other and sought to engage only by means of domestication: by translation in the imperial sense. The intention is to dialogize dominant monologues, indeed, to show that dialogue is not an abstract ideal, nor is it only realized in—to refer specifically to Bakhtin's work—the "novel" in literature or "carnival" in society, but that it is everywhere. A multicultural commitment, then, does not particularly encourage one to urge additions to the curriculum or the canon in the name of (as I shall try to show) "diversity" or "tolerance" (important as these are), but, rather, to urge the deconstruction of all dichotomized paradigms of the us/them, West/Rest type, and so to undo manichean allegories at every level. It should be fairly obvious that to proceed in this way has strong implications for a variety of possible reorganizations of the institutionalized pedagogical curriculum, and, too, for the reorganization of the social order. Sociopolitically, as I have said, the multicultural perspective finds expression in a commitment to cosmopolitan values as these do not only propose an ideal vision of what might be, nor an option strictly for a privileged class of intellectuals (this is another point to which I shall return), but, rather, as they claim to be implicit, in varying degrees, in all social interaction.

Why multiculturalism is opposed to all notions of Western cultural purity with its attendant arrogance should already be more than abundantly clear; why it is opposed to opposing monoculturalism in the name of such things as "diversity" and "tolerance" may not, however, be so clear. Let me try to explain by reference to Linda Kerber's paper, "Diversity and the Transformation of American Studies," which appeared not long ago in *American Quarterly*. Originally presented as the Presidential Address at the 1988 American Studies Association meeting, Kerber's views have more than personal authority.

Kerber notes that the sixties and seventies insisted "on the importance of race" while "the insistence of the eighties is [now "was"] on the importance of ethnicity" (423). She does not hesitate to recognize that this "valorization—even romanticization—of ethnicity has been energized in part as a backlash against black people's claims for equity and for power. 'Nobody here but us ethnics,' " she shrewdly notes, "has been a parochial slogan used to mask real issues of race and power" (423). Kerber's considerations of the issues of power in regard to race and gender—questions of class, in the manner typical of American academic liberalism, are not taken seriously as influences on identity, cultural or social, or as constituents of literary value—are all aspects of some unspecified but positive value Kerber names "diversity." Kerber never uses the term multiculturalism, and its absence from her discourse seems not merely a preference for one rather than another of two generally synonymous terms, but, instead, signals a difference in values.[3]

Kerber associates the "diversity" she approves in "American Studies" with the broader ethical and epistemological values (the political as such is, again, off limits) of "cosmopolitanism." Her understanding of the term comes most immediately from an essay by David Hollinger. But Hollinger's "*liberal* cosmopolitan" (my emphasis) is rather different from the cosmopolitanism I have been linking to multiculturalism and ethnocriticism.

We encourage diversity, Kerber affirms, to " 'move toward . . . a *cosmopolitanism* that is *both* a more complete human experience and a more [comprehensive] under-

3. The term "multiculturalism," that is to say, by the time Kerber composed her address, was commonly enough available in the contexts she addressed so that one might, indeed, expect to find it mentioned. This conclusion itself, for example, was first conceived as a presentation for a panel at the 1989 meeting of the American Studies Association whose title was "Is Multiculturalism Enough?" I thank Constance Coiner, organizer of that panel, for prodding me to think about the particular valences of multiculturalism as the term differs from other, apparently synonymous terms. More recently, I read in the February 21–7, 1990, edition of *In These Times* that "On February 11, the new East German Green Party adopted a program for a 'multicultural, non-violent society' " (Johnstone 3). I don't know what the German original for the word translated here as "multicultural" was—whether, that is, it might have been differently translated, or whether it is quite distinct from parallel terms. Still, it is interesting to think that the East German Greens were working toward "multiculturalism"—and interesting to wonder what they will do now, as part of a reunified Germany.

standing of that experience' " (Kerber 423). These words are from Hollinger, whom, in an endnote, Kerber quotes more fully. Hollinger writes:

> The "cosmopolitanism" to which I refer is the desire to *transcend* the limitations of any and all particularisms in order to achieve a more complete *human* experience and a more complete understanding of that experience. The *ideal* is decidedly counter to the eradication of cultural differences, but counter also to their preservation in *parochial* form. Rather, particular cultures and subcultures are viewed as *repositories* for insights and experiences that can be drawn upon in the interests of a more comprehensive outlook on the world. (Hollinger, in Kerber 430, my emphases)

Now, this is to resurrect for our time a "cosmopolitanism"—as Hollinger explains in the article from which Kerber quotes—embraced by "the *Liberal* Intelligentsia" (emphasis mine) roughly from the 1920s to the 1950s. I want to offer a brief critique of this liberal cosmopolitanism as defined by Hollinger and endorsed by Kerber, one that anyone left (or right) of liberalism can easily develop for her or himself. What I want to remark is a diction that, apparently innocent enough if taken abstractly—e.g., in terms, more or less, of the dictionary's generalized meanings for these words—in historical context has some very specific and, I think, not so innocent implications.

First, there is "the desire to transcend" actual cultural differences that, as "particularisms," are taken to be inherently limited. That the maintenance of the "boundary," as Fredrik Barth in a classic study of 1969 noted, is the essence of ethnic insularity (Barth would say identity), I do not dispute. But "particularisms" of whatever kind cannot in practice be *transcended* inasmuch as they are the pervasive and inevitable codes of culture in its situated and concrete social practice. There is, then, no moving beyond them—what I take Hollinger to mean by "transcend." Rather, one can only imagine their incorporation into more complex systems—complex not in the sense of some inherently greater sophistication, but, rather, complex in that they presume the interaction of several, many "particularisms," and presume this interaction in ways that have no historical antecedent, indeed, in ways that may not even have an existing referent. But however "complex" this larger system, it will inevitably have particularities—and so, also inevitably, limitations—of its own.

One would not, thus, be able to indulge any illusions of moving in the direction of a "more complete human experience," which, as Hollinger invokes it, appears to be an already known, fully articulated category. As such, this could be none other than the old Western humanistic ideal projected as a universal. Instead, one would be tentatively attempting to actualize new combinations of "particularisms," combinations which are brought into play only because they seem conducive to *forms* of "human experience" one takes as desirable. These could not claim a "more complete" human-ness—unless, that is, one believes in a point at which the human project would, indeed, be "completed" in history—but only alternative forms of human-ness, forms of cultural and social life that might be presented as "larger," better, whatever. Hollinger does, indeed, say that his form of cosmopolitanism would preserve "cultural differences," but, repeating the point about the limitations of particularisms, he says they would not do so "parochially." The question one might raise is who gets to decide which differences are "parochial" and which are somehow in the interest of that "more complete human experience" so much desired. "[P]articular cultures and subcultures" (but, again, "sub-" from whose vantage point, in whose definition? forever sub- or with a potential for parity or dominance, etc.) are to become museums, or, more literally, savings banks of significant difference, "repositories . . . that can be drawn upon in the interests of a more comprehensive outlook on the world." But I think this comprehensiveness, like the aforementioned completeness Hollinger projects, suspiciously recalls the sort of unselfcritical humanistic universalism one had thought quite thoroughly discredited by now.

In an introductory note to his essay, Hollinger remarks that

> Adherents of the cosmopolitan ideal have often made supportive references to cultural pluralism in the interests of promoting the common cause of "tolerance." (57)

The difference between "cultural pluralism" and liberal cosmopolitanism is

> the commitment of the former to the survival and nurturing of the ethnic group as such. While cosmopolitanism is inherently suspicious of ethnic particularism, cultural pluralism actually prescribes it and envisions a society full of particular groups, each respecting one another. (57)

Linda Kerber's "diversity," I suspect, is the 1980s–1990s version of 1920s "tolerance." To the extent that this is so, it is indeed useful as a defense against the "Americanizers"— of the 1860s, of 1915–1922, or of 1980–1992—but it is quite empty as a positive program in its own right. Rather than

the liberal cosmopolitanism of Hollinger and Kerber, sometimes consistent with "cultural pluralism" and "ethnic par-
ticularism" in the name of "tolerance" and "diversity," I
would propose, as more nearly consistent with multiculturalism and ethnocriticism, the somewhat more radical cosmopolitanism defined by Paul Rabinow. I have discussed
Rabinow's cosmopolitanism in a different context elsewhere,[4] and foreshadowed my understanding of it above, so
here I will try to be as brief and as little repetitious as I can.

In an essay called "Representations Are Social Facts: Modernity and Postmodernity in Anthropology," Rabinow proposes what he calls a "critical cosmopolitanism," one which
would, in a variety of contexts, have a force "oppositional"
(258) to the determinations of monoculturalists foremost,
but also to those of liberal cosmopolitans. Rabinow's "critical cosmopolitanism" is

> suspicious of sovereign powers, universal truths, overly relativ-
> ized preciousness, local authenticity, moralisms high and low.
> Understanding is its second value ["The ethical is the guiding
> value"], but an understanding suspicious of its own imperial
> tendencies. It attempts to be highly attentive to (and respectful
> of) difference, but it is also wary of the tendency to essentialize
> difference. (258)

As cosmopolitans,

> We live in between . . . insider's outsiders of a particular his-
> torical and cultural world; not members of a projected universal
> regime (under God, the imperium, or the laws of reason). (258)

4. See *The Voice in the Margin: Native American Literature and the Canon*, in
particular chapter 5, "Local, National, Cosmopolitan Literature." I knew very
little, when I wrote that chapter, about the history of the subject in the twenties.

Rabinow's ethical and epistemological cosmopolitanism has a wider—a global—frame of reference than that of the tolerance, diversity, or "cosmopolitanism" of the "liberal intelligentsia." For all that Rabinow says little about any politics his cosmopolitanism might found beyond the academy, its model of cultural mapping has implications not only for understanding but also, I believe, for changing the world.

In this regard, I should note that Hollinger has remarked with considerable realistic acumen that "Full-blown cosmopolitanism"—and, I would assume this might, on the face of it, hold both for "liberal" or more radical versions of cosmopolitanism—from the twenties to the fifties "was understood to be a realistic ideal primarily for intellectuals" (57). Liberal cosmopolitanism, and, surely, any other cosmopolitanism, represents a conscious *choice* of values on the part of those who have experienced, or, at least read widely. To the extent that this is so, cosmopolitan values are not, therefore, likely to appeal to many outside the "intelligentsia." In a period like our own, when most people's experience of anything very much beyond their immediate surroundings is experience presented by television—which, of course, has replaced reading as the primary source of other than immediately personal experience, and of information—it certainly is not easy to have wider hopes for cosmopolitan values than those Hollinger historically describes. About the only populist hope a radical cosmopolitanism (as I have tried to define it in relation to Bakhtin, progressive translation, multiculturalism, and ethnocriticism) might have beyond that of a liberal cosmopolitanism resides in the fact that it doesn't quite ask people simply to discard ethnic and local attachments for more global ones, but, rather—to appropriate a recent catchphrase—to try to see how the local is *already* global, the ethnic and regional *already* shot through with other and distant perspectives.[5] Nonetheless, as I think of the major news stories during the time I have worked on this book—the election of Violeta Chamorro in Nicaragua, the unification of the two Germanies, and a war in the Persian Gulf determined to produce and sustain the illusion of victory no matter the cost in Arab lives—it is indeed difficult to be optimistic in regard to any form of cosmopolitan social order. But this is not to say that nothing can be done.

Without overestimating the potential of curricular multiculturalism or ethnocritical discourse as politically functional in any direct or immediate manner—indeed one must remember in a cautionary fashion the example of those deconstructionists or postmodernists who affirmed or continue to affirm each of their readings as radical, subversive, transgressive, revolutionary, while the walls of Jericho showed no sign of tumbling down—still, one must not underestimate the possibilities of cultural work either. Yes, as Rabinow writes, and as James Clifford agrees, we are all

5. For all this, it is necessary to take into account Fredrik Barth's insistence that "ethnic distinctions do not depend on an absence of social interaction and acceptance" (10) and that what is important is "the ethnic *boundary* that defines the group, not the cultural stuff that it encloses" (15). Barth traces the tendencies of peoples, however easily they move back and forth across boundaries, to persist in their identification as "A's" not "B's," declaring "their allegiance to the shared culture of A's" (15) on the basis of "criteria of origin and commitment" (28). Barth is most interested in regional diversities not necessarily influenced by colonialism; these he takes as culturally and historically the more usual case (36), for all that studies of the subject, in his view, have been dominated by attention to the colonial context. My own sense is that perhaps not colonialism but most certainly imperialism of a cultural, if not overtly political, sort reaches almost everywhere. Barth knows more about these matters than I do: but, as I think any reader may note, he also seems to *like* the idea of maintaining boundaries more than I do.

already cosmopolitans: the problem is that many in power have yet to accede to that fact—a fact which, obviously enough, threatens their power.

Moreover—and this to me is more important even than the opinion of "those in power"—many marginalized people wish to maintain the ethnic "boundary" in the interest of, in Werner Sollors's phrase, "generating feelings of *dissociative belonging*" (1990 299 my emphasis), feelings which, however "dissociative," nonetheless serve to promote positive constructions of "minority" identity and worth. Inasmuch as ethnic and minority groups regularly suffer the representational and material disdain of the dominant society, it is not casually that one would recommend to them cosmopolitan values that may well seem a luxury beyond their current means. Nonetheless, for reasons I hope have become clear throughout this book, for the long term I believe exclusionary or "dissociative" strategies are inherently limited. Indeed, I find it of considerable interest (and admirable, too) that, although Werner Sollors's reputation as a critic rests on his assertion of the importance of ethnicity as a category, he nonetheless concludes the recent essay from which I have just quoted as follows:

> Although ethnicity remains potentially one of the most interesting aspects of modern literature around the world and opens many new possibilities for examining great [!] texts on a comparative basis, it is hardly an exaggeration to state that it may also bring out the worst in readers of literature. (1990 304)

Thus it seems to me that culture workers have more than merely abstract incentive to encourage multiculturalism and to practice ethnocriticism in the interest of promoting those cosmopolitan values that socially may found what I have elsewhere called the polyvocal polity:[6] the material-ization of dialogic values in institutions other than *carnival*.

To say these things is, admittedly and unfortunately, to be no more than generally hortatory, and I confess to being unable to describe more specifically the shape those in-stitutions might take. But it would be a mistake to assume that my own limitations are exactly those of ethnocriticism, multiculturalism, cosmopolitanism, and polyvocal politics: these name possibilities yet to be realized, neither fantasies nor daydreams, but, rather, plans for the future.

I began this conclusion by quoting Emerson at—on? against?—the Indians. I will end it by quoting the Indians at—on? against?—Emerson: by closing, that is, with some lines from no Sioux or Iroquois or cannibal, but from two contemporary Native American poets, Wendy Rose, of Hopi-Miwok background, and Jimmie Durham, a Chero-kee. Wendy Rose writes:

> It's not that your songs
> are so much stronger
> or your feet more deeply
> rooted, but that
> there are
> so many of you
> shouting in a single voice
> like a giant child. (38)

And Jimmie Durham:

> In school I learned of heroic discoveries
> Made by liars and crooks. The courage

6. See note 4, above.

of millions of sweet and true people
Was not commemorated.

Let us then declare a holiday
For ourselves, and make a parade that begins
With Columbus' victims and continues
Even to our grandchildren who will be named
In their honor. (11)

Gardiner, New York
October 1990

Works Cited

Alcoff, Linda. "Cultural Feminism Versus Poststructuralism: The Identity Crisis in Feminist Theory." *Signs* 13(1988): 405–36.

Allen, Gay Wilson. *Waldo Emerson: A Biography*. New York: Viking Press, 1981.

Allen, Paula Gunn. "The Sacred Hoop: A Contemporary Indian Perspective on American Indian Literature." Chapman, 111–36.

Anzaldúa, Gloria. *Borderlands/La Frontera: The New Mestiza*. San Francisco: Spinsters/Aunt Lute, 1987.

Apes, William. *Eulogy on King Philip, as Pronounced at the Odeon in Federal Street, Boston, by the Reverend William Apes, an Indian, January 8, 1836*. Boston, 1836; rpt. Brookfield, Mass.: Lincoln Dexter, 1985.

———. *The Experiences of Five Christian Indians: Or the Indian's Looking Glass for the White Man*. Boston: James B. Dow, 1833.

———. *Indian Nullification of the Unconstitutional Laws of Massachusetts, Relative to the Marshpee Tribe, or, The Pretended Riot Explained*. Boston: Jonathan Howe, 1835.

———. *A Son of the Forest: The Experience of William Apes, a Native of the Forest*. New York: Published by the Author, 1829.

Applebee, Arthur. *A Study of Book-length Works Taught in High School English Courses*. Albany: Center for the Learning and Teaching of Literature, 1989.

Arac, Jonathan. "The Politics of *The Scarlet Letter*." *Ideology and Classic American Literature*, ed. S. Bercovitch and M. Jehlen. Cambridge: Cambridge University Press, 1986, 247–66.

Ardener, Edwin. "Social Anthropology and the Decline of Modernism." *Reason and Morality*, ed. J. Overing. London: Tavistock, 1985, 47–70.

Armstrong, Virginia, ed. *I Have Spoken: American History Through the Voices of the Indians*. New York: Pocket Books, 1972.

Asad, Talal. "The Concept of Cultural Translation in British Social An-thropology." Clifford and Marcus, 141–64.

Bahr, Donald. *Collected Poems of Oriole*. Unpublished manuscript.

———. "Indians and Missions: Homage to and Debate with Rupert Costo and Jeannette Henry." *Journal of the Southwest* 31(1989): 300–29.

———. *Pima and Papago Ritual Oratory: A Study of Three Texts*. San Francisco: The Indian Historian Press, 1975.

Bakhtin, Mikhail. *The Dialogic Imagination: Four Essays by Mikhail Bakhtin*, ed. Michael Holquist. Austin: University of Texas Press, 1981.

Bandelier, Adolph. *The Delight Makers: A Novel of Prehistoric Pueblo Indians*. New York: Harvest/Harcourt, 1971 [1890].

Barnouw, Victor. *Culture and Personality*. Homewood, Ill.: Dorsey, 1985.

Barth, Fredrik, ed. *Ethnic Groups and Boundaries: The Social Organi-zation of Culture Difference*. Boston: Little, Brown, 1969.

Baudrillard, Jean. "Marxist Anthropology and the Domination of Na-ture." *The Mirror of Production*. St. Louis: Telos Press, 1975.

Beckett, Samuel. *Waiting for Godot*. New York: Grove Press, 1967 [1953].

Benedict, Ruth. *Patterns of Culture*. New York: Mentor, 1946 [1934].

Benjamin, Walter. "The Task of the Translator." *Illuminations*, ed. Han-nah Arendt. New York: Schocken, 1969, 69–82.

Berkhofer, Robert. *The White Man's Indian: Images of the American Indian from Columbus to the Present*. New York: Vintage, 1979.

Berman, Judith. "Oolachan-Woman's Robe: Fish, Blankets, Masks and Meaning in Boas' Kwakw'ala Texts." Swann, 1991.

Bernstein, R. J. *Beyond Objectivism and Relativism*. Philadelphia: Uni-versity of Pennsylvania Press, 1983.

Bevis, William. "American Indian Verse Translations." Chapman, 308–23.

———. "Native American Novels: Homing In." Swann and Krupat (1987b), 580–620.

Bieder, Robert. *Science Encounters the Indian, 1820–1880: The Early Years of American Ethnology*. Norman: University of Oklahoma Press, 1986.

Biolsi, Thomas. "The American Indian and the Problem of Culture. A Review of *The American Indian and the Problem of History*." *American Indian Quarterly* 13(1989): 261–9.

Black Elk. *Black Elk Speaks*, ed. John G. Neihardt. Lincoln: University of Nebraska Press, 1979 [1932].

Black Hawk. *Black Hawk: An Autobiography*, ed. Donald Jackson. Urbana: University of Illinois Press, 1964 [1833].

Blanchot, Maurice. "Translating," tr. Richard Sieburth. *Sulfur* 26(1990): 82–6.

Boas, Franz. "The Aims of Anthropological Research." *Race, Language, and Culture*. New York: Macmillan, 1940 [1932], 243–59.

———. "The Aims of Ethnology." *Race, Language, and Culture* [1888], 626–38.

———. "The Limitations of the Comparative Method in Anthropology." *Race, Language, and Culture* [1896], 270–80.

———. "Recent Anthropology II," *Science* 98(October 15, 1943): 334–7.

———. "The Study of Geography." *Race, Language, and Culture* [1887], 639–47.

Bock, Philip K. *Continuities in Psychological Anthropology*. San Francisco: W. H. Freeman, 1980.

Bohannon, Laura. "Shakespeare in the Bush." *National History Magazine* 45(1966): 560–77.

Bradford, William. "Of Plymouth Plantation." *The Norton Anthology of American Literature*, ed. Nina Baym et al. New York: Norton, 1985, 50–80.

Brightman, Robert. "Tricksters and Ethnopoetics." *International Journal of American Linguistics* 55(1989): 179–203.

Brodbeck, May. "Introduction." *Readings in the Philosophy of the Social Sciences*, ed. May Brodbeck. London: Collier-Macmillan, 1968.

Brown, Catherine. *Memoirs of Catherine Brown a Christian Indian of the Cherokee Nation*, ed. Rufus B. Anderson. Philadelphia: American Sunday School Union, 1824.

Brumble, H. David. *American Indian Autobiography*. Berkeley: University of California Press, 1988.

———. *An Annotated Bibliography of American Indian and Eskimo Autobiographies*. Lincoln: University of Nebraska Press, 1981.

Caroll, David. "Narrative, Heterogeneity, and the Question of the Political: Bakhtin and Lyotard." *The Aims of Representation*, ed. Murray Krieger. New York: Columbia University Press, 1987.

Carrithers, Michael, Steven Collins, and Steven Lukes, eds. *The Category of the Person: Anthropology, Philosophy, History*. Cambridge: Cambridge University Press, 1985.

Castro, Michael. *Interpreting the Indian: Twentieth-Century Poets and the Native American*. Albuquerque: University of New Mexico Press, 1983.

Chapman, Abraham, ed. *Literature of the American Indians: Views and Interpretations*. New York: New American Library, 1975.

Cheyfitz, Eric. *The Poetics of Imperialism: Translation and Colonization from "The Tempest" to "Tarzan."* New York: Oxford University Press, 1991.

Clements, William M. "Faking the Pumpkin: On Jerome Rothenberg's Literary Offenses." *Western American Literature* 16(1981): 193–204.

Clifford, James. "On Ethnographic Authority." *Representations* 2(1983): 132–43.

———. *The Predicament of Culture: Twentieth-Century Ethnography, Literature, and Art*. Cambridge: Harvard University Press, 1988.

———, and George Marcus, eds. *Writing Culture: The Poetics and Politics of Ethnography*. Berkeley: University of California Press, 1986.

Clifton, James A., ed. *Being and Becoming Indian*. Chicago: The Dorsey Press, 1989.

Codere, Helene, ed. *Kwakiutl Ethnography: Franz Boas*. Chicago: University of Chicago Press, 1966.

Coltelli, Laura, ed. *Native American Literatures*. Pisa: SEU, 1989.

Crane, Stephen. "The Open Boat." *Stories and Tales*. New York: Vintage, 1955 [1896], 215–41.

Cuffe, Paul. *Narrative of the Life and Adventures of Paul Cuffe, Pequot Indian: During Thirty Years Spent at Sea, and in Traveling to Foreign Lands*. Vernon: Horace N. Bill, 1839.

Darnell, Regna. *Daniel Garrison Brinton: The "Fearless Critic" of Philadelphia*. Philadelphia: University of Pennsylvania Anthropology Monograph Series 3, 1988.

———. *Edward Sapir: Linguist, Anthropologist, Humanist*. Berkeley and Los Angeles: University of California Press, 1990.

Dauenhauer, Nora, and Richard Dauenhauer, eds. *Haa Shuka, Our Ancestors: Tlingit Oral Narratives.* Seattle: University of Washington Press, 1987.

DeGeorge, F., and R. DeGeorge, eds. *The Structuralists from Marx to Lévi-Strauss.* Garden City, N.Y.: Anchor/Doubleday, 1972.

Deloria, Ella Cara. *Waterlily.* Lincoln: University of Nebraska Press, 1988.

DeMallie, Raymond. "Afterword" to *Waterlily.* Deloria, 233–44.

De Man, Paul. "Autobiography as De-Facement." *Modern Language Notes* 94(1979): 919–30.

Derrida, Jacques. "Otobiographies: The Teaching of Nietzsche and the Politics of the Proper Name." *The Ear of the Other: Texts and Discussions with Jacques Derrida*, ed. Christie McDonald. Lincoln: University of Nebraska Press, 1985, 1–38.

———. "Structure, Sign, and Play in the Discourse of the Human Sciences." Macksey and Donato, 247–64.

de Tocqueville, Alexis. *Democracy in America*, ed. J. P. Mayer. Garden City, N.Y.: Doubleday/Anchor, 1969 [1838–9].

Devereux, George. *From Anxiety to Method in the Behavioral Sciences.* The Hague: Mouton, 1967.

———. *Reality and Dream: Psychotherapy of a Plains Indian.* Garden City, N.Y.: Anchor, 1969 [1951].

Dippie, Brian. *The Vanishing American: White Attitudes and United States Relations.* Middletown, Conn.: Wesleyan University Press, 1982.

Dorris, Michael. "The Grass Still Grows, the Rivers Still Flow: Contemporary Native Americans." *Daedalus* 110(1981): 43–69.

Dumont, Louis. "A Modified View of Our Origins: The Christian Beginnings of Modern Individualism." Carrithers, Collins, and Lukes, 93–122.

Durham, Jimmie. *Columbus Day.* Minneapolis: West End Press, 1983, 10–11.

Eakin, Paul John. *Fictions in Autobiography.* Princeton: Princeton University Press, 1985.

Eastman, Charles Alexander. *From the Deep Woods to Civilization: Chapters in the Autobiography of an Indian.* Lincoln: University of Nebraska Press, 1977 [1916].

Emerson, Ralph Waldo. "The Adirondacs." *Poems by Ralph Waldo Emerson*, vol. IX. New York: William H. Wise and Co., 1929 [1867], 182–95.

Erikson, Eric. *Childhood and Society*. New York: Norton, 1963 [1950].

Fajans, Jane. "The Person in Social Context: The Social Character of Baining 'Psychology.' " White and Kirkpatrick, 367–400.

Fanon, Frantz. *Black Skins, White Masks*. New York: Grove Press, 1967 [1952].

———. *The Wretched of the Earth*. New York: Grove Press, 1968 [1963].

Fish, Stanley. "Being Interdisciplinary Is So Very Hard to Do." *Profession 89*, The Modern Language Association of America, 15–22.

Foster, Michael. *From the Earth to Beyond the Sky: An Ethnographic Approach to Four Longhouse Iroquois Speech Events*. Ottawa: National Museum of Canada, 1974.

Freud, Sigmund. "One of the Difficulties of Psychoanalysis." *Collected Papers of Sigmund Freud*, vol. 4, tr. by Joan Riviere. London: The Hogarth Press, 1925, 347–56.

Frye, Northrop. *The Anatomy of Criticism*. New York: Atheneum, 1967 [1957].

Gates, Henry Louis, Jr. "Editor's Introduction: Writing, 'Race' and the Difference It Makes." *Critical Inquiry* 12(1985): 1–20.

———. "Introduction: Tell Me, Sir . . . What *Is* 'Black' Literature?" *PMLA* 105(1990): 11–22.

Geertz, Clifford. " 'From the Native's Point of View': On the Nature of Anthropological Understanding." *Local Knowledge: Further Essays in Interpretive Anthropology*. New York: Basic Books, 1983, 55–72.

———. "Thick Description: Toward an Interpretive Theory of Culture." *The Interpretation of Cultures*. New York: Basic Books, 1973, 3–32.

———. *Works and Lives: The Anthropologist as Author*. Stanford: Stanford University Press, 1988, 147–53.

Genette, Gerard. *Figures of Discourse*. New York: Columbia University Press, 1982.

Gill, Sam D. *Mother Earth: An American Story*. Chicago: University of Chicago Press, 1987.

Gingerich, Willard. "The Southwest as Spiritual Geography in the Work of Simon Ortiz, Rudy Anaya, and John Nichols." Unpublished manuscript.

Goldman, Emma. *Living My Life.* New York: Dover, 1970 [1931].

Goldman, Irving. "Boas on the Kwakiutl: The Ethnographic Tradition." *Theory and Practice: Essays Presented to Gene Weltfish*, ed. Stanley Diamond. The Hague: Mouton, 1980.

———. "A Conversation with Irving Goldman." Ed. Enid Schildkraut. *American Ethnologist* 16(1989): 551–63.

Goldschmidt, Walter, ed. *The Anthropology of Franz Boas: Essays on the Centenary of His Birth.* The American Anthropological Association, Memoir no. 89, 1959.

Graff, Gerald. *Professing Literature: An Institutional History.* Chicago: University of Chicago Press, 1987.

Guttmann, Allen, and Van R. Halsey, eds. *States Rights and Indian Removal: The Cherokee Nation V. The State of Georgia.* Boston: D.C. Heath, 1965.

Habermas, Jurgen. *Communication and the Evolution of Society.* Boston: Beacon Press, 1979.

Hale, Horatio. *The Iroquois Book of Rites*, ed. William Fenton. Toronto: University of Toronto Press, 1963 [1883].

Hallowell, A. I. "The Self and Its Behavioral Environment." *Culture and Experience.* Philadelphia: University of Pennsylvania Press, 1955, 75–111.

Haraway, Donna. "Teddy Bear Patriarchy: Taxidermy in the Garden of Eden, New York City, 1908–36." *Social Text* (1985): 20–63.

Hardy, Thomas. *The Dynasts.* London: MacMillan, 1954 [1908].

Harris, Marvin. *Cultural Materialism: The Struggle for a Science of Culture.* New York: Vintage, 1980.

———. *The Rise of Anthropological Theory.* New York: Crowell, 1968.

Hartsock, Nancy. "Rethinking Modernism: Minority vs. Majority Theories." *Cultural Critique* 7(1987): 187–206.

Heelas, Paul. "The Model Applied: Anthropology and Indigenous Psychologies." Heelas and Lock, 39–64.

———, and Andrew Lock, eds. *Indigenous Psychologies: The Anthropology of the Self.* London: Academic Press, 1981.

Hemenway, Robert. *Zora Neale Hurston: A Literary Biography.* Urbana: University of Illinois Press, 1977.

Hirsch, E. D. *The Aims of Interpretation.* Chicago: University of Chicago Press, 1978.

Hollinger, David. "Ethnic Diversity, Cosmopolitanism, and the Emergence of the American Liberal Intelligentsia." *In the American Province: Studies in the History and Historiography of Ideas.* Bloomington: Indiana University Press, 1985, 56–73.

Hopkins, Gerard Manley. "As Kingfishers Draw Fire Dragonflies Draw Flame." *Collected Poems of Gerard Manley Hopkins.* London: Oxford University Press, 1937 [1918], 53.

Hopkins, Sarah Winnemucca. *Life Among the Piutes: Their Wrongs and Claims.* Ed. Mrs. Horace Mann. Bishop, Calif.: Chalfant Press, 1969 [1883].

Hurston, Zora Neale. *Mules and Men.* Bloomington: Indiana University Press, 1978 [1935].

———. *Tell My Horse.* Berkeley: Turtle Island Press, 1981 [1938].

———. *Their Eyes Were Watching God.* Urbana: University of Illinois Press, 1978 [1937].

Hymes, Dell. *'In Vain I Tried to Tell You': Essays in Native American Ethnopoetics.* Philadelphia: University of Pennsylvania Press, 1981.

Jakobson, Roman. "Concluding Statement: Linguistics and Poetics." *Style in Language*, ed. Thomas A. Sekeok. Cambridge: MIT Press, 1960, 350–77.

———, and Claude Lévi-Strauss. "Charles Baudelaire's 'Les Chats.' " *The Structuralists from Marx to Lévi-Strauss*, ed. R. and F. DeGeorge. Garden City, N.Y.: Anchor/Doubleday, 1972, 124–46.

James, Henry. *The American Scene.* Bloomington: Indiana University Press, 1963 [1907].

———. *Hawthorne.* Ithaca: Cornell University Press, 1963 [1879].

Jameson, Fredric. "Postmodernism, or the Cultural Logic of Late Capitalism." *New Left Review* 146(1984): 53–93.

JanMohamed, Abdul R. "The Economy of Manichean Allegory: The Function of Racial Difference in Colonialist Literature." *Critical Inquiry* 12(1985): 59–87.

Jay, Nancy. "Gender and Dichotomy." *Feminist Studies* 7(1981): 38–56.

Jefferson, Thomas. "The Declaration of Independence." *The Norton Anthology of American Literature*, ed. Nina Baym et al. New York: Norton, 1985, 639–44.

————. "Notes on the State of Virginia." *The Norton Anthology of American Literature*, ed. Nina Baym et al. New York: Norton, 1985, 617–23.

Jennings, Francis. *The Invasion of America: Indians, Colonialism, and the Cant of Conquest*. New York: Norton, 1975.

Johnstone, Diana. "German disunification on issue of reunification." *In These Times*. February 21–7, 1990, 3.

Kahn, Victoria. "Rhetoric and the Law." *Diacritics* 19(1989): 21–34.

Kaiser, Rudolf. "Chief Seattle's Speech(es): American Origins and European Reception." Swann and Krupat (1987b), 497–536.

Keats, John. "Ode on a Grecian Urn." *The Complete Poetry and Selected Prose of John Keats*, ed. H. E. Briggs. New York: Modern Library, 1951, 294.

Kerber, Linda. "Diversity and the Transformation of American Studies." *American Quarterly* 41(1989): 415–31.

Kilpatrick, J. F., and A. G. Kilpatrick, eds. *New Echota Letters: Contributions of Samuel A. Worcester to the Cherokee "Phoenix."* Dallas: Southern Methodist University Press, 1968.

————. *The Shadow of Sequoyah: Social Documents of the Cherokee, 1862–1964*. Norman: University of Oklahoma Press, 1965.

Kroeber, Alfred. "Preface." Goldschmidt, v–vii.

Kroeber, Karl. "An Introduction to the Art of Traditional American Indian Narration." *Traditional American Indian Literatures: Texts and Interpretations*. Lincoln: University of Nebraska Press, 1981, 1–24.

————, ed. *Traditional American Indian Literatures: Texts and Interpretations*. Lincoln: University of Nebraska Press, 1981.

————. "Turning Comparative Literature Around: The Problem of Translating American Indian Literatures." Coltelli, 39–52.

Kropotkin, Peter. *Memoirs of a Revolutionist*. Gloucester, Mass.: Peter Smith, 1967 [1899].

Krupat, Arnold. "The Dialogic of Silko's *Storyteller*." Vizenor, 1989, 55–68.

————. "Fiction and Fieldwork: A Review of *Waterlily*." *The Nation* 247 (July 2/9 1988): 22–3.

————. *For Those Who Come After: A Study of American Indian Autobiography*. Berkeley: University of California Press, 1985.

———. "Introduction" and "Afterword" to *Crashing Thunder*. Paul Radin, 1983.

———. *The Voice in the Margin: Native American Literature and the Canon*. Berkeley: University of California Press, 1989.

LaCapra, Dominick. "On the Line: Between History and Criticism." *Profession 89*. The Modern Language Association of America, 4–9.

Lakoff, George, and Mark Johnson. *Metaphors We Live By*. Chicago: University of Chicago Press, 1980.

Lazere, Donald. "Literary Revisionism: Partisan Politics and the Press." *Profession 89*. The Modern Language Association of America, 49–54.

Lee, Dorothy. "The Conception of Self Among the Wintu Indians." *Freedom and Culture*. Englewood Cliffs, N.J.: Prentice-Hall, 1959, 131–40.

———. "Autonomy and Community." *Valuing the Self: What We Can Learn from Other Cultures*. Prospect Heights, Ill.: Waveland Press, 1986, 28–41.

Lincoln, Kenneth. *Native American Renaissance*. Berkeley: University of California Press, 1983.

Lock, Andrew. "Universals in Human Conception." Heelas and Lock, 19–38.

Lovejoy, Arthur. *The Great Chain of Being*. Cambridge: Harvard University Press, 1936.

Lukes, Steven. "Conclusion." Carrithers, Collins, and Lukes, 282–301.

Lutz, Hartmut. "The Circle as Philosophical and Structural Concept in Native American Fiction Today." Coltelli, 85–100.

Lyotard, Jean-François. *The Post-Modern Condition: A Report on Knowledge*. Minneapolis: University of Minnesota Press, 1984.

Lytle, Donovan. "Validating a Native American Text." Unpublished manuscript, 1989.

Macksey, Richard, and Eugenio Donato, eds. *The Structuralist Controversy: The Languages of Criticism and the Sciences of Man*. Baltimore: Johns Hopkins University Press, 1972.

Macquet, Jacques. "Objectivity in Anthropology." *Current Anthropology* 5(1964): 37–57.

Manganaro, Marc, ed. *Modernist Anthropology: From Fieldwork to Text*. Princeton: Princeton University Press, 1990.

Marcus, George, and Michael Fischer. *Anthropology as Cultural Critique*. Chicago: University of Chicago Press, 1986.

———, and Dick Cushman. "Ethnographies as Texts." *Annual Review of Anthropology* 11(1982): 25–69.

Marsella, Anthony J., George DeVos, and Francis L. K. Hsu, eds. *Culture and Self: Asian and Western Perspectives*. New York: Tavistock, 1985.

Martin, Calvin, ed. *The American Indian and the Problem of History*. New York: Oxford University Press, 1987.

Matthews, F. H. "The Revolt Against Americanism: Cultural Pluralism and Cultural Relativism as an Ideology of Liberation." *Canadian Review of American Studies* 1(1970): 4–31.

Matthews, Washington. "The Mountain Chant: A Navajo Ceremony." *Bureau of American Ethnology Fifth Annual Report*. Washington: Government Printing Office, 1887, 385–468.

Mattina, Anthony. "William Charley's Speech." Unpublished manuscript, 1989.

Mauss, Marcel. "A Category of the Human Mind: The Notion of Person, the Notion of Self." Tr. W. D. Halls. Carrithers, Collins, and Lukes, 1–25.

Mead, Margaret. *Coming of Age in Samoa*. New York: Mentor, 1953 [1928].

Momaday, N. Scott. *The Names*. New York: Harper and Row, 1976.

———. *The Way to Rainy Mountain*. New York: Ballantine, 1973 [1969].

Murra, John, ed. *American Anthropology: The Early Years*. St. Paul, Minn.: West Publishing Company, 1976.

Murray, David. *Forked Tongues: Speech, Writing, & Representation in North American Indian Texts*. Bloomington: University of Indiana Press, 1990.

Nabokov, Peter. *Native American Testimony: An Anthology of Indian and White Relations*. New York: Crowell, 1978.

Norman, Howard, ed. *Northern Tales: Traditional Stories of Eskimo and Indian Peoples*. New York: Pantheon, 1990.

Norris, Christopher. *The Contest of Faculties: Philosophy and Theory After Deconstruction*. London: Methuen, 1985.

O'Brien, Lynne Woods. *Plains Indian Autobiographies*. Boise: Boise State College Press, 1973.

Occom, Samson. "A Short Narrative of My Life." *The Elders Wrote: An Anthology of Early Prose by North American Indians 1768–1931*. Ed. Bernd Peyer. Berlin: Dietrich Reimer Verlag, 1982 [1762], 12–18.

O'Connell, Barry, ed. *The Complete Works of William Apess*. Amherst: University of Massachusetts Press, forthcoming.

Ortner, Sherry. "Theory in Anthropology Since the Sixties." *Comparative Studies in Society and History* 26(1984): 126–66.

Parsons, Elsie Clews, ed. *American Indian Life*. Lincoln: University of Nebraska Press, 1967 [1922].

Peacham, Henry. *The Garden of Eloquence*. Gainesville, Flor.: Scholars Facsimiles, 1954 [1593].

Pearce, Roy Harvey. "From the History of Ideas to Ethnohistory." *Journal of Ethnic Studies* 2(1974): 86–92.

———. *Savagism and Civilization: a Study of the Indian and the American Mind*. Berkeley: University of California Press, 1988 [1967].

Peters, Richard, ed. *Cases Argued and Decided in the Supreme Court of the United States*, Book 8. Rochester: The Lawyers Co-Operative Publishing Co., 1970.

Porush, David. "Cybernetic Fiction and Postmodern Science." *New Literary History* 20(1989): 373–96.

Pratt, Mary Louise. "Fieldwork in Common Places." Clifford and Marcus, 27–50.

Purchas, Samuel. *Hakluytus Posthumus, or Purchas His Pilgrimes*. New York: AMS Press, 1965.

Rabinow, Paul. "Representations Are Social Facts: Modernity and Postmodernity in Anthropology." Clifford and Marcus, 234–61.

Radin, Paul. *The Autobiography of a Winnebago Indian*. New York: Dover, 1963 [1920].

———. *Crashing Thunder: The Autobiography of an American Indian*. Lincoln: University of Nebraska Press, 1983 [1926].

———. "Personal Reminiscences of a Winnebago Indian." *Journal of American Folklore* 26(1913): 293–318.

Ramsey, Jarold. "From 'Mythic' to 'Fictive' in a Nez Perce Orpheus Myth." Kroeber, 25–44.

————. *Reading the Fire: Essays in the Traditional Indian Literatures of the Far West*. Lincoln: University of Nebraska Press, 1983, xiii–xxi.

Revard, Carter. "History, Myth, and Identity Among Osages and Other Peoples." *Denver Quarterly* 14(1980): 84–97.

Ridge, John. "Essay on Cherokee Civilization." *Harper Anthology of American Literature*, vol. 1, ed. D. McQuade et al. New York: Harper, 1987, 730–37.

Robinson, Harry. *Write It On Your Heart: The Epic World of an Okanagan Storyteller*, ed. Wendy Wickwire. Vancouver: Talon/Theytusbooks, 1989.

Rogin, Michael Paul. *Fathers and Children: Andrew Jackson and the Subjugation of the American Indian*. New York: Knopf, 1975.

Rohner, Ronald, and Evelyn P. Rohner. "Introduction." *The Ethnography of Franz Boas*, ed. Rohner and Rohner. Chicago: University of Chicago Press, 1969.

Root, Deborah. "The Imperial Signifier: Todorov and the Conquest of Mexico." *Cultural Critique* 9(1988): 197–219.

Rorty, Amélie O. *The Identities of Persons*. Berkeley: University of California Press, 1976.

Rorty, Richard. *Consequences of Pragmatism*. Minneapolis: University of Minnesota Press, 1983.

————. *Contingency, Irony, and Solidarity*. Cambridge: Cambridge University Press, 1989.

————. *Philosophy and the Mirror of Nature*. Princeton: Princeton University Press, 1979.

Rose, Wendy. "Backlash." *The Halfbreed Chronicles*. Minneapolis: West End Press, 1985, 38.

Rothenberg, Jerome. *Shaking the Pumpkin: Traditional Poetry of the Indian North Americas*. Garden City, N.Y.: Doubleday, 1972.

————. "Total Translation: An Experiment in the Presentation of American Indian Poetry." Chapman, 292–307.

————. " 'We Explain Nothing, We Believe Nothing': American Indian Poetry & the Problematics of Translation." Swann, forthcoming.

Rousseau, Jean-Jacques. *The Confessions*. Tr. J. M. Cohen. Harmondsworth, England: Penguin, 1953 [1781].

Said, Edward. "Identity, Negation, and Violence." *New Left Review* 171(1988): 226–47.

———. *Orientalism*. New York: Vintage, 1979.

———. "Traveling Theory." *The World, the Text, the Critic*. Cambridge: Harvard University Press, 1983, 226–47.

Sale, Kirkpatrick. "How Paradise Was Lost: What Columbus Discovered." *The Nation* 251(1990): 444–6.

Sanders, Thomas, and Walter Peek, eds. *Literature of the American Indian*. New York: Glencoe, 1973.

Sangren, P. Steven. "Rhetoric and the Authority of Ethnography: 'Postmodernism' and the Social Reproduction of Texts." *Current Anthropology* 29(1988): 405–23.

Sapir, Edward. *Dreams and Gibes*. Boston: Poet Lore Co., 1917.

Schildkraut, Enid. "A Conversation with Irving Goldman." *American Ethnologist* 16(1989): 551–63.

Sebeok, Thomas, ed. *Style in Language*. Cambridge: MIT Press, 1960.

Sequoya, Jana. "The American Indian as Fetish Object: Cultural Revitalization and the Literature of Difference." Unpublished manuscript.

Shakespeare, William. *The Tempest*. New York: Penguin, 1970 [1623].

Shakur, Assata. *Assata*. Westport, Conn.: Lawrence Hill, 1987.

Shelley, Percy Bysshe. *A Defence of Poetry*. Indianapolis: Bobbs-Merrill, 1965 [1821].

Shweder, Richard A. "Rethinking Culture and Personality Theory Part I: A Critical Examination of Two Classical Postulates." *Ethos* 7(1979): 255–78.

———. "Rethinking Culture and Personality Theory Part II: A Critical Examination of Two More Classical Postulates." *Ethos* 7(1979): 279–311.

———. "Rethinking Culture and Personality Theory Part III: From Genesis and Typology to Hermeneutics and Dynamics." *Ethos* 8(1980): 60–94.

———, and Edmund J. Bourne. "Does the Concept of the Person Vary Cross-culturally?" *Culture Theory: Essays on Mind, Self, and Emotion*, ed. Richard A. Shweder and Robert LeVine. Cambridge: Cambridge University Press, 1984, 158–99.

Silko, Leslie Marmon. "An Old-Time Indian Attack Conducted in Two Parts." *Shantih* 4(1979): 3–5.

————. *Ceremony*. New York: Viking, 1977.

————. *Storyteller*. New York: Seaver Books, 1981.

Smith, Marion. "Boas' 'Natural History' Approach to Field Method." Goldschmidt, 46–60.

Smith, M. Brewster. "The Metaphorical Basis of Selfhood." Marsella, DeVos, and Hsu, 56–88.

Smith, Paul. *Discerning the Subject*. Minneapolis: University of Minnesota Press, 1988.

Sollors, Werner. "Ethnicity." *Critical Terms for Literary Study*, ed. Frank Lentricchia and Thomas McLaughlin. Chicago: University of Chicago Press, 1990, 288–305.

————. "Introduction: The Invention of Ethnicity." *The Invention of Ethnicity*, ed. Werner Sollors. New York: Oxford University Press, 1989, ix–xx.

Sontag, Susan. "The Anthropologist as Hero." *Claude Lévi-Strauss: The Anthropologist as Hero*, ed. E. N. Hayes and T. Hayes. Cambridge: The MIT Press, 1970, 184–96.

Soper, Kate. *Humanism and Anti-Humanism*. London: Hutchison, 1986.

Spindler, George D., and Louise S. Spindler. "American Indian Personality Types and Their Sociocultural Roots." *Annals of the American Academy of Political and Social Science* 311(1957): 147–57.

Spivak, Gayatri C. "The Making of Americans: The Teaching of English and the Future of Culture Studies." *New Literary History* 21(1990): 781–98.

Stocking, George. *Race, Culture, and Evolution: Essays in the History of Anthropology*. New York: Free Press, 1968.

————. *Victorian Anthropology*. Chicago: University of Chicago Press, 1988.

Strachey, William. *The History of Travaile into Virginia Britannia*, ed. R. H. Major. London: The Hakluyt Society, 1954 [1612].

Strathern, Marilyn. "Out of Context: The Persuasive Fictions of Anthropology." Manganaro, 80–122.

Strickland, Rennard. *The Fire and the Spirits*, Norman: University of Oklahoma Press, 1975.

Swaffar, Janet. "Curricular Issues and Language Research: The Shifting Interaction." *Profession 89*. The Modern Language Association of America, 32–8.

Swagerty, W. R., ed. *Scholars and the Indian Experience: Critical Reviews of Recent Writing in the Social Sciences.* Bloomington: University of Indiana Press, 1984.

Swann, Brian. *Song of the Sky: Versions of Native American Songs and Poems.* Ashvelot Village, N.H.: Four Zoas Night House, 1985.

———, ed. *Essays on the Translation of Native American Literatures.* Washington: The Smithsonian Institution Press, 1991.

———, and Arnold Krupat, eds. *I Tell You Now: Autobiographical Essays by Native American Writers.* Lincoln: University of Nebraska Press, 1987a.

———, and Arnold Krupat, eds. *Recovering the Word: Essays on Native American Literature.* Berkeley: University of California Press, 1987b.

Tedlock, Dennis. *The Spoken Word and the Work of Interpretation.* Philadelphia: University of Pennsylvania Press, 1983.

Thoreau, Henry David. *Walden.* New York: Norton, 1966 [1854].

Timberlake, Lt. Henry. *Memoirs: 1756–65.* Salem, N.H.: Ayers, 1971 [1767].

Todorov, Tzvetan. *The Conquest of America: The Question of the Other.* Tr. Richard Howard. New York: Harper and Row, 1984.

———. " 'Race', Writing, and Culture." *Critical Inquiry* 13(1986): 171–81.

Turner, Frederick J. "The Significance of the Frontier in American History." *American Ground: Vistas, Visions & Revisions*, ed. R. H. Fossum and J. K. Roth. New York: Paragon House, 1988 [1893], 153–63.

Turner, Victor. *The Anthropology of Performance.* New York: PAJ Publications, 1986.

———. *The Forest of Symbols.* Ithaca: Cornell University Press, 1967.

Tyler, Daniel, ed. *Red Men and Hat-Wearers: Viewpoints in Indian History*, papers from the Colorado State University Conference on Indian History, 1974. Boulder: Pruett, 1976.

Tyler, Stephen. "PostModern Ethnography: From Document of the Occult to Occult Document." Clifford and Marcus, 122–40.

———. "The Vision Quest in the West or What the Mind's Eye Sees." *Journal of Anthropological Research* 40(1984): 23–40.

Underhill, Ruth. *Hawk Over Whirlpools.* New York: J. J. Augustin, 1940.

————. *Social Organization of the Papago Indians*. New York: AMS Press, 1969 [1939].

Vanderwerth, W. C. *Indian Oratory*. Norman: University of Oklahoma Press, 1971.

Veeser, H. Aram, ed. *The New Historicism*. New York: Routledge, 1989.

Vizenor, Gerald. "A Postmodern Introduction." *Narrative Chance: Postmodern Essays on Native American Indian Literature*. Albuquerque: University of New Mexico Press, 1989a, 3–16.

————. *Crossbloods: Bone Courts, Bingo, and Other Reports*. Minneapolis: University of Minnesota Press, 1990a.

————. *Earthdivers: Tribal Narrative on Mixed Descent*. Minneapolis: University of Minnesota Press, 1981.

————. *Interior Landscapes: Autobiographical Myths and Metaphors*. Minneapolis: University of Minnesota Press, 1990b.

————. "Trickster Discourse: Comic Holotropes and Language Games." Vizenor, 1989a, 187–212.

————. "Trickster Discourse." *Wicazo Sa Review* 5(1989): 2–7.

————. *The Trickster of Liberty: Tribal Heirs to a Wild Baronage*. Minneapolis: University of Minnesota Press, 1988.

Wallace, Anthony. "The Modal Personality Structure of the Tuscarora Indians as Revealed by the Rorschach Test." Bureau of American Ethnology Bulletin, no. 150, 1952.

Washburn, Wilcomb, ed. *The American Indian and the United States, a Documentary History*. New York: Random House, 1973.

White, Allon. "The Struggle for Bakhtin: Fraternal Reply to Robert Young." *Cultural Critique* 8(1987–8): 217–41.

White, Geoffrey M., and John Kirkpatrick. "Exploring Ethnopsychologies." White and Kirkpatrick, 3–34.

————, eds. *Person, Self, and Experience: Exploring Pacific Ethnopsychologies*. Berkeley: University of California Press, 1985.

White, Hayden. *The Content of the Form: Narrative Discourse and Historical Representation*. Baltimore: Johns Hopkins University Press, 1987.

————. " 'Figuring the Nature of the Times Deceased': Literary Theory and Historical Writing." *The Future of Literary Theory*, ed. Ralph Cohen. New York: Routledge, 1989, 19–43.

————. *Metahistory*. Baltimore: Johns Hopkins University Press, 1973.

White, Leslie. *The Ethnography and Ethnology of Franz Boas*. Bulletin of the Texas Memorial Museum, no. 6 (1963).

Whiteley, Peter M. "Naming, Intentionality, and Personhood in Hopi Society: A Critique of Mauss." Paper presented to the American Anthropological Association symposium, "Persons and Selves in Pueblo and Northwest Coast Societies," 1988.

————. "*Hopitutungwni*: Hopi Names as Literature." Swann, 1991.

Wilden, Anthony. *System and Structure: Studies in Communication and Exchange*. London: Tavistock, 1972.

Williams, Raymond. *Keywords*. New York: Oxford University Press, 1976.

————. *Marxism and Literature*. Oxford: Oxford University Press, 1977.

Williams, Robert A., Jr. "Documents of Barbarism: The Contemporary Legacy of European Racism and Colonialism in the Narrative Traditions of Federal Indian Law." *Arizona Law Review* 31(1989): 231–78.

Williams, Thomas R., ed. *Psychological Anthropology*. New York: Oxford University Press, 1976.

Williams, William Carlos. *In the American Grain*. New York: New Directions, 1956 [1925].

————. "To Elsie." *Selected Poems*. New York: New Directions, 1968, 28–30.

Woodward, Grace Steele. *The Cherokees*. Norman: University of Oklahoma Press, 1963.

Index

Designer: Cynthia Krupat
Compositor: Wilsted & Taylor
Text: Caledonia
Display: Bulmer and Poster Bodoni
Printer: Bookcrafters, Inc.
Binder: Bookcrafters, Inc.